Story Structure and Development

A Guide for Animators, VFX Artists, Game Designers, and Virtual Reality

Story Structure and Development

A Guide for Animators, VFX Artists, Game Designers, and Virtual Reality

Craig Caldwell

CRC Press
Taylor & Francis Group
Boca Raton London New York

CRC Press is an imprint of the
Taylor & Francis Group, an **informa** business

A FOCAL PRESS BOOK

CRC Press
Taylor & Francis Group
6000 Broken Sound Parkway NW, Suite 300
Boca Raton, FL 33487-2742

International Standard Book Number-13: 978-1-4987-8173-2 (Paperback) 978-1-138-70835-8 (Hardback)

Library of Congress Cataloging-in-Publication Data

Names: Caldwell, Craig, author.
Title: Story structure and development : a guide for animators, VFX artists, game designers, and virtual reality / Craig Caldwell.
Description: Boca Raton : Taylor & Francis, a CRC title, part of the Taylor & Francis imprint, a member of the Taylor & Francis Group, the academic division of T&F Informa, plc, [2017] | Includes bibliographical references.
Identifiers: LCCN 2016048892| ISBN 9781498781732 (pbk. : alk. paper) | ISBN 9781138708358 (hardback : alk. paper)
Subjects: LCSH: Video games--Authorship. | Virtual reality. | Online authorship. | Computer animation.
Classification: LCC GV1469.34.A97 C35 2017 | DDC 794.8--dc23
LC record available at https://lccn.loc.gov/2016048892

Visit the Taylor & Francis Web site at
http://www.taylorandfrancis.com

and the CRC Press Web site at
http://www.crcpress.com

Dedicated to
Dee, Ryan, and Joanna

Contents

Part 2   Story Elements

Part 3   Character Development

Part 4   Idea Development

Author

Craig Caldwell is USTAR (Utah Science Technology and Research) professor in digital media, University of Utah. Having worked for Walt Disney Feature Animation and Electronic Arts games he has extensive experience in the industry approach to creating animation and games. Caldwell has been a co-founder and arts director for one of the top-ranked interactive games programs, Entertainment Arts and Engineering (EAE – University of Utah) with its numerous award winning games. He has served as head of the largest film school in Australia—Griffith Film School, Griffith University as well as chair of the Media Arts Department and associate director of the New Media Center at University of Arizona; as well as having been selected as a DeTao Master, Institute of Animation and Creative Content on the SIVA campus, Shanghai, China. Caldwell speaks frequently on story at major conferences such as SIGGRAPH, FMX, Sundance, CCG Expo, and Mundos Digitales. He earned his PhD from the Advanced Computing Center for Art and Design, Ohio State University.

PART 1
Story Structure
(the Plot)

1

Plot: The Structure

What Is a Dramatic Story?

Every day we tell each other stories, but these are not the dramatic stories we see in the movies or encounter in interactive games. Dramatic stories are more than just *what* is happening... they are about *why* things are happening and *how* it affects the viewer.

The dictionary definition of story is *a sequence of events*. Dramatic stories are still a sequence of events, but the fundamental difference is that they are a sequence of *connected* events. Many years ago, E. M. Forster (Figure 1.1) indicated that a story can be about *"the king died and then the queen died"* but a dramatic story is *"the king died and then the queen died of grief."*[1] The emphasis moves from *what* happened to *why* it happened.

Figure 1.1

E. M. Forster, novelist.

Stories connect audiences to what individuals think, and what cultures value. The important questions in a story are: *What* do people want? *Why* do they want it? *How* do they go about getting it? *What* stops them? *What* are the consequences?[2] These are fundamental. Dramatic stories are about a main character, who goes after something but it gets increasingly difficult (conflict)... and by the end, they are changed, and see the world differently.

The *Why* underscores how we use a story to understand life; why things work the way they do. Stories aid human beings in their search for meaning; to make sense of why we are alive. They give us a perspective on priorities in our lives. For generations, cultures have proposed answers to these questions through myths (Figure 1.2): Greek plays, Shakespearean plays, Chinese proverbs, folk tales, and interpreted dreams.[3] Today, we get this information through novels, movies, animation, and interactive games. In dramatic stories, we see a main character that (1) has a problem which can't be avoided, (2) is faced with difficult choices, and (3) which has serious consequences if they are not successful.

Figure 1.2

Ancient mythology.

Today, audiences have even higher expectations from dramatic stories. Joseph Campbell, author of the *Hero's Journey* story structure, emphasizes that audiences have evolved from searching for clues on the meaning of life to additionally seeking an *"experience of being alive"* in stories.[4] The key is to engage audiences emotionally, by linking the external action to the internal emotions of the characters. Joe Ranft emphasizes that connecting a viewer's internal emotions with the main character enhances their ability to identify with the story (Figure 1.3).

Linda Seger (Figure 1.4) asks the question: *What is a story?* She indicates that it sounds like an obvious question but believes that many films, animations, and games are released every year where there is not a story... but episodes. Episodes are defined as the daily events that happen in our lives. The difference is that *episodes* are how we live most of our lives; we get up, go to work, see friends, go to lunch, but none of these events are intrinsically linked to each other.[5]

All dramatic stories have a similar set of elements—*connected actions, with conflict that intensifies*, which force *difficult choices* with *consequences*. Along the way the ever-increasing conflict results in a *crisis* that leads to a *climax*, with a *surprise* along the way that the audience didn't anticipate. This leads to a *resolution* (gives meaning to the story) and in the end the character is *changed*. These are the universal components of a story today.

We are trying to find what we hope the audience will feel while watching this movie. Every other department is on board... the environment, the coloring, the lighting, the animation, to make the strongest possible statement; that when people are in a theatre they are going to... Wow, this is something special, this is something that affected me.

Figure 1.3

Joe Ranft, Head of Story, Pixar, 1990–2005.

Figure 1.4

Linda Seger, story consultant and author of *Making a Good Script Great*, Samuel French Trade, 1987.

Plot... What Is It?

What is Plot? Plot is the sequential arrangement of the story elements (i.e., character, setting, and theme); *what* happens and *when* it happens in the story. It is the arrangement of which events come before (or after) something else... that results in *increasing conflict*, leading to a *climax*, to produce a *particular ending* to the story. In *The Three Little Pigs*, the order of the houses getting blown down sets up increasing tension in the telling of the story (Figure 1.5).

Figure 1.6

Alfred Hitchcock on suspense, https://www.youtube.com/watch?v=md6 folAgGRU

Plot is to story as composition is to art and music. The hard work of story is not just selecting the correct story elements but also putting them in the right order—this is just as important. While the terms story and plot are often used interchangeably ... *they are not the same thing.*

The more familiar an audience is with a particular *plot structure* (i.e., mystery, horror, comedy, etc.) the better an audience understands what is happening in the story. A plot connects the events in a story, to not only grab an audience/player's interest, but also to keep them interested in what happens next. This arrangement of events uses plot devices such as suspense, surprise, coincidences, reversals, emotional moments, etc. Alfred Hitchcock (Figure 1.6) explains that the difference between *suspense* versus *shock/surprise* depends on what the audience knows ahead of time. The most critical information in a scene where a bomb has been planted is whether or not the *audience knows* about the bomb *before it goes off* (5 minutes of suspense) or *after it goes off* (5 seconds of surprise).[6] Such plot devices directly impact the level of emotional engagement of the viewer/player.

Figure 1.5

The Three Little Pigs by Francis Glebas, *Directing the Story.*

Story Elements

- *Character—who* the audience identifies with—Maximus (Figure 1.8).
- *World/Setting—where*, ancient Rome, its territories, and the Roman Coliseum.
- *Goal—what* the main character wants—revenge, to kill the emperor.
- *Theme—why*—to be with his family. This is the meaning of the story. The theme is realized at the climax as a result of the choices the character makes.
- *Conflict/Obstacle—the things that prevent* the character from reaching their goal—he is injured, becomes a slave, the guards protect the emperor. Collectively, these result in….
- *Change*—the main character goes through or they bring to the world around them. Maximus frees Rome from the emperor's tyranny, frees his fellow slaves, joins his family.

Plot is the writer's choice of events and their design in time.[7]

Figure 1.7

Robert McKee.

Robert McKee clarifies that what a plot organizes are story elements (Figure 1.7). Paradoxically, if the plot is well done… it won't be remembered. What is remembered is the *story* (the characters and situation). Successful story telling is when the audience is so engrossed with the story—nothing else is noticed. The audience is unaware of how the story is being told. Similar to VFX (visual effects); when VFX is done really well, it is invisible.

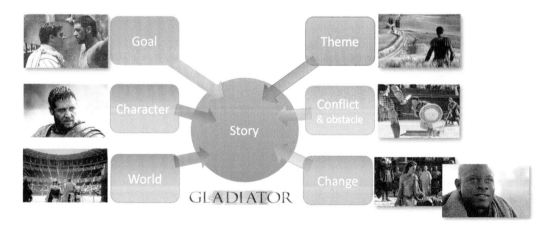

Figure 1.8

Story elements in *Gladiator*.

3 Act Structure

The classic plot structure is often referred to as 3 acts, corresponding to setup, increasing conflict, and resolution. Even something as short as a scene, or interactive game level, has a similar 3-part structure (Figure 1.9):

Act 1—*the setup* introduces the characters and the rules of the world. The audience/player learns where the story takes place (the setting), what the main character wants (motivation), and the dramatic question (what the story is really about, that the audience can relate to). This act contains only the minimum amount of information the audience needs to start the story.

Act 2—*Increasing Conflict* forces the main character to confront obstacles that stand between them and what they want, their goal. These conflicts build until the final crisis that has to be resolved… one way or another. This act is where the bulk of the conflict takes place.

Act 3—*Resolution* follows the Climax that is the transition to Act 3. Here, the conflict is resolved, the big questions are answered, and a new status quo is established. It's the shortest act, with a resolution which gives the story its meaning.

Each act has a different purpose, but what that purpose is can vary depending on the author's point of view. The terminology and the style depend on what is most important in how the story is told (Figure 1.10):

- Conflict/crisis, climax, and resolution[8]
- Departure, tests/choices/change, and return[9]
- Setup, confrontation, and resolution[10]

Ridley Scott, director of *The Martian* (referring to the screenplay for *Gladiator*) … *I needed all this information converted into a good 3-Act play… drama.*[11]

Figure 1.10

Ridley Scott, director, *The Martian, Alien, Gladiator.*

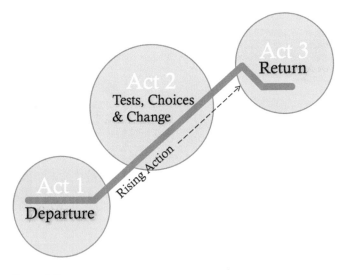

Figure 1.9

3-Act plot structure.

Aristotle[12] (352 BC) originally defined plot as having beginning, middle, and end. Today, stories continue to have a beginning, middle, and end… just not necessarily in that order. Today, the traditional link between beginning, middle, and end and the 3-act structure has been decoupled. This is evident in films such as *Memento* (Figures 1.11) and *Edge of Tomorrow: Live, Die, Repeat* which don't follow the traditional linear order of beginning, middle, and end. This is possible because viewers have seen so many stories they innately understand the 3-act structure and can reassemble a 3-act story sequence in their mind… even when it is not presented in a linear order.

This enhanced capability of the viewer/player permits game designers to break story elements into narrative blocks. These blocks are distributed across a variety of sequences, with the player piecing together the narrative as they interact with a game or virtual reality (VR).

Figure 1.11

Christopher Nolan, director, *Memento*, *Inception*.

Screen media (i.e., video games, VR, film, and animation) is expanding its use of narrative blocks. Such narrative blocks are an extension of the axiom that *All stories start in the middle*. Action movies (i.e., James Bond, *Mission Impossible*) always start the story in the *middle* of the action. In Act 1, the conflict has always begun earlier than when the story opens. Although the viewer didn't see that beginning action, they use their innate story knowledge to puzzle their way through and put the pieces together. This innate capability has permitted directors to shift narrative information from its traditional sequence (i.e., beginning, middle, and end) to dispersing these narrative elements throughout the plot structure (Figure 1.12).

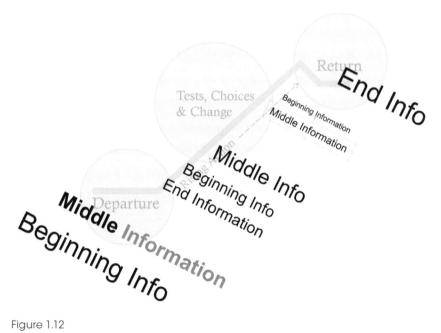

Figure 1.12

Narrative elements distributed throughout the plot.

Act Structures

Although the beginning, middle, and end structure is the standard today, there can be more, or less, than just 3 acts in a story. The number of acts varies. It depends on story length, cultural standard (Bollywood vs. Hollywood), and screen media (i.e., film, VR, games, novel, etc.).

History tells us that the ancient Greek dramas were conceived in a 3-act structure[13] (Aristotle). This expanded the concept of beginning, middle, and end to 5-acts[14] (Horace in ancient Rome). Five acts were the norm for classic Renaissance dramas and Shakespearean plays.[15] In the late nineteenth century, there was a resurgence of 3-acts. The early twentieth century saw an 8-Act[16] (Sequences) structure emerge, corresponding to the number of film reels that had to be changed every 10–15 minutes for a movie. Television had an even greater impact on act structure—ranging from one act for cartoons to many acts for a miniseries. The 3-act structure is synonymous with Aristotle's *beginning, middle, and end;* yet, where it can get confusing is that stories, whether they have one act or eight acts, also have a beginning, middle, and end structure. That continues to be the standard starting point for a story... even as the number of acts changes to fit various lengths in screen media.

Figure 1.13

One act stories.

Figure 1.14

Two act stories.

Figure 1.15

Three act stories.

1-Act stories (Figure 1.13) are found in cartoons, commercials, shorts, cut-scenes in games... anything with a 1–8-minute length. One act stories are best limited to two characters, one location setting, one familiar social situation, and one turning point ending the story (i.e., *Bugs Bunny, Pixar Shorts, SpongeBob*).

2-Act stories (Figure 1.14) are found in television shows and situation comedies, 30 minutes or less. These work best within the constraints of a limited number of characters, only a few location settings, familiar social situations, and a limit of two major turning points before the resolution (i.e., *Friends, The Big Bang Theory*).

3-Acts (Figure 1.15) are traditionally found in movie genres (i.e., Mystery, Action, Romance, Comedy...). 3-Act plots communicate stories that can connect the audience to their more personal experiences. This format includes three major turning points... at a minimum. Epic movies often require a larger number of acts to tell their story. Narrative interactive games often have a 3-act structure within each distinct level.

4-Acts are commonly found in television dramas, 60 minutes in length—*Law & Order, NCIS* (Figure 1.16), with the commercial breaks signaling the change to the next act. Such shows are primarily centered around the inherent conflict found in crime and medical shows. While these shows have a formulaic structure, audiences relate to the drama due to their own legal or medical encounters. These stories offer much in the way of life's lessons with potential situations. The 4-act structure relates to those story theorists who advocate breaking Act 2 into 2A and 2B (e.g., Trottier, Snyder, and Hauge).

5-Acts are seen in emotional dramas such as Shakespearean plays and contemporary relationship stories with their multiple points-of-view and multitude of turning points—*Silver Linings Playbook, Four Weddings and a Funeral* (Figure 1.17). A 5-act plot has a structure that is broken into the following acts: *exposition, rising action, climax, falling action,* and *resolution.*[17] This 5-act structure also parallels the 3-act structure as Act 1 is exposition, Act 2 is comprised of rising action and climax, and Act 3 includes both falling action and resolution.

8-Acts (and more) are found in epic movies, video games levels, and stories with numerous characters—*Breaking Bad, Game of Thrones* (Figure 1.18). Eight acts are the standard in the USC story theory *Sequence Approach* which evolved in the early days of cinema when film reels had to be changed every 10–15 minutes. Robert McKee warns that multiple acts can reduce the impact of the final crisis and invites clichés.[18] Phil Parker encourages seeing acts as dramatic movements, as opposed to structural units. As movements, story development will be more effective in seeing "[the viewer's] *engagement with the narrative as a whole....*"[19]

Figure 1.16

Four acts with a middle Act II [2A + 2B].

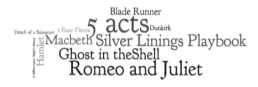

Figure 1.17

Five act stories.

Figure 1.18

Eight + act stories.

Plot: The Hero's Journey

There are different plot structures that lay out the basic steps of a dramatic story. One of the more popular today is the Hero's Journey[20] credited to Joseph Campbell (Figure 1.19). This structure has gone on to become one of the most familiar structures for action movies and first person shooter (FPS) games today (*Mission Impossible, Star Wars, Battlefield*). Viewers see it so often they now expect it, but at the same time, they want to see it in fresh configurations (*Avatar, Suicide Squad, Call of Duty*). Ironically, the Hero's Journey is based on some of

the oldest cultural stories… yet is also one of the more recent story structures to have emerged. It heavily influenced the plot for *Star Wars* which has a direct correspondence with the Hero's Journey structure (see Figure 1.20).

This structure is derived from Joseph Campbell's research on common narrative patterns in myths handed down from generation to generation. Campbell detected that the principal myths from numerous cultures around the world share a fundamental structure; the *monomyth*[21] (one great story). Campbell summarized this structure as…

A hero ventures forth from the world of common day into a region of supernatural wonder: fabulous forces are there encountered and a decisive victory is won: the hero comes back from this mysterious adventure with the power to bestow boons on his fellow man.[22]

Figure 1.19

Joseph Campbell, author, *A Hero with a Thousand Faces*.

Most people want to be the hero in their own story, so they readily identify the hero motif. With the increased popularity of this structure, it's common to refer to the main character as the *hero*.

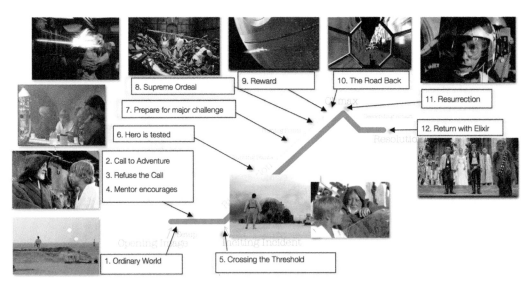

8. Supreme Ordeal

9. Reward

10. The Road Back

7. Prepare for major challenge

11. Resurrection

6. Hero is tested

12. Return with Elixir

2. Call to Adventure
3. Refuse the Call
4. Mentor encourages

1. Ordinary World

5. Crossing the Threshold

Figure 1.20

Analysis of *Star Wars* as the Hero's Journey.

The Hero's Journey is made up of a number of stages that the main character goes through in a story.[23] Joseph Campbell broke it down into 12 stages. The Hero's Journey pattern of stages is familiar in many of the world's spiritual narratives (i.e., Buddha and Jesus) which in turn influenced *The Matrix* (see Figure 1.21).

Do movies and games have all these stages? No... but all dramatic stories have some of them, in one form or another. Christopher Vogler, in *the Writer's Journey*, consolidated them into 12 stages for the film industry. He stresses that *"the order of the stages... is only one of many possible variations. The stages can be deleted, added to, and drastically shuffled without losing any of their power."*[24]

There are a number of examples where writers tried to follow this structure as a template only to come to ruin (i.e., *Delgo: A Hero's Journey*). The Hero's Journey continues to evolve across cultures and with the times we live in. Those who have built on the stages of the Hero's Journey include (8-point arc [Watts],[25] 22 steps [Truby],[26] and 31 functions [Propp][27]). Which ones to consider depend on the content and story to be told. These stages provide familiar points of reference that a viewer uses to track where they are in the story and gain insights into the character's motivation as well as enhancing the entertainment through anticipation.

MATRIX as Hero's Journey

1. Neo shown working in his office cubicle *(show ordinary life, current status quo)*.	
2. Neo gets phone call *(call to adventure)* from mentor Morpheus.	
3. Neo changes his mind on the building ledge *(refuse the call)*.	
4. Morpheus encourages Neo *(Mentor convinces hero to make the change and begin the journey)*	
5. Neo swallows the red pill, ejected from Matrix. *(crosses the 1st threshold into the new world)*	
6. Neo is *tested* and meets ship's crew *(allies)* and Agent Smith *(enemies)*	
7. Get "*Guns*" *(prepare for challenge)* and go back into the Matrix *(cross 2nd threshold, inner cave)*	
8. Fight agents as they rescue Morpheus *(endure supreme ordeal)*	
9. Rescue Morpheus *(take possession of reward)*	
10. Agent Smith stops Neo returning. *(pursued on the Road Back, leading to Climax)*	
11. Neo returns to life, and is the "one". *(cross 3rd threshold, resurrection and transformation)*	
12. Neo returns to expose Matrix. *(Returns with Elixir [benefit] to establish new status quo)*	

Figure 1.21

Analysis of the Hero's Journey in *The Matrix*.

Plot Structures: The Short

While the Hero's Journey works well for epic stories, there are other plot structures that are better adapted for short stories. These structures differ from the Hero's Journey in that they have a fewer number of stages and use contemporary terms. Even if not used in each story's plot structure, these stages can serve as a checklist to be considered. It is important that each person select (and assemble), their own set of plot stages that match their sensibilities and media (i.e., animation, film, games, VR, etc.). For each stage has its strengths as well as its tradeoffs.

Nigel Watts proposes that all classic plots pass through eight stages—similar to the Hero's Journey (Figure 1.22).[28] Stories pass through predictable points: the beginning of a story that sets up the basic problem (everyday life and trigger), the middle that build the story's rising conflict (quest), and the end that provides a resolution (surprise, critical choice, reversal, climax, and resolution [the meaning]).

1. Stasis (everyday life)
2. Trigger (inciting incident)
3. Quest (middle)
4. Surprise (obstacles)
5. Critical choice (leading to crisis)
6. Climax (climax)
7. Reversal (change of status quo)
8. Resolution (change is visible)

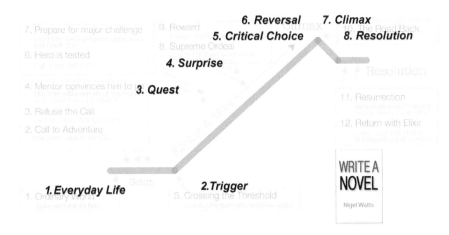

Figure 1.22

8-Point arc.

A comparable 8-point structure has emerged for Karen Sullivan in *Ideas for the Animated Short* (Figure 1.23).[29] This also echoes the stages of the Hero's Journey but is a more realistic plot structure adapted for animated shorts—under 5 minutes and scoped to fit within the time allotted. This structure can also be seen in the successful Pixar shorts (i.e., *Presto, Luxo Jr., For the Birds*) as well as award winning shorts found in the major competitions (i.e., Oscars, Emmys, SIGGRAPH, Film Festivals [e.g., Tropfest]).

Short stories work best when limited to no more than two primary characters, one setting, and one theme (i.e., *Looney Tunes* [Bugs Bunny]). There is limited time to establish what a character wants and the obstacle(s) that are preventing the character from getting it. Sullivan proposes in "*Ideas for the Animated Short*" that shorts are more successful when the stories are direct, simple, and have an economy of structure and plot (Figure 1.24).

1. A character wants something badly
2. Something happens that moves the character to action
3. The character meets with conflict
4. Things gets worse until the character is in crisis
5. Almost all is lost
6. Lesson is learned
7. Hard choice must be made
8. Success

Figure 1.23

8-Point structure, *Ideas for the Animated Short*, Karen Sullivan.[29]

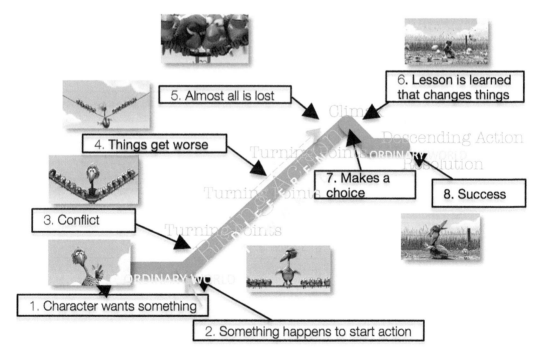

Figure 1.24

Analysis of *For the Birds* as 8-point structure.

Structure Comparisons

There are two major categories of plot structure: *Hero's Journey* and an *(updated) Aristotelian* paradigm. Hero's Journey is today's most well-known story structure based on Joseph Campbell's research, *The Hero with a Thousand Faces*, on the commonalities between narratives found in myths from around the world[30] (Figure 1.25).

Popular story theorists that ascribe to the Hero's Journey structure include Christopher Vogler[31] and John Truby[32] (Figure 1.26). This approach took off when Vogler's 7-page summary, written when he worked at Disney, was distributed and embraced by the Hollywood studios in the 1990s. Vogler expanded his summary into the definitive book— *The Writers Journey: Mythic Structure for Writers*.

Figure 1.25

The Hero with a Thousand Faces by Joseph Campbell.[30]

The Hero's Journey Structure

Christopher Vogler - *The Writer's Journey*

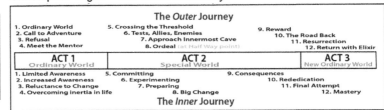

John Truby - *The Anatomy of a Story*

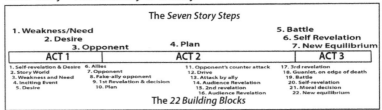

Linda Seger - *The Story Spline*

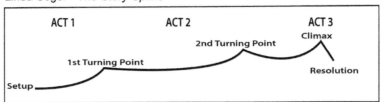

Figure 1.26

Hero's Journey story theorists.

The updated-Aristotelian plot approach is built on Aristotle's story theories, *Poetics*, derived from the structure of Greek plays in 300 BC[33] (Figure 1.27). This approach has been time tested as well as enhanced with new emphases on characters and their free will. Originally, Aristotle put the emphasis on *what* happens as opposed to today with audiences wanting to more about the *why*.

The story theorists that ascribe to the updated-Aristotelian plot structure include Syd Field,[34] Michael Hauge,[35] Robert McKee,[36] and Linda Seger[37] (Figure 1.28). Their approaches codify the recognized standards of story in screen media. Syd Field was the first to lay out the contemporary story concepts for film writers in his 1979 book *Screenplay*. Since that time, the Aristotelian structure has been further expanded by McKee (*Story, Principles of Screenwriting*). Pixar's writers and directors credit their attendance at McKee's *Story Seminar* in the early 1990s as instrumental in their structuring of *Toy Story*.[38]

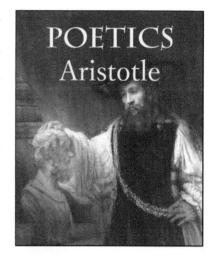

Figure 1.27

Poetics by Aristotle. [33]

The Aristotelian Structure

Robert McKee - *The Central Plot*

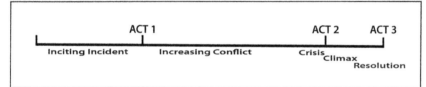

Michael Hauge - *Six Stage Plot Structure*

Syd Field - *Story Paradigm*

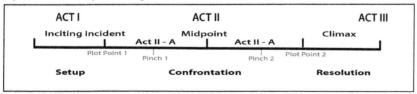

Figure 1.28

Updated-Aristotelian story theorists.

What They All Have in Common?

Each story theorist has their own terminology but their structures include many of the same plot components (Figure 1.29). The common plot pattern is a 3-act structure:

1. Act 1—story *setup, ordinary world, everyday life* (background information).
2. Act 2—increasing conflict: *complications, higher stakes, supreme ordeal, quest, confrontation.*
3. Act 3—*resolution, aftermath, realization, resurrection.*
4. Within Act 1 (often near the end), there is a significant event: *inciting incident, catalyst, trigger, cross the threshold* where the story really starts.
5. End of Act 1 moves the character to take action (start the quest), which signals transition into Act 2. This transition into Act 2 involves a location change… with the hero crossing into a new world.
6. Act 2 shows the conflict intensifying. Things increasingly get worse with a *reversal* (of fortune).
7. Story theories split 50/50 between Act 2 as one act versus Act 2 divided into Act 2A and 2B, with a distinct midpoint.
8. Midpoints have a variety of characteristics: point of no return, conflict becomes personal, rite of passage, lovers or buddies commit to each other, next stage of growth, reveal, ticking clock to increase tension.[1]
9. Act 2 results in a *crisis* that leads to the *climax.*
10. Act 3 has a climax with a turning point and twist.
11. There is an ending that gives meaning to the story.

In comparing story structures, the terminology may vary, but those variations are far more idiosyncratic. The structures all have roughly the same story points in common. However, while there is a consensus on these major points, there are distinct differences in how and where the structures place the emphasis. These structures might be most useful as a story *editing* tool in the rewriting phase.

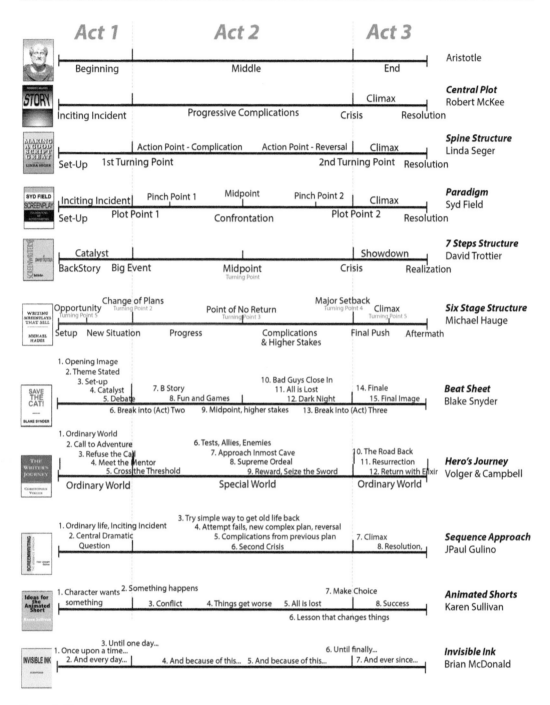

Figure 1.29

What they all have in common.

References

1. E. M. Forester, *Aspects of the Novel*, (USA, Harcourt, 1927), 83.
2. R. McKee, *Story, Substance, Structure, Style, and the Principles of Screenwriting* (New York, Harper-Collins Publisher, 1997), 19.
3. J. Campbell, *The Hero with a Thousand Faces* (New York, New World Library, 2008).
4. Ibid, 129.
5. L. Seger, *How to Make a Good Script Great* (Hollywood, California, Samuel French Trade, 1987), 101.
6. A. Hitchcock, *Quotes about Hitchcock*, http://www.goodreads.com/quotes/728496-there-is-a-distinct-difference-between-suspense-and-surprise-and
7. R. McKee, Audio CD on Story. Plot section.
8. D. Trottier, *Screenwriter's Bible*, 6th edition (New York, Silman-James Press, 2014), 14.
9. B. Snyder, *Save the Cat* (Chelsea, Michigan, Michael Wiese Productions, 2005), 24.
10. M. Hauge, *Writing Screenplays that Sell, the Complete Guide to Turning Story Concepts into Movie and Television Deals* (New York, Harper Collins Publisher, 1988), 34.
11. "Story," *Gladiator* directed by Ridley Scott (DreamWorks Video, 2000), Gladiator Signature Selection (Two-Disc Collector's Edition), 2nd Disc.
12. A. K. Aristotle, *Poetics* (London, Oxford University Press, 2013), 25.
13. A. K. Aristotle, *Poetics*, 24.
14. H. Rushton Fairclough (Transl.), *Horace: Satires, Epistles and Ars Poetica* (Boston, Massachusetts, Harvard University Press, 1929).
15. J. H. Lawson, *Theory and Technique of Playwriting and Screenwriting* (Estate of John Howard Lawson, 2014), 14, http://wwwjohnhowardlawson.com.
16. R. Gulino, *Screenwriting: The Sequence Approach* (London, Bloomsbury Academic, 2004), 54.
17. G. Freytag, Die Technik des Dramas, *Wikipedia*, last modified April 23, 2016, https://en.wikipedia.org/wiki/Dramatic_structure
18. R. McKee, *Story*, 14.
19. P. Parker, *The Art and Science of Screenwriting* (New York, Intellect Ltd., 1999), 27.
20. J. Campbell, *Hero with a Thousand Faces* (New York, New World Library, 2008).
21. J. Campbell, *Hero with a Thousand Faces*, 44.
22. J. Campbell, A Hero with a Thousand Faces, *Wikipedia*, last modified May 17, 2016, https://en.wikipedia.org/wiki/The_Hero_with_a_Thousand_Faces
23. J. Campbell, *Hero with a Thousand Faces*, 44.
24. C. Vogler, *The Writer's Journey* (Ann Arbor, Michigan, Michael Wiese Productions, 1992), 26.
25. N. Watts, *Write a Novel and Get It Published* (New York, Teach Yourself Publisher, 2012).
26. J. Truby, *The Anatomy of Story* (New York, Faber and Faber, Inc., 2007).
27. V. Propp, *The Russian Folktale* (Detroit, Michigan, Wayne State University Press, 2012).
28. N. Watts, *Write a Novel*, 55. http://www.writersfriend.com/post/30580376166/how-to-structure-a-story-nigel-watts
29. K. Sullivan, *Ideas for the Animated Short* (Boston, Massachusetts, Focal Press, 2008), 24.
30. J. Campbell, *Hero with a Thousand Faces* (New York, New World Library, 2008).
31. C. Vogler, *The Writer's Journey*.
32. J. Truby, *Anatomy of Story*, 22.
33. C. Vogler, *The Writer's Journey*, 114.
34. S. Field, *Screenplay—The Foundations of Screenwriting* (New York, Delta Publisher, 2005).
35. M. Hauge, *Writing Screenplays that Sell* (New York, Harper-Collins, 1991).
36. R. McKee, *Story*, 14.
37. L. Seger, *How to Make a Good Script Great*, 88.
38. E. Catmull, *Creativity, Inc.* (New York, Random House, 2014), 44.

2

Setup: Act 1

Types of Setup

The setup serves several important functions: the first is to tell the viewer what they need to know to get the story started (who it is about, where, when?) and introduces the type of story (comedy, drama…). A second function is to elicit emotion in the viewer; to get them to identify with the plight of the characters. If the viewer doesn't care what happens next, they won't stay for the rest of the story.

A setup has three components (1) to provide enough information to orient the viewer to what is happening, (2) to introduce the inciting incident that forces the main character to take action, and (3) to raise the central question (theme) that must be answered by the end of the story. *Will they get the Shark or will the Shark get them first? (Jaws).*

The setup prepares the viewer (Figure 2.2). Where do stories start?—*in media res*, in the middle of the conflict.[1] *The Three Little Pigs* doesn't start when the pigs are born, but when they leave home. Viewers don't need everything laid out for them. We have been exposed to thousands of stories and have an innate sense of story structure.

Figure 2.1

What's at stake? *Oktapodi,* www.oktapodi.com. (Courtesy of Emud Mokhberi.)

Figure 2.2

Setup.

Where to Start

1. **Start where the conflict begins.** Conflict begins in most action films and FPS games. These beginnings are most dramatic with physical action; confrontation, a chase, a gun fight, a discovery, hanging from a plane, etc. Dramatic conflict (action) is found in James Bond films, *Assassin's Creed* games, Jason Bourne, *Call of Duty,* etc.

2. **Start with a decision or choice that begins the conflict.** *Wreck-It-Ralph* decides he doesn't want to be the bad guy any more. He decides he is going to get a medal to earn the admiration of the other characters in the game. Such big decisions change the course of the character's life.

3. **Start at a turning point in life.** There are certain times in life when there are dramatic turns that set out lives in a different direction: divorce, marriage, new girl/boyfriend, first baby, death, money, medical, new job…. These changes result in a whole new set of challenges in life.

4. **Start with what is a stake/risk.** Show what is being risked in the conflict the character is going through: life or death (Figure 2.1), love, safety, respect…. These immediately get the viewer's empathy. It isn't enough to show that a character can fail but to let the viewer know what that will mean. What are the consequences for failure in the character's life?

Traditional Setup Sequences

1. *Show everyday life, character in their normal environment...* before their life is changed (i.e., *Matrix, Ratatouille*). If something unfair happens, then the viewer empathizes with the character. The viewer becomes emotionally engaged because they can identify with the unfairness of life. By starting with ordinary life, the viewer anticipates things are going to change.

2. *Arriving or departing to somewhere new...* character landing in a new location; airport, train station, apartment, etc. (i.e., *Titanic [setting sail, reaching the Titanic on ocean floor], The Graduate [coming home]*) (Figure 2.3).

3. *Action sequence* (blockbuster). Story starts in mid-conflict with action. Danger gets the viewer's attention, they become emotionally invested... *will the character survive*? It's the emotion that grabs a viewer (i.e., *Raiders, Mission Impossible, Star Wars*).

4. *Something bad happens* (murder, robbery, accident), followed characters responding as part of their job; crime or emergency (i.e., *Law and Order, Grey's Anatomy, CSI, Déjà Vu*).

5. *Open the story in the past, then fast forward to today.* To create anticipation, a life changing event is shown that happened before the story starts. The viewer wonders where the story is going? This setup uses more in-depth exposition: establishes setting, gives background details, and then jumps to present day (i.e., *Fugitive, Shawshank Redemption, Red Death Redemption*).

6. *Open in the middle of conflict... today, then flashback to past.* Show their life today in conflict, then cut back to life events earlier in the story. Generates curiosity for viewer (i.e., *The Hangover*).

7. *Open with the ending, then jump back to before the conflict starts.* The viewer knows what is going to happen, but not *how* it happens. They empathize with characters who don't know what is going to happen to them (i.e., *Titanic, Sunset Boulevard, Lawrence of Arabia*).

Figure 2.3

Departing as opening. (*Titanic*. Copyright 1999, 20th Century Fox.)

Opening Image(s)

The setup begins with an opening image(s). These are visuals that give a strong sense of where the story takes place. The eye is quicker at grasping details as opposed to using dialog which takes longer. The images that open the story focus the viewer's attention. The purpose is to quickly orient the viewer and transport them into the setting, with sufficient details to make it believable. Effective opening images create a metaphor, used to connect the viewer to the theme (what the story is really about... emotionally).

These images take several forms. One form is a *wide shot* of the world and then the camera moves to something specific. In *Star Wars* (Figure 2.4), it starts with a shot above a planet, then a small ship followed by a big ship that fills the frame. Next, it cuts to the small ship being pulled into the big ship. This is a metaphor of a big fish eating a little fish, which immediately grabs the viewer's attention; gets them involved in the action.

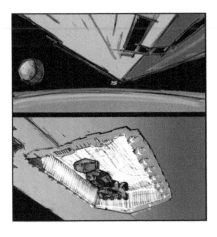

Another option is a *close-up*. The camera then pulls back to reveal the setting where the action occurs. *Touch of Evil* is famous for its opening sequence of a close-up of hands setting a bomb (Figure 2.5) before pulling back to reveal the action... immediately creating curiosity in the viewer.

There is also the option of *no image* (Figure 2.6). A black screen with sounds of the environment opens *Close Encounters of the Third Kind*. This approach focuses the viewer's attention by eliminating any distractions.

The opening image establishes the *before* picture of the main character's life that connects with the *after* picture at the end of the story. This contrast communicates how the main character has been changed or has changed the world around them. The purpose of the opening images is to insert the needed *before* picture in the viewer's mind.

Figure 2.4

A dynamic opening, *Star Wars*. (Copyright 1977, 20th Century Fox.)

Figure 2.5

Opening with a close up of something that can cause harm immediately captures a viewer's curiosity as to what might happen next.

Figure 2.6

No image, just sound—*Close Encounters of the Third Kind*.

Michael Arndt shared that while working on *Toy Story 3*, he had a hard time setting up the story. It is common to focus on the ending when having problems but he suggests that the real seeds of failure are planted at the beginning. To solve this problem, he decided to go back and look at *Toy Story, Finding Nemo,* and *The Incredibles* to learn how Pixar had set up their characters in the past. His first observation revealed that "*usually what you do when you are introducing your main character is that you show them doing the thing they love the most. … their grand passion, that is the center of their whole universe. So in Woody's case he is playing with Andy (Figure 2.7). That's his favorite thing, the thing that defines who he is as a person. With Marlin (Finding Nemo), Marlin is a family man, he has just moved into a new house, with his wife, a brood of eggs and he couldn't be happier. With the Incredibles you introduce Mr. Incredible being a super hero. So you start with your main character, you introduce the universe (their world) they live in, and you show your hero doing the thing they love the most….*"[2]

Figure 2.7

Toy Story opens with Andy playing with Woody. (Copyright 1995, Disney • Pixar.)

For the opening of the *Titanic*, Director James Cameron initially story-boarded a sequence of workmen building the Titanic. He came to the realization that version wasn't going to emotionally engage the viewer. After re-watching a number of opening sequences of successful movies, he decided to use a sequence of modern submersibles (Figure 2.8) discovering the Titanic on the bottom of the ocean. The contrast of the two images echoes the contrast in the story between perceptions today versus in the past when the Titanic first sailed.

Figure 2.8

Ghosts of the Abyss, an MIR submersible observing the bow of the Titanic wreck, 2003. (Copyright Walt Disney/Courtesy Everett Collection.)

Exposition

Exposition is the background information needed by the viewer so they can understand what is going on in the story. The majority of this information comes in Act 1... as the story starts. The viewer is given *only* what is necessary to understand the characters and their situation.

Exposition is a balance between revealing too much information or not revealing enough information. Dumping all the exposition at the beginning can kill the momentum; it will dampen the viewer/player's curiosity as to what will happen next. On the other hand, holding back too much information in the story leaves the viewer confused.

> *Exposition serves two ends: it's primary purpose is to further conflict, it's secondary purpose is to convey information.*[4]

Exposition isn't all revealed in the beginning but dispensed across the story (Figure 2.9). Information is first introduced in the setup (just enough to start the story), then next more important information is revealed at the first turning point, then finally by the second turning point the critical information is revealed—the secrets.[3] Exposition can be thought of as breadcrumbs left along a path leading the viewer forward as they assemble the pieces mentally.

Tip. Revealing information adds surprises in the first half of the story, but not so much in the latter half of the story. The viewer feels manipulated, not surprised, when essential information has been withheld too long (there are exceptions... *Luke, I am your father*).

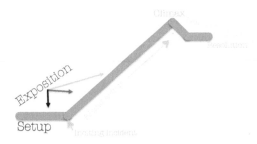

Figure 2.9

Exposition is distributed throughout the story.

Figure 2.10

Use text as exposition only as a last resort. *Star Wars* is the exception to the rule.

Exposition comes in a variety of forms: text, narration, dialog, and visuals. There is exposition as text seen on screen (letters, text messages, and newspaper headlines). Text is kept to a minimum as viewers don't come to *read* a movie/game. Screen text is used only when it is the fastest way to move the story forward, or as in a special case, the *Star Wars* opening (Figure 2.10).

Characters close to the main character often deliver exposition. These characters are useful for revealing what the main character wants and needs. James Bond's commander, M, serves this purpose. For Austin Powers, his superior is named Basil *Exposition*, with his surname used as a gag on his function in the film.

In animation, the sidekick character frequently serves this purpose (Olaf, the snowman in *Frozen*). There is even a specific archetype (see archetypes), the Herald, who serves this function in the Hero's Journey stories. If exposition is going to be delivered by dialog, it's more interesting to have the characters arguing or solving problems than just saying it. Minor conflicts between them get information across with humor and feels less *expository*. In *The Incredibles*, there is the added entertainment to exposition, when the culprit almost makes good on his escape while the characters are arguing (exposition for the viewer) (Figure 2.11).

Exposition can also be accomplished through *narration* (voice overs, unseen character speaking). Narration is generally reserved for dramatic stories focused on individual character growth (i.e., any movie with Morgan Freeman) as well as, documentaries, and educational stories. *Tip:* narration doesn't work when it is repeating the obvious; that which can be seen clearly in the scene.

Figure 2.11

Exposition works well with two characters in conflict. *The Incredibles*. (Copyright 2005, Disney • Pixar.)

Show Don't Tell

The frequently repeated axiom *Show Don't Tell* speaks to the effectiveness of images over words for exposition. *Star Wars* very effectively didn't resort to dialog to tell the viewer that Darth Vader is evil—showing Darth Vader choking someone (Figure 2.12). It isn't an image that is forgotten quickly. To communicate a character as a good person, they must be shown doing something good (i.e., *saving a cat*). It defines who they are; someone for the viewer to root for and like. In video games/VR, there is an additional option for getting information besides *showing*, there is *interacting*. Instead of the player being told or shown the story world, the player becomes oriented by interacting with the characters and environment.

Exposition is frequently thought of as a necessary evil. This perception originates from the writer's problem in differentiating what to include and what not to include. The evil part comes from when one doesn't know they put it in anyway which weighs down the story's pacing. Exposition falls into three categories:

Figure 2.12

Showing, not telling the audience that Darth Vader is evil. *Star Wars*. (Copyright 1977, 20th Century Fox.)

Figure 2.13

Iron Man, Robert Downey Jr. (Copyright 2008, Paramount.)

1. *Need to know now*! What is the critical information needed to start the story? Pete Docter, director of UP, asked himself "*What do you need to tell the story?*" The exposition challenge was "*that for the audience to really care and invest in this guy (Carl) through all of act 2 and 3, we needed to have a really strong reason for him to be doing what he's doing—and that's where the montage came in.*"[4] The exposition, showing Carl and Ellie from childhood to old age... resulted in one of the most memorable scenes of the movie.

2. *Need to know but not just yet...* information that is important to know later, when it will have the maximum effect. Previsualization Supervisor of the *Iron Man* movie, Kent Seki said "*Originally Tony Stark getting into the Iron Man Suit wasn't in the film. Director Jon Favreau, felt something was missing, that they needed to show the audience how the suit gets on*"[5] (Figure 2.13). This exposition became one of the highlights of the film. It added dramatic action as well as anticipation for what was to follow.

3. *Nice to know but not necessary information* (the bulk of information), it would add richness to the story but isn't relevant to the main story and most likely would slow the pacing. Most likely destined for the cutting room floor. No examples, because this information never makes it into a story.

When done well, exposition builds a foundation for a payoff that comes later in the story. Showing Neo, *The Matrix*, doing something out of the ordinary—

dodging bullets (Figure 2.14), sets up the viewer to accept that Neo can do something extraordinary later (*come back to life*). The viewer wouldn't have accepted this resurrection without the earlier exposition. It is important to lay the foundation so the viewer is already clued in for making connections subsequently in the story. It can be as simple as a match stick planted by Sid in Woody's Holster in *Toy Story*, used at the climax to light the rocket strapped to Buzz's back.

Early exposition also serves to maintain the flow of the story. If the viewer already knows crucial information about the situation or characters, then it doesn't interfere with the pacing as the action speeds up toward the end of the story. In *Burning Safari* (Figure 2.15), the directors opted for a slower exposition so the viewer would empathize with the characters before the roller-coaster action starts.

Exposition can be utilized to become a feature of how the story is told. In interactive games, this is the purpose of cut-scenes. With complex plots such as *Inception*, the first hour of the movie is exposition. In *Mission Impossible*, the exposition has become an integral part of the story… how will the new mission be communicated to Ethan Hunt and then self-destruct in a way the viewer hasn't seen before?

Figure 2.14

The Matrix, Keanu Reeves, 1999. (Copyright Warner Bros./Courtesy Everett Collection.)

Figure 2.15

Burning Safari. (Copyright 2006, William Trebutien.)

Inciting Incident

The inciting incident is the unexpected event or catalyst that throws the main character's life out of whack[6] (Figure 2.16). In Act 1, this sets the story in motion as the main character has to take action. The inciting incident is the first major turning point in the story. This signals the viewer that the story is moving from the setup in Act 1 to the increasing conflict of Act 2. It moves the story forward in three important ways:

Figure 2.16

The audience is shown the house flying which leads to Dorothy landing in *The Wizard of OZ*.

Figure 2.17

Inciting incident sets up the central question—Will Dorothy get back home in *The Wizard of OZ*?

- *It pushes the character out of their comfort zone into a different world.* The viewer has seen the character in their ordinary life and now witnesses the main character leave that life behind and move into a distinctly different world. Following the inciting incident, the main character makes a decision to take action—follow the yellow brick road.
- *Establishes what is at stake.* Shows the risk to the character and their world. Will the murderer be caught? (Crime Dramas); Will the patient live? (Medical Shows). Knowing what the consequences are triggers empathy in the viewer/player so they care about the main character and what could happen next.
- *Sets up the central question.* Which must be answered by the end of the story. Will Dorothy return home? (*The Wizard of OZ*). This is linked to the theme *There is no place like home* (Figure 2.17). The rest of the movie is Dorothy on her journey trying to get home.

Inciting incidents traditionally take place in the setup, near the end of Act 1, but can really take place anywhere in the Act I setup (Figure 2.18). In *Pacific Rim*, there are two inciting incidents; one of the inciting incidents takes place before the movie starts (world invaded by the Kaiju years earlier) and again after the movie starts with the final battle for earth with the Kaiju.

Figure 2.18

Location of the inciting incident, near the end of Act I.

The inciting incident corresponds with where the conflict is painful, where the external goal for the main character becomes clear, and when the story moves to a new location ("*Toto, we're not in Kansas anymore*").

Types of Inciting Incidents

- ***Action***—something happens… death, accident, assault, someone gets taken. *Toy Story* (Buzz falls out of window) (Figure 2.19), *Pacific Rim* (Kaiju invade earth), *Taken* (daughter kidnapped).
- ***New information***—this information changes a character's world; things will never be the same because of this information. *The Hobbit* (Bilbo Baggins is needed); *Mission Impossible* (new mission); *A Bug's Life* (grasshoppers want food) (Figure 2.20); *The Matrix* (red pill).
- ***Situational***—a series of incidents that orient the viewer. *Ratatouille* (gets separated and things get complicated) (Figure 2.21); *Hangover* (can't find friend); *Wedding Crashers* (get further entangled); *Finding Nemo, Office Space, Stripes* (fed up with their current life).

For additional examples, see *Inciting Incident Types* by Eric Bork[7] and *Inciting Incident Supercut—50 Movie Moments* by Paul Forte.[8]

Figure 2.19

Action—Buzz falls out window. (*Toy Story.* Copyright 1995, Disney • Pixar.)

Figure 2.20

Information—Grasshoppers want food. (*A Bug's Life*. Copyright 1997, Disney • Pixar.)

Figure 2.21

Situational—Remy gets separated from his rat pack. (*Ratatouille*. Copyright 2007, Disney • Pixar.)

What's at Stake?

The viewer needs to know *What's at stake?*[9] Why they should care about the character and their situation. What is the main character risking by not taking action... or by taking action? These fall into the categories of what human beings need to survive as well as thrive. Psychologist Abraham Maslow devised a hierarchy of human needs (Figure 2.22) that catalogs what we as human beings want and need.[10] While some of these are more important than others, they are all interrelated. *What's at stake* falls into two distinct categories: physical and emotional.

Survival (Figure 2.23)—life and death; the most basic instinct that the viewer can identify within a story. Human beings require air, food, water, shelter, clothing, and sleep. Health can also fall into this category. A viewer immediately relates with this self-preservation instinct (*Wile E. Coyote, Action Movies [James Bond], First Person Shooter [Battlefield]*). *Mad Max: Fury Road... "I'm reduced to a single instinct, survival."*[11]

Safety/Security—after survival comes the need to feel safe. This is a broad concept that is thought of as personal/physical safety and protection from accidents/injury. This can also include feeling safe from mental abuse or financial jeopardy.

Love/Belonging—humans have evolved a need to be socially connected; to be loved by family and friends, as well as belong to and be accepted in a social group. These groups may be religious, gangs, clubs, or cultural. Many sitcoms center around the need to belong (*Modern Family, Friends, Big Bang*). In *Toy Story 2*, the viewer could assume that Pixar wasn't about to kill off Woody or Buzz, so to keep the emotional connection the stakes were about being loved. Even if life and death is not at stake, it needs to feel that way. For not being loved can *feel* like life and death.

Figure 2.22

Abraham Maslow's *Hierarchy of Human Needs*.

Figure 2.23

Survival. (*Battlefield 4*. Copyright 2013, Electronic Arts.)

Respect is similar to love/belonging but respect must be earned. There are two versions of respect. First is external recognition which manifests itself as attention, appreciation, admiration, and status; to be respected for what one does. The second, more critical version, is self-respect that relies on competence, mastery, and self-confidence. Characters seek external fame and glory but this doesn't suffice until human beings can accept who they really are inside (internally). *Toy Story* (Woody loss of status when Buzz arrived), *Ratatouille* (Linguini, the cleanup boy, who wants to be a real chef), *Kung Fu Panda, She's Out of your League,* and *How to Train your Dragon.*

Self-Realization/Freedom—fulfilling our potential. To realize our talents and skills. It takes a certain level of freedom to become all we can be. *Ratatouille* (Remy, wants to really cook, what does it take to realize his dream?) (Figure 2.24), *Finding Nemo* (to become the best parent).

Self-transcendence—this is a higher form of self-realization. A person can't become fully realized until they give themselves to something higher. This may be altruism or spirituality. Connecting with a sense of order, something greater than ourselves. *Star Wars* (the force), *James Bond* (willing to sacrifice for the country and queen).

Need to know/understand—the innate curiosity of how things function. How things work? Why people do what they do? How society really works. A knowledge that makes things possible. *CSI, Back to the Future, Detective and Medical Stories, Inception, North by Northwest.*

Figure 2.24

Ratatouille. (Copyright 2007, Disney • Pixar.)

Story World

Crossing the Threshold, from the Hero's Journey, is the transition where the main character leaves their *ordinary world* and crosses over into a *different world* where the real story takes place. This changeover comes at the end of Act 1, following the inciting incident. The main character has to leave home (often reluctantly) to get their life back under control. This moves the story into a new world where the majority of the action takes place. Subconsciously, viewers expect this story world; they want to be taken to places they have never been before.

This new story world visually reinforces the change in direction that was started by the inciting incident. Stories in screen media are told through pictures; changing the setting reinforces a viewer's awareness that things are truly different.

Though the story generally takes place in a new setting, a new story world can result from a significant change in the original world (i.e., new perception, enemies arrive, finding love, and job change). A monster appearing is not uncommon: *Jaws* (a shark comes to town), *Pacific Rim* (the Kaiju come to earth), *Avengers: Age of Ultron*, *Jurassic World* (dinosaur escapes). Crossing into this different story world may be blocked by Threshold Guardians (external), our fears (internal), or physical barriers such as doors, gates, bridges, walls, or landscapes. This has a long tradition going back to the classic *Odyssey* by Homer (Figure 2.25) as well as the childhood favorite, *Three Billy Goats Gruff*, with the troll blocking their way across the bridge.

Figure 2.25

Odysseus and the Sirens by J. W. Waterhouse.

The viewer innately understands that when the main character leaves home and enters into this new story world, it comes with new conflict. In *Avatar*, Jake, a paraplegic Marine, continues to not only jump back and forth from the mining base's medical bay to Pandora's (the planet) surface but also alternates between his human form and his Na'vi hybrid form (Figure 2.26). Location and character transformations are used frequently to signal emotional changes in the story. In *Mass Effect 3* (Figure 2.27), the video game utilizes level changes as narrative opportunities. The physical challenges of a location change can delineate its own narrative in video games.[13]

Figure 2.26

Moving between the character's ordinary world and the story world. *Avatar*. (Copyright 2009, 20th Century Fox.)

Figure 2.27

Levels as narrative opportunities. *Mass Effect 3*. (Copyright 2012, Electronic Arts.)

Story Question

The inciting indent raises the *central story question* (What is the story really about?). Everything that happens in the story relates to a central question/theme that keeps the story focused. The central question is raised in the beginning, and this central question must be answered by the end of the story. Knowing the central question clarifies for the writer where the story starts and stops. In the movie *Jaws*, the central question is more than who will survive, Brody or the Shark? (Figure 2.28). At its core is the question... *Are we really safe (to go back in the water)?* The action ends when this central dramatic question has been answered.

The most important questions are linked to the *What's at stake question...* life/death, safety, love, self-respect, etc. *E.T.*, Will he get home? *Gravity*, Will she get back to earth, alive? *The Little Mermaid*, Will Ariel become a real girl? In *Inception*, the goal, will they successfully plant an idea by using dreams, is not the central question. The central dramatic question is *will Cobb get to see his kids again*? When Cobb was reunited with his kids, then the movie can end. If the central question is not answered at the end of the story, it results in one of the major sins of storytelling... that the story lacks meaning. If this occurs, the viewer will feel that their time has been wasted and that the story had no point.

The most common types of story questions are... Will they succeed? Will they reach their goal? Will they get what they want? Most narrative questions are variations of this type which revolve around external goals. The secondary questions, the more emotional questions (internal) can often be most important to the story: What will happen when they find out the truth? How will they react? What will people think of me?

Francis Glebas advocates that question-asking is a powerful persuasion device because questions structure our decision-making process. They do this by directing our thoughts about the issues at hand and by implying the range of possible answers—*We are going to need a bigger boat (Jaws)*.[14]

Figure 2.28

The fundamental question in Jaws is... who will survive? Brody or the Shark? (Copyright 1975, Universal.)

The central question drives the story forward but it is the *narrative questions* that keep a viewer's interest during the story: How will they escape? Will they find each other? Will they do it? Will they fight or flee? Narrative questions are a fundamental story tool to focus the viewer's attention. In *Oktapodi*, the central question may be the fate of the Octopus but the real strength of the piece is that there are narrative questions asked and answered throughout the animation (Figure 2.29).

Narrative questions are asked and answered throughout the story. Raising questions stimulates curiosity in the viewer, especially when the answer is not revealed immediately. Delaying the answer[2] is such an effective technique that it is now routine to raise a question just before going to a commercial on television. Questions that are asked but not immediately answered keep the viewer emotionally engaged. How narrative questions are poised is unique to each medium (books, plays, films, games, and VR) as well as each story.

Act I is just that… the first act. Steven Spielberg cautions *"People have forgotten how to tell a story. Stories don't have a middle or an end any more. They usually have a beginning that never stops beginning."*[15]

Narrative Questions   Narrative Answers

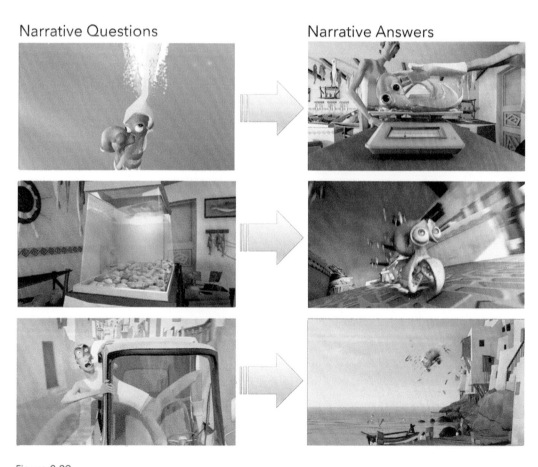

Figure 2.29

The question the audience wants answered—Will the Octopus be saved? Oktapodi, http://www.oktapodi.com, Courtesy of Emud Mokhberi.

References

1. A. K. Aristotle, *Poetics* (London, Oxford University Press, 2013).
2. M. Arndt, *Beginnings: Setting a story in motion, Toy Story 3* (Pixar Animation Studios, Walt Disney Pictures, 2014), Blu-Ray Edition, Supplemental Disc.
3. R. McKee, *Story: Substance, Structure, Style and the Principles of Screenwriting* (New York, Harper-Collins, 1997), 336.
4. P. Docter, Up—Pete Docter and Jonas Rivera interview by Rob Carnevale, *indieLONDON*, 2001, http://www.indielondon.co.uk/Film-Review/up-pete-docter-and-jonas-rivera-interview
5. K. Seki, *Visual Effects, Iron Man* (Paramount Studios, 2008), DVD Supplemental Disc.
6. J. H. Lawson, *Theory and Technique of Playwriting* (New York, Hill & Wang, 1960), 44.
7. E. Bork, Inciting Incident Types, *flying wrestler*, November 3, 2012, http://www.flyingwrestler.com/2012/11/inciting-incident/
8. P. Forte, Inciting Incident Supercut—50 Movie Moments, *YouTube*, May 24, 2012, https://www.youtube.com/watch?v=uXbALHEEjxg
9. C. Vogler, *The Writer's Journey: Mythic Structure for Storytellers & Screenwriters* (Ann Arbor, Michigan, Michael Wiese Productions, 1992), 110.
10. A. Maslow, The instinctual nature of basic needs, *J. Personality*, 1954, 22, 326–47.
11. T. Hardy, *The Making of Mad Max: Fury Road* (Mad Max: Fury Road, Warner Brothers Distribution, 2015), Blu-Ray Disc.
12. P. Docter, Pete Docter on making 'Inside Out' work: 'How do I make this resonate?' by Drew McWeeny, Hitflix, May 27, 2015, http://www.hitfix.com/motion-captured/pete-docter-on-making-inside-out-work-how-do-i-make-this-resonate
13. H. Jenkins, Game design as narrative architecture, In: N. Wardrip-Fruin and P. Harrigan (eds), *First Person: New Media as Story, Performance, and Game* (Cambridge, Massachusetts, MIT Press, 2004), 44.
14. F. Glebas, *Directing the Story, Professional Storytelling and Storyboarding Techniques for Live Action and Animation* (Boston, Massachusetts, Focal Press, 2009), 52.
15. S. Spielberg, *Masterclass with Spielberg—On His Films and Film Techniques*, *Jamuura*, October 14, 2015, http://www.jamuura.com/blog/steven-spielberg-on-his-films-and-film-techniques/

3
Middle

Middles

What happens in the *middle* of the story? … rising conflict, this is the key. After the inciting incident, the story enters Act II, the longest act. The challenge is to keep moving the story forward while holding the audience's interest (wondering what will happen next). The primary story tools in this act include anticipation, curiosity, suspense, and surprise. These keep the audience wondering what will happen next.

This is all done while also maintaining continuity through cause-and-effect action: a character does something, encounters conflict, reacts, tries something new, encounters conflict, reacts … (cause-and-effect). The biggest challenge is delivering story information to the audience and at the same time connecting the action to the central dramatic question. Act II is defined by increasing levels of difficulty:

Figure 3.1

Linguini teams up with Remy and everyone loves their food, *Ratatouille*. (Copyright 2007, Disney • Pixar.)

1. Main character enters a new setting, tries to figure out what is going on, and makes a plan (must be specific and visual). As the main character continues to pursue their goal, the viewer learns about the main character's inner baggage they are carrying around with them. This baggage is making life difficult in moving forward, causing all sorts of complications.
2. Next comes a new conflict, things don't go well and main character abandons the plan they thought would work. For the benefit of the viewer, these conflicts are "tests" to show what the character is made of. The journey now requires a change of plans as a new course of action is decided upon.
3. At the midpoint of the story the conflict escalates but there is some success with this new plan. The main character now sticks with this new direction and passes the point of no return (Figure 3.1). Unfortunately, the success is short lived; things get worse instead of better.
4. Approaching the end of Act II, a crisis is reached as everything hits rock bottom. The villain, the adversary/opposition, has the upper hand with the main character having no choice but to risk everything. This results in a crisis that has the story heading straight for a climax in the next act.

The viewer needs to feel the conflict (keep them hooked). It isn't necessary to have the world coming to an end... just that the main character believes that *their* world will end (*...if she leaves me then what will I do?*). To keep their interest, "what's at stake" must be *progressively increased* in Act II.

Using the right story tools makes all the difference. Suspense (dictionary) not knowing, sustains interest and makes the viewers ask "what happens next?" Surprise, just when an audience thinks they have a handle on the story something they hadn't anticipated happens (example). These gaps keep opening between our expectations and the result—the way things actually turnout.[1] In the middle the viewer should be cluing in to the realization that *Things are not what they seem* (the foundation of all stories).

A checklist for the middle will include the following: (1) a reaction to a new situation, (2) main character has formulated a plan (and then had to change it), (3) conflict is increasing, (4) not only the conflict but also the stakes are getting higher, (5) midpoint is the point of no return, and (6) everything culminates in a crisis (Figure 3.2).

The midpoint of the story serves a solid checkpoint: this is a physical (or emotional) point of no return, conflict has become personal, there has been (or about to be) a new revelation, there has been another opportunity for the character to change (don't forget change only comes about through failure), and time is running out to really reach the goal (this increases tension). All the while, the goal continues to be specific and visual for the viewer.

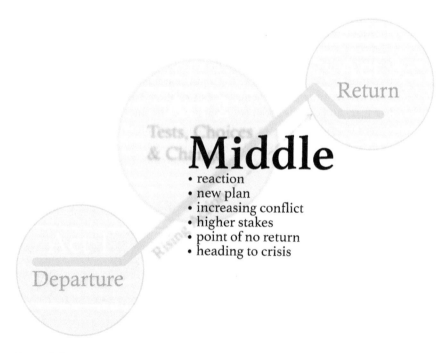

Figure 3.2

The Middle of the story.

Types of Conflict

Conflict is whatever stands in the way of the main character and their goal[2]... it can be a person, a physical barrier, even themselves. Conflict creates the drama and action; it is the key ingredient that drives the story forward. No conflict—no story. There are various levels of conflict that range from incompatibility (viewpoints, ideas), quarrels (discord), physical collisions, to all out fighting escalating to war. The seriousness of conflict is directly linked to motivation, the causes, what starts it.

- **Conflict with others**—(1) a character, (2) a group, or (3) the supernatural. In *Guardians of the Galaxy*, Peter Quill has conflict in every possible way; with characters—Rocket, Gamora, Drax, etc., with groups—the Ravagers and Nova Corps, and with a supernatural power—the Infinity Stone. It is inevitable that two characters that have mutually exclusive goals (only one person can get what they want) will butt heads. Conflict with a group may involve a bureaucracy, a gang, their family, the military, or the government (Luke and the Evil Empire). Conflict that plays out on multiple levels—simultaneously—generates more interest, increases the complexity in the story.
- **Conflict with nature** can be as straightforward as trying to get from one place to another (games—*Monument Valley, Portal 2, Journey*—Figure 3.3) or as epic as disaster films *Gravity, Titanic* (Figure 3.4). Disaster films result in an intense situation with the audience glued to how the character will react. Often embedded in such situations is the relational conflict (will they leave someone behind?) *The Revenant, Gravity, Ice Age, Titanic, Call of Duty*, etc.
- **Conflict within themselves**—inner conflicts are psychological barriers that must be dealt with before the main character can confront the external barriers in front of them. We can relate to this because we all have had fears and doubts about confrontation. The internal conflict is almost always the result of character flaws, and unhealed insecurities from the past. The challenge in digital media is to design these conflicts visually (Peter Quill lost his mother) *Batman, Deadpool, The Matrix*.

Figure 3.3

Journey. (Copyright 2012, thatgamecompany. com)

Figure 3.4

Conflict with nature. *Titanic*, 1997. (TM & Copyright 20th Century Fox Film Corp. All rights reserved/Courtesy Everett Collection.)

Elements of Conflict[3]

1. *Conflict must build* throughout the story. It has to develop, get more intense.
2. *Conflict must be engaging* for the viewer; we need to care. The viewer wants to know how committed the main character is to their goal (*more than anything else in their life* works best). Are the stakes high enough... do they feel like life and death? The main character is only as interesting as the conflict they struggle against.
3. *Conflict must be well-matched...* like a tug-a-war. One side cannot be stronger than the other; there would be no suspense as to outcome.[1]
4. *Conflict must be nasty!* Most people are fundamentally good so it is difficult to create stories that really treat the characters badly. Eric Edson says "*it is your job to figure out the very worst things that can possibly befall your hero, then find the most shocking ways to make those very bad things happen*"[4] (Figure 3.5).
5. *Conflict must be visual.* If the conflict can't be shown, then it is the type of conflict that works best in a novel.
6. *Conflict must not be predictable.* Every story must offer unexpected turns, twists, and surprises.
7. *Conflict must be believable.* Stories start to fall apart when they have lost touch with the rules of the story's fictional world. Audiences will believe many things if they have been set up to accept that the story world really operates that way. Being clever is not a substitute for consistency in this new story world.
8. *Conflict resolved in a meaningful way.* What did it all mean? Conflict is linked to a motivation.

Figure 3.5

Gladiator, Russell Crowe (right), 2000. (Copyright DreamWorks/ Courtesy Everett.)

Increasing Conflict

The middle is where each succeeding conflict becomes more intense. Each conflict reveals a bit more about the characters and their situation. For if there is no increase in the conflict… it is just another conflict among many; viewers learn nothing new, the conflict stays at the same level. A story will lose its momentum when the conflict becomes repetitive. Each subsequent crisis must rise on an ascending scale or it becomes redundant and the viewer/player loses interest. There isn't much point to additional levels in video games if their difficulty is pretty much the same. Successful stories incorporate *Increasing Conflict*. This is also known as rising action or progressive complications where the conflicts get increasingly more difficult to overcome.

In *The Martian*, the main character (Mark) is assumed to have died and has been left behind… stranded on Mars. However, he wakes up and must survive. He devises a way to grow food but then his food supply is destroyed; next he must leave everything behind to get to a different rocket module but he has limited time; next he must blast off into space with little guidance or protection… each trial comes with greater and greater risk (as well as less time to complete each task) (Figure 3.6).

Story pioneer Lajos Egri states that *"each conflict causes the one after it. Each is more intense than the one before."*[5] Such conflicts increase not just the drama but also reveal increasingly more about the characters, their values, and stakes just keep getting higher. These include complications along the way that expose personality clashes—characters who hit heads because they both want the same thing or find they are stuck with each other wanting different things in life (unity of opposites). In *The Martian*, his crew's priorities are to save Mark Watney, while the NASA program director's priority is to keep the space program safe.

There is a fundamental story axiom—*a character's true self is only revealed by their response to conflict.*[6] No character will expose more than they have to. Thus it is only by increasing the conflict, making the choices harder and harder, that the viewer learns more and more about the characters. As the viewer learns more, so too does the story's meaning deepen. In *Jaws,* the emotion intensifies (characters and viewer) as the conflict becomes increasingly personal… when the shark first eats a swimmer the Sheriff doesn't risk anything; when they find a great white shark tooth in a sunken boat he is obliged to risk his job; but it is not until the shark almost eats his son is he compelled to put his own life on the line.

Figure 3.6

The challenges to survive get increasingly difficult in *The Martian*. (Copyright 2015, 20th Century Fox Film Corp.)

Increasing the conflict doesn't automatically mean it must get violent or physical. For the viewer will stop caring if it is exclusively violent (and in turn tiresome). Personality conflicts can be just as emotionally draining as physical conflicts. Audiences respond to emotional conflict for they can relate to the friction inherent in their own day-to-day encounters with others.

It isn't always the case that conflict is unpleasant (though that is generally the case). Conflict can have a positive outcome. Ed Hooks suggests that to get out of a negative mindset about conflict, think of conflict as a *negotiation*.[7] The outcomes from a negotiation can be good, bad, and all shades of gray, which makes it less likely the viewer can predict how the things will be resolved.

Conflict isn't a series of obstacles to be checked off a list or hurdles to be overcome before the hero reaches their goal. There must be doubt in the mind of the viewer how things will turn out. If all the obstacles are successfully overcome, then the viewer ceases to stay engaged since the character apparently can overcome anything thrown at them.

Video games inherently have challenges, goals, and obstacles[8] with varying degrees of difficulty built into the game play. Progress always remains in doubt as players have at one time or another been stymied by some obstacle they couldn't overcome, at least initially. These seemingly unsurmountable barriers in FPS or Run & Gun add to the potential narrative directions (Figure 3.7).

> *Does the conflict build or does it just become repetitive?*

Figure 3.7

Narrative elements *Cuphead*. (Copyright 2016, StudioMDHR.)

Turning Points/Reversals

Turning points are those unexpected twists that turn the direction of the story. They keep the viewer engaged, wondering what will happen next. Turning points are also known as reversals, action points (Seger),[9] plot points (Field)[10]... but all perform the same functions.

Figure 3.8

Turn a scene with action—Lightsaber duel. *Star Wars.* (Copyright 1977, 20th Century Fox.)

- *Change the direction* of the story. This can be a little or a lot—the Reversal, a 180° change in direction; one of the more powerful story devices.
- Fuel *insight* into the character. How committed is the main character to their goal? Must achieve the goal at all costs, or it would be nice to achieve the goal.
- Increase *curiosity* which results in the viewer wondering what will happen next.
- *Raise the stakes* which intensifies the action as the consequences of failure just got higher.
- Add *surprise* (what just happened?).
- Reaffirm the *central question* (love, home, revenge) to keep the viewer focused on what it all means in the end. The strongest stories incorporate this reminder to the audience.

There can be many turning points in a major movie or game but even small stories have two turning points that need to happen... the *Inciting Incident* (forces character out of their ordinary life) and *crisis/climax* (forces character to take final action to resolve the story). These turning points come at the end of Acts: Act 1 (Inciting Incident) and end of Act II (crisis [leading to climax]). A minor turning point is a complication (things get tougher). It increases complexity but it is more a diversion as opposed to a dramatic turning point that changes story direction.

To turn a scene, there are only two routes[11]:

Figure 3.9

Turn a scene through revelation—*Luke, I am your father.* The Empire Strikes Back. (Copyright 1980, 20th Century Fox.)

- *Action* (i.e., a lightsaber duel) (Figure 3.8)
- *Revelation* ("*Luke, I am your father*") (Figure 3.9)

If choosing revelation, look at the backstory for past secrets to reveal at a critical juncture in the story. A couple start to fight, they argue, she slaps him, "*It's over*" (action), he responds "*I've been seeing someone else*" (revelation).

Today, reversals are a part of the Hollywood narrative structure anticipated by the viewer. Thus, they can easily become a cliché if they are not integrated into the story or if a sufficient amount of preparation (hinting earlier) isn't setup for the viewer.[12] For turning points are carefully planned, not sprinkled to add interest. They are effective strategies for transitioning between scenes and acts.

In *Jaws*, the shark punches a hole in boat and it starts to sink. Up until that point they were chasing the shark, now the shark is after them. This turning point highlights the central question in this story... *are humans really in charge of their world or is it all an illusion?* Viewers match their life experiences against their story expectations and the inevitable twists and turns that emerge.

Five Story Turning Points[13] (Figure 3.10)

- *Inciting incident*—the main character is compelled to change their current life and undertake a new direction as they deal with new circumstances as well as a new environment. This marks the transition from Act I into Act II. (Bilbo Baggins leaves his home and village [*The Hobbit, the Unexpected Journey*]; Katniss volunteers and is whisked away from District 12 [*The Hunger Games*].)
- *Change of plans*—main character thought getting what they want would entail just completing a few tasks… but it has become a bit more difficult than they thought. Now, there is the need to come up with an entirely new plan… Remy and Linguini agree to work together.
- *Point of no return* (midpoint)—new plan seems to be working, main character burns the bridges to their past which means there is no going back now. They commit wholeheartedly to their new direction, which means the risk is now greater if they don't succeed. (Gladiator—Maximus is winning the crowd over in the arena.)
- *Major setback*—things have gotten more complicated. The stakes have changed; things are now even riskier than at the midpoint. Things are definitely not going well. Their adversary/villain has gained the upper hand and the plan that was supposed to lead to success has fallen apart. There is only one choice… to risk it all and confront their adversary.
- *Crisis/Climax*—final turning point that speeds up the action and forces the biggest confrontation. (Final fight [*Gladiator*], meal served to food critic [*Ratatouille*].)

At these major turning points, reversals, 180° change in direction, are most effective. Whether it be physical or emotional, the change in direction goes from good to bad or bad to good (*Jaws*, beach is safe, then the shark shows up). Such changes are so dramatic that viewers will experience the same emotions as the characters.

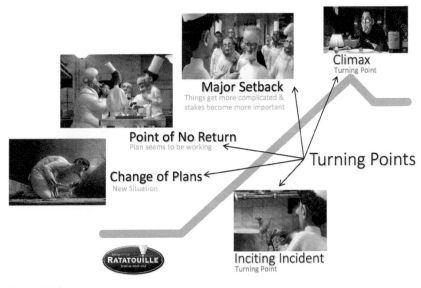

Figure 3.10

Turning points in a story, *Ratatouille*. (Copyright Disney • Pixar.)

Cause and Effect

Things don't happen randomly in a story. There is always a cause (even if not immediately seen) to every result, the effect; which in turn becomes the next cause for the next effect. Keeping a story on track boils down to cause-and-effect relationships. This is so fundamental that it is given in almost all dramatic story definitions. This strong cause-and-effect relationship is played out from beginning to end—otherwise it would be "*just one damn thing after another.*"[14]

Viewers use these cause-and-effect exchanges to understand the story. It is their toolbox when they get confused, anticipating that everything will become clear shortly. There is always a reason, whether the viewer can immediately pinpoint it or not. It will make sense in hindsight to the viewer... if it has been set up well. Stories are said to be *driven by emotion, but organized by logic.*

Well told stories are a balancing act. They can't be so logical that the story is predictable (viewer rapidly loses interest), while at the same time not so arbitrary, that the lack of cause-and-effect confuses the viewer. There must be a logic at the story's core as the emotional and physical events unfold. Can't just put something in "*because it's a cool idea.*"[15] This is where stories often fall apart... where things just happen out of the blue.

Cause-and-effect is where dramatic stories and real life differ. In real life, there are a million unrelated things happening at the same time. But in a story (animation, VFX, games), only those things that are related, that are pertinent to story, are revealed. For there is a limited time frame for the viewer to engage with the media. Everything included must be there for a reason. Every scene must lead to the next one, which in turn leads to the next one and so on (Figure 3.11).

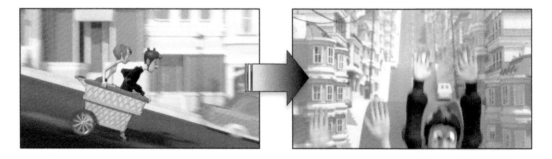

Figure 3.11

Cause and Effect, *Jinxy Jenkins, Lucky Lou* created by Michael Bidinger, Michelle Kwon, and Sarah Kambara.

Just because the cause may result in an expected effect doesn't mean that *effect* must happen. There are a myriad of different reactions and subsequent responses a cause might evoke. This innate sense of cause-and-effect is often used to set up a gap between what the viewer anticipated was going to happen and what really happened instead.[16] Creating anticipation in the viewer and then switching the outcome is a powerful tool.

There is also an internal cause-and-effect—the *Why* a character does what they do. A character's flaws, desires, fears, choices all impact the *action, the* specific *cause* and in turn the myriad of different reactions that action might cause. Audiences embrace that appearance of free will, though cause and effect has an inevitability to it in hindsight. In *Star Wars: Episode VII*, we see Rey approach Luke at the end of the movie. This leaves the audience imaging a myriad of reactions that will open the next *Star Wars: Episode VIII* (Figure 3.12).

Every scene generates momentum when connected in a cause-and-effect relationship... when one thing leads to another, that thing leads to another, and so on. Linda Seger suggests looking at momentum as more than just cause-and-effect, but as *action-reaction* sequences.[17] That *action* comes out of a conflict that is not just visual and dramatic, but demands a *reaction*. It is the reaction that grabs a viewer's attention—they want to know what the character will do next. It is the resultant curiosity, crucial to the story's momentum, that is always challenging to sustain in Act II.

Figure 3.12

What will happen next? Rey and Luke, *Star Wars*: Episode VIII. (Copyright 2015, Walt Disney Pictures.)

Crisis

Near the end of Act II, the conflict builds to a definitive crisis. It is the point where a decision must be made by the main character, it can't be avoided and everything is at stake. The final crisis forces the main character to take one action or another to achieve their objective.[18] All the options having been exhausted… but *one*. In turn, this unavoidable decision reveals not only more about who the character really is but also reinforces the story's theme—what the story has been about.

There are several purposes to the crisis (1) raise the stakes, (2) force a decision, (3) reveal more about the characters, and (4) push the story from the middle (Act II) into the resolution stage (Act III) of the story. The crisis is the anticipated precursor to the climax. Although more often than not they are separate, it's common for crisis and climax to coincide in short stories.

The crisis is the low point before the climax. Where the main character will feel the most disillusioned, disheartened, cynical, angry, betrayed, and vulnerable.[19] To pull out of this descent,[2] the main character is forced to make a choice, that forces this crisis, requiring them to confront their internal demons before they can go on.

In an action genre, the expectation is that things will continue to fall apart and the main character will face overwhelming odds. At which point they must decide to risk it all or give up. At this crisis point, the worst thing that could happen in the story should happen. How will the Incredibles family defeat Syndrome when he has apparently already defeated them? (Figure 3.13). In *Avatar*, the Na'vi's home/tree is destroyed; how will they fight such superior forces? The crisis is the biggest turning point of the story.

Figure 3.13

The Incredibles, Syndrome, 2004. (Copyright Walt Disney/Courtesy Everett Collection.)

3. Middle

For Lajos Egri[20] and William Archer,[21] the structure of story is as a series of mini-crises. These are not the do or die situation of the final crisis but conceived as a succession of "should I continue or give up" barriers, external or internal obstacles along the way. These mini-crises require the main character to decide, again and again, what course of action to take next. At each mini-crisis, the audience learns a little bit more about the main character: are they really committed to their goal, will they fight or flee? The middle can be seen as a series of (increasing) crises, climaxes, resolutions. One crisis begets another crisis. These escalate and intensify the action until the final crisis is reached. The final crisis is the sum total of all the preceding crises, confirming the theme.

Lajos Egri goes as far to assert that stories must open with a crisis.[22] That the most engaging stories start at that point in one's life where they have reached a level of crisis. Where a *crisis decision* is imminent and the characters are ready to take *action*. A young couple may threaten to break up but the story doesn't really start until one of them *is about to make that decision; when the point of crisis is reached.* Though starting at the moment of crisis in a person's life is frequently considered a cliché; it is effective. It quickly catches the viewer's attention, every time. To mitigate it feeling like a cliché, the character must be compelled to take action—Luke must rescue the princess who has been taken, James Bond must stop the potential carnage by various villains (Figure 3.14), or Marlin must protect Nemo after his family is killed (*Finding Nemo*).

Complications are not as severe as a crisis. A complication doesn't pose an immediate threat. However, a sufficient number of complications does add up to a crisis. Complications are something that just makes it tougher, more difficult, for the main character to move forward—their car has broken down. Like a crisis, unexpected complications add suspense as to whether this will be the straw that breaks the camel's back with the main character giving up. Complications come in the form of characters, circumstances, events, mistakes, misunderstandings, or discoveries.

Figure 3.14

A James Bond always opens with some form of crisis. *Casino Royale.* (Copyright 2006, Columbia.)

References

1. K. T. Rowe, *Write That Play* (New York, Funk & Wagnalls Company, 1939), 27.
2. M. Hauge, *Writing Screenplays That Sell* (New York, Harper Collins, 2011), 62.
3. P. Lucey, *Story Sense: Writing Story and Script for Feature Films and Television* (New York, McGraw-Hill, 1996), 53.
4. E. Edson, *The Story Solution* (Saline, Michigan, Michael Wiese Productions, 2011), 37–48.
5. L. Egri, *The Art of Dramatic Writing* (New York, Simon & Schuster, 1960), 219.
6. M. Hauge, *Writing Screenplays That Sell* (New York, Harper Collins, 2011), 44.
7. E. Hooks, *Acting for Animators* (London, Routledge, 2011), 44.
8. E. Skolnick, *Video Game Storytelling* (Berkeley, California, Watson-Guptill Publications, 2014),
9. L. Seger, *Good Script Great*, 62.
10. S. Field, *Screenplay*, 10.
11. R. McKee, *Story*, 243.
12. L. J. Cowgill, *Plotting*, 71.
13. M. Hauge, *Writing Screenplays*, 115.
14. K. Schulz, *Being Wrong* (TED 2011).
15. E. Coats, Pixar's 22 Rules of Storytelling, *Aerogramme Writers' Studio*, March 7, 2013, http://www.aerogrammestudio.com/2013/03/07/pixars-22-rules-of-storytelling
16. L. Cron, *Wired for Story* (Berkeley, California, Ten Speed Press, 2012), 152.
17. L. Seger, *Good Script Great*, 62.
18. R. McKee, *Story*, 303.
19. D. Marks, *Inside Story*, 285.
20. L. Egri, *The Art of Dramatic Writing*, 219.
21. W. Archer, *Play-Making* (New York, Dover Publications, 1960), 183.
22. L. Egri, *The Art of Dramatic Writing*, 34.

4
Endings

Endings

Successful stories require an ending that feels *satisfying* for the audience. There is an implicit understanding between director and viewer that the ending will be worth the viewer's time. Viewers today tolerate chronological displacement, disruptive editing, and fourth-wall breaking but they still "*want closure, a catharsis, some kind of assurance that what we have seen has meaning and takes place within a morally ordered imaginative universe.*"[1] Stories require an ending that is not ambiguous. A clear ending as to whether the goal has been achieved or not is needed. One where all relevant narrative questions have been answered—a once and for all outcome.

Act III's elements include a final twist, climax, completion of the character arc, a climax/obligatory scene, and a resolution. Together these make up Act III, the story's ending. At this point, there is no time to introduce anything new (i.e., new characters, new locations). To do so would disrupt the pacing and lessen the emotional impact. There should be a final twist, a surprise, that is both logical and not completely unexpected. Woody and Buzz have a rocket to propel them back to the moving van… as well as a match and Buzz's helmet as magnifying glass. Groot has the capacity to grow himself around the characters to protect them (*Guardians of the Galaxy*) (Figure 4.1).

Act III is the final confrontation. Everything has been tried, all plots and subplots collide, there is only one option left for the main character. This comes together in the climax. A sequence in which the main character faces their greatest challenge (needs to be visual). Frequently, the big showdown is between the main character and their archrival. This is the scene that the viewer has been waiting to see, often referred to as the *Obligatory Scene*.[2] Ever since the thematic problem was introduced, the viewer has anticipated this scene, which is needed to resolve the situation once and for all.

ACT III should be the peak emotional scene in the story. In an ideal scenario, this climax/obligatory scene will both symbolize and reinforce the theme (family, love, etc.). The climax isn't typically the final scene, there is still a resolution to follow, though in short films (and certain feature films) they are one and the same scene (i.e., *Thelma & Louise, Butch Cassidy*). In short films, there isn't time for a full climax and this is usually omitted in favor of a final twist or revelation.[3]

Figure 4.1

Guardians of the Galaxy, from left: Dave Bautista, Zoe Saldana, Groot (voice: Vin Diesel), Chris Pratt, 2014. (Copyright Walt Disney Studios Motion Pictures/Courtesy Everett Collection.)

At the Resolution, it is expected that the viewer will see how the character has changed and that this transformation has made their final triumph possible. The viewer is shown the new world of the character (Figure 4.2). Relevant plot threads are tied up.

Act III will often contain a major reveal—something the audience or character hasn't known, triggering degrees of insights for the viewer. Which in turn stimulate realizations by the viewer that unify earlier story elements. At the end of *Guardians*, the viewer is shown Gamora and Will together (love has triumphed), Will's mom left him another tape, and Groot can regrow himself from a twig… everyone is now back together, as an extended family (Figure 4.3).

It is only at the end of the story, when everything comes together, that the viewer truly understands what has only been hinted at earlier—the real motivation behind the actions taken by characters. Alma Coin's selfish reason behind her support of Katniss and the resistance (*Hunger Games*)? Kyle Reese was John Connor's real father, which is why he was selected to go back in time to protect Sarah Connor (*The Terminator*). Only by trusting the force will Luke be able to destroy the Death Star (*Star Wars*).

Not necessarily a happy ending, but at a minimum… redemptive. Linda Cowgill stresses that "*Given a choice, give your movie a happy ending: Audiences go to movies and watch television to see problems solved, and to identify with characters that overcome the seemingly insurmountable obstacles they face.*"[3] If there is not a happy ending, then it must not be a defeated ending… "*The audience is willing to hear that life is hard, life is sad, or even that life is tragic, but they don't want to hear that life is s**t.*"[4] At the end, the viewer doesn't just realize what the story has been about all along, they feel it to.

Figure 4.2

Up. (Copyright 2009 Disney • Pixar.)

Figure 4.3

The theme is realized at the end; *family is where you find it—Guardians of the Galaxy,* from left: Groot (voice: Vin Diesel), Dave Bautista, 2014. (Copyright Walt Disney Studios Motion Pictures/Courtesy Everett Collection.)

Climax

The final conflict, the climax, follows on the heels of the crisis (end of Act II). For the main character to reach their goal, their archrival, who *"stands in the way, must be beaten, outsmarted, overcome, knocked out, killed, destroyed, won over, or neutralized in some way."*[5] The climax—a showdown, a confrontation—is when the main character and their adversary square off. It is the final battle between the Incredibles and Syndrome (*The Incredibles*).

At the climax all the action is concentrated into a specific event—a scene with the greatest intensity. There are exemptions but the climax will invariably involve the final confrontation between the main character and their adversary (Po and Tai Lung [*Kung Fu Panda*], Harry Potter and Voldemort, Iron Man and Captain America [*Civil War*] Figure 4.4).

If done well, the climax integrates all the previous conflicts while at the same time reinforcing the theme (i.e., love, family, revenge). The purpose of the climax is to make the theme tangible as it focuses all the previous action to complete the story.

The climax is the obligatory scene, the *"one which the audience foresees and desires, and the absence of which it may with reason resent."*[6] An obligatory scene is the event the audience knows it must see before the story can end. The scene is obligatory because the viewer has been anticipating this moment. This expectation, is both a powerful device to keep the viewer engaged as well as an obligation. It is so important that by omitting it will not only incur the viewer's resentment but also stigmatizes the writer as having chosen the undramatic or less dramatic way of completing the story. Thus, to bring that closure, the climax must be both visual and emotional for the audience. It doesn't have to be violent (fight or battle), but the action must be a *definitive*; someone walking out of the door (for the last time)—a clear, and memorable scene. In keeping it visual, focus on showing a character's emotion. This is effective in enabling the viewer to relate to the conflict.

Figure 4.4

Final confrontation—Po and Tai Lung in *Kung Fu Panda*. (Copyright 2008, DreamWorks Animation.)

In cinematic stories, there is often a revelation, just before the climax, where the main character learns why they have been encountering so many difficulties. This will either create further doubt in themselves, or strengthen their resolve to free themselves and confront the problem straight on. It is here the main character must confront their flaws and inner demons, and make a change. This transformation is not without a price to be paid, a sacrifice… a shedding of their former persona in order to become a new person.

Sometimes only the viewer is let in on the reason why this new insight has aroused this final act of courage.[7] This reveal serves two purposes: how and why the main character can now succeed as well as reminding the viewer of the theme (again). While dialog can support this change, it needs a visible image. *Theme:* Gru has an epiphany about what is valuable in life (*Despicable Me*), William figures out what really defines him (*The Hurt Locker*), and Neo realizes that the matrix is just computer code (*The Matrix*) (Figure 4.5).

The climax becomes a reference point for the efficacy of every element in the plot. If any of the scenes are not leading to this climax, they need to be reworked or discarded.[8] Marks emphasizes *"there can be no ambiguity to the climax of your screenplay, your hero achieves her outer motivation, or she doesn't, but you can't leave the issue unresolved."*[9] The climax is the ultimate test which brings the conflict to a resolution. It is at the climax, we look for the defeated hero to turn victorious—Neo obliterates Agent Smith. For further specifics on climax, go to pages 133–145, *Writing Short Films*, Linda Cowgill.[10]

Figure 4.5

The Matrix, 1999. (Copyright Warner Bros./Courtesy Everett Collection.)

Resolution

The resolution (falling action, the realization) follows the climax. The fates of the main characters are resolved as the unfinished subplots are wrapped up. A new status quo is revealed confirming this new world order in this story. To show how all the characters have been affected (i.e., happy, angry, grieving), it is not uncommon to end with a social event (i.e., airport departure, ceremony [*Star Wars*], weddings [*Bridesmaids*], funerals [*Spiderman*]). It is here the viewer fully appreciates the extent to which main character has changed (character arc is completed), or the main character has changed the story world (i.e., *Gladiator*).

Linda Cowgill underscores that the best resolution presents one last revelation or insight (realization).[11] The realizations translate into a literal, and emotional, *resurrection* of the hero. In *Despicable Me*, the realization that he loves Margo, Edith, and Agnes resurrects Gru, turning him from a sinner to a saint (Figure 4.6). Syd Field believes it is more effective to not think of resolution as an end to the story but as a *solution*, the main character has to come up with, to the story problem.[12]

Do not underestimate the extent to which the viewer expects emotional satisfaction for staying through to the end. This does not necessarily mean a happy ending, but one that at a minimum has meaning. There needs to be a take away for the viewer, some sense of what did it all mean? McKee believes that at the end, if there has been a great emotional high (terror to tears) it is appropriate to provide a "slow curtain" so the audience can gather their thoughts and come back to their true identities before leaving.[13]

Figure 4.6

Despicable Me. (Copyright 2013 Illumination Entertainment.)

Deus ex Machina

In ancient Greece, at the end of a play, it was not uncommon to have their gods enter and solve all the character's unresolved story problems. This is referred to as Deus ex Machina, translated as "the god from the machine." Only a handful of such stories have survived because viewers resent such endings. Deus ex Machina is considered a contrived plot device, an unexpected intervention to force an ending. The resolution might be a (1) character (the biggest dinosaur, Figure 4.7), (2) an event (a car accident), (3) supernatural ability (previously unknown), or (4) object (a gun happens to be handy). Such plot devices strip the story of any meaning it might have had.

Closure, that feels true, comes from the *character rescuing themselves* (this is how it is in real life), and which provides an answer to the central story question.

> I'll tell you a secret. The last act makes a film... You can have flaws, problems, but wow them in the end, and you've got a hit. Find an ending, but... don't you dare bring in a Deus ex Machina. Your characters must change, and the change must come from them. Do that, and you'll be fine.[14]
>
> (Robert McKee character to Charlie [*Adaptation*])

There are exceptions: *Wizard of OZ* (it was so real... *was it really a dream*?), *Life of Pi* (he rescued himself in the dream?), last episode of *Newhart* (dream as comedic device, 1990), *The Usual Suspects* (real or dream—was it all part of the deception). However even *Call of Duty: Black Ops* III succumbs to the temptation to use Deus ex Machina—for the Mission Reports indicate that the player died during the operation in the second level. Is everything after the first level just in the player's mind...?[15]

Figure 4.7

Resolution achieved through character action. *Jurassic World*. (Copyright 2015, Universal Pictures.)

Meaning

The meaning is the reason viewers watch. Can't emphasize this too strongly. It provides more than the prerequisite satisfaction expected by the viewer; it offers something the viewer can take away… to reflect upon. In Act III, the main character confronts not only their external adversary but also confronts who they really are. *"To go to those places inside ourselves that have been hidden… where we send our hurt, our shame, our ugliness, our sorrow, our loneliness."*[16] For the ending to work something must occur for the viewer to see, and feel, the depth of the emotional loss the character suffers at the crisis.[17] To go from lowest depths, and be able to rise up and come out on the other side.

Meaning is contained in the emotional change from negative to positive (or in the case of a tragedy, positive to negative).[18] It is this transition going from good to bad, or bad to good, that moves viewers. It clarifies what the story has been about… whether it ends up, ends down, or there is some mixture of both. The viewer now has a final context of everything that has preceded it—the decisions, actions, obstacles, complications, crises. Not just *who* succeeds, but *why* which determines the meaning of the story.

Producer Dan Lin (Sherlock Holmes) indicated that *"What shocked us (was) we had thought what was most important was the lead character winning at the end of the movie… but what makes an audience happy is not the moment of victory but the moment afterwards when the winner shares that victory (meaning) with someone they love."*[19] What viewers value *most* in their characters is *resilience*. That despite the character suffering loss (*Obi-Wan* dies, *Gandalf* dies, Jack dies [*Titanic*]…), the main character has learned from their experience and will go on stronger than before. Though it feels that the character being alive at the end should be sufficient, viewers know subconsciously it has to mean more—they must embrace life versus just existing (e.g., *Gravity*) (Figure 4.8).

The ending is the key to unifying the story.

Figure 4.8

The meaning in Gravity is that to live means more than just existing. Ryan had to embrace life again by the end of *Gravity*. (Copyright 2013, Warner Brothers.)

Viewers will endure a down ending; it doesn't have to be a happy ending to be satisfying (i.e., *Gone with the Wind, Casablanca, Gladiator*) but it has to be meaningful. Lawson qualifies that stories can even *"end on a question-mark, but we* (the viewer) *must know what the question-mark means."*[20] There are viewers who will tolerate endings that are depressing, unfair, sad (Thelma and Louise) but even those viewers will not accept an ending that says that life doesn't matter, that life has no meaning. Meaning (love, family, choice) is the whole point of story.

If the ending does not work; if it lacks impact and inevitability, it is because the theme hasn't been woven into the story's progression.[21] Somewhere along the way the meaning has been derailed in favor of clever or cool. It is possible to have both, but the theme must be at the core. In *Guardians of the Galaxy*, the decisive confrontation against Ronan (for control of the Universe) will only succeed if the main characters join together... as family.

Figure 4.9

James Gunn, director, *Guardians of the Galaxy.*

> For me this movie is about family... It's about a bunch of people that don't have a family and they learn to love each other... this is a movie that says it's really OK to give a sh*t.[22]

James Gunn, director (Figure 4.9)

Such stories are universal because they contain universal truths. The endearing stories that always resonate with viewers are about families, growing up, sacrifice, learning who you are... and for that reason those stories survive because they tap into our universal desires, feelings, and symbols.[23] To make this connection with the audience, the conflict culminates in (1) a final revelation for the character and (2) a final realization by the audience—linking the meaning to the story's theme.

To learn more about universal meanings that speak to everyone go to the classic text The Hero with a Thousand Faces by Joseph Campbell, or his more accessible interviews in The Power of Myth, DVD. In addition, there is Man and His Symbols by Carl Jung with his often-cited ideas on meaning in life.

References

1. A. O. Scott, Critics' Forum: Thresholds of shock, *New York Times*, Arts, September 19, 2012, http://www.nytimes.com/interactive/arts/art-shock.html?_r=0#/#critics1

2. W. Archer, *Play-Making: A Manual of Craftsmanship* (London, Chapman & Hall, 1912), 172, https://archive.org/details/playmakingmanual00archiala

3. L. Cowgill, *Writing Short Films* (New York, Lone Eagle Publishing Company, 2005), 110.

4. D. Lin, Perfectly happy, even without happy endings, Lindsay Doran by Carrie Rikey, *New York Times*, January 13, 2012, http://www.nytimes.com/2012/01/15/movies/lindsay-doran-examines-what-makes-films-satisfying.html?pagewanted=all&_r=3&

5. D. Marks, *Inside Story: The Power of the Transformational Arc* (Studio City, California, Three Mountain Press, 2007), 297.

6. W. Archer, *Play-making*, 172.

7. L. Cowgill, *Writing Short Films*, 140.

8. D. Trottier, *Screenwriter's Bible*, KL 672.

9. D. Marks, *Inside Story*, 297.

10. L. Cowgill, *Writing Short Films* (New York, Lone Eagle Publishing Company, 2005), 133–145.

11. L. Cowgill, *Writing Short Films*, 144.

12. S. Field, *Screenplay: The Foundations of Screenwriting* (New York, Delta, 2005), 55.

13. R. McKee, *Story*, 312.

14. *Adaptation* (film), *Wikiquote*, last modified January 18, 2016, https://en.wikipedia.org/wiki/Adaptation_(film)

15. D. Billy, Call of duty: Black ops 3 ending explained, *One Angry Gamer*, November 6, 2015, http://blog-job.com/oneangrygamer/2015/11/call-of-duty-black-ops-3-ending-explained/

16. D. Marks, *Inside Story*, 287.

17. Ibid, 292.

18. R. McKee, *Story*, 309.

19. D. Lin, Perfectly Happy, 2012.

20. J. H. Lawson, *Theory and Technique of Playwriting and Screenwriting*, 176.

21. L. Cowgill, *Writing Short Films*, 141.

22. J. Gunn, 'Guardians of the Galaxy' is a Movie about Love, Family & Caring by Andrew Dyce, *Screenrant*, January 17, 2014, http://screenrant.com/guardians-of-the-galaxy-story-themes-james-gunn-interview-2014/

23. J. Yorke, *Into the Woods*, 228.

5

Story Types

Genres

Genres are *types* of stories (i.e., *comedy, science fiction*) which are an indicator of content as well as structure. The structure of a genre is composed of elements specific to the genre that not only appeal to viewers (horror—desire to be scared) but also are expected.[1] If these expectations are not satisfied, a storyteller runs the real risk of leaving the viewer confused or worse—inviting their resentment. At the same time, there must be some element of the unexpected or the viewer becomes bored.[2] This goes back to the twentieth century film axiom... *give them the same thing, only different.*

Why bother learning genres? Because viewers have become *genre experts* through a lifetime of watching. Within each genre are specific types of characters, settings, and values which have become systemized over time. Such information serves as a *toolbox* for satisfying a viewer's expectations.

There are universal genres: *Fantasy, Romance/Love, Action/Adventure, Mystery/Crime, Drama, Horror, Science Fiction, and Comedy*. In addition, there are other useful subsets—the Western, Disaster, Historical, Thriller, War, Redemption, Sports, Musical, Film Noir... not to mention the genres in games: FPS, RPG (Role Playing Games), racing, sports, etc.

- *Fantasy*—its focus is on the *world* of the story; not just the physical setting, but also the rules that govern it. Because there isn't necessarily a specific narrative tied to this genre it often *"needs to be paired with a strong 'story' genre (i.e. Science Fiction) in order to flesh out the narrative."*[3] This works best when the narrative choices exploit the strengths of each medium: TV (*The Walking Dead*), Film (*Night of the Living Dead*), and Game (*The Walking Dead: The Game*). Fantasy thrives in the media of interactive games and virtual reality (i.e., *Journey, Diablo, Mass Effect*).
- *Romance/Love*—is about more than just *finding love*; it is a story about the journey of love (which is never smooth). It includes such variations as *wanting love, losing love, regaining love,* and *learning to love again* (i.e., *Casablanca, When Harry met Sally, Gone with the Wind, Bridget Jones...*). The conflict involves misunderstandings, mistrust, as well as navigating the different value systems each person brings to the relationship. A popular subset in this genre is the Buddy relationship; not about love but trust (often they start off as enemies)—*Bridesmaids, Toy Story* (Figure 5.1).
- *Action/Adventure*—the hallmarks of this genre are rapid paced editing and nonstop action often coupled with physical stunts, chases, rescues, battles, fights, escapes, and disasters. The hero is motivated by a moral compass (duty), destiny, even arrogance (not limited to just the villain) (i.e., James Bond and Superheroes).
- *Crime*—murder, kidnappings, robbery often make up the story content with expectations of a detective/investigator, a variety of suspects, and the solution that must be revealed by the end.

- *Drama*—a reality-based story... true-to-life characters, in real settings, and real situations. A focus on characters at unavoidable turning points in their lives; where things cannot go on the way they have been. The main character is an *everyman* or *everywoman* that the viewer can identify with (this is a key element). Content revolves around high-pitched emotions, neurosis, addictions, hopes, dreams which are all brought to the surface.[4] A recurring premise is the vulnerability of man at the mercy of a corrupt system—*Godfather, Hunger Games.*

- *Horror*—comes with an expectation of being manipulated psychologically, as the viewer experiences disturbing, anxious, and frightening scenes. It is an examination of evil as the genre explores our deep-seated fears—while being both revolted and entertained.[5]

Figure 5.2

Mike Myers (*Austin Powers*).

- *Science fiction*—what interests viewers about science fiction is the desire *to understand* the possibilities of science (dark, evil, or good). This is combined with our desire to have some semblance of control in our lives.[6] In creating science fiction, the question to ask is *What If* ... dinosaurs could be brought back to life? There is a supernatural force in the universe? Be wary of Sci-Fi clichés—technical dystopias of tyranny and chaos, combined with the subtext of man against a corrupt society empowered by technology in the future.[7]

- *Comedy*—is most often built on flawed characters, in painful situations, who must grow internally to rise above the pain, and make a difference in their own destiny. Mike Myers (Figure 5.2) says he sees himself as an *"architect of (painful) embarrassment"*[8] Screenwriter/director Audrey Wells believes the key is to *"Steep characters in pain—make them miserable. Then after they've really suffered, make them happy."*[9] Comedy lives in these painful events of life. David Bordwell advises that *"Comedy is not so much a genre as a way of looking at the world."*[10] Jule Selbo, does an excellent job of tracing the steps in the comedy genre in her book, *Film Genre for the Screenwriter*, pages 114–120.[11]

Genres today are often mixed and matched. Disney's *Frozen* is an adventure/ romance/fantasy/musical. *Game of Thrones* is a fantasy/epic/war/drama. *Dances with Wolves* has all the appearances of a Western but incorporates fantasy and historical genre patterns. *Avatar* incorporates Western genre patterns but none of its artifacts (i.e., cowboy hats). At the same time, genres generally have a negative connotation, for they can easily degenerate into formulas that break down— *Delgo, A Hero's Journey.*

Story Concepts

An alternative to genre labels is categorizing stories by what the stories have in common. Blake Snyder advocates using story categories—concepts which reflect universal experiences. These stories embrace a variety of characters who find themselves in special situations dealing with the inevitable conflict: *Monster in the House, Out of the Bottle, Dude with a Problem*, etc.[12] To work, it is necessary (1) to match characters to situations, that are relatable to the viewer, and (2) identify a viewer's expectations within each category.

Monster in the House—don't get killed (or in this case, eaten). The monster can range from dinosaurs, sharks, ex-lovers, ghosts, snakes (on a plane) to even yourself. It takes place in a specific location (e.g., Dinosaur Park, Gotham City) and "*There must be a sin committed—usually greed (monetary or carnal)—prompting the creation of a supernatural monster that comes like an avenging angel to kill those who have committed that sin and spare those who realize what that sin is.*"[13] The *Resident Evil* series, *Jurassic World,* and its namesake *Monster House* (the House itself) (Figure 5.3).

Don't Mess with My Family—shows the character in their normal life, and then someone harms their family. They must do something extraordinary to save their family members or embark on a course of revenge/vengeance. An ordinary person (with unseen potential) rising to the challenge (i.e., *Josey Wales, Spartacus, Star Wars*) or drawing upon hidden capabilities (often lethal) from an earlier life they wanted to leave behind (i.e., *John Wick, Gladiator, Taken*).

Out of the Bottle[14]—a genie, a potion, a fairy godmother, sword (mythical)… changes the character's life, dramatically. Story opens with the main character oppressed by the unfairness of life, then something incredible happens, their life looks up, but only for a little while (i.e., *Cinderella*). However, now that they have seen what life could be like, the audience is rooting for them (and a little luck) to change their life forever. A lesson is learned and a moral revealed (i.e., *Pretty Woman, How to Train Your Dragon*). The reverse is the comeuppance tale; the rich, insensitive person who loses it all.

What the f*** (*Dude with a Problem*[15])—an *ordinary* person in an *extraordinary* situation (i.e., *Die Hard*). What makes this category work is the size of the problem—the greater the odds against them the better (i.e., the worst villain, the biggest volcano). They succeed because of their uniqueness, to defeat powers far greater than their own: the right person, in the right place, at the right time, with the right skills. Timing is everything.

Figure 5.3

Monster House, D.J., 2006. (Copyright Sony Pictures/Courtesy Everett Collection.)

Coming of Age—a life in change (i.e., transition from childhood to adulthood).[16] A character grapples with their insecurities—virginity, leaving home, breakups, mortality. These rites of passage stories are often fundamental in the classics *Jane Eyre, Huckleberry Finn, 21 Jump Street*. The transition is marked by a life-changing event, or major realization that allows them to embrace who they can become. *Ferris Bueller's Day Off* (everyone is changed but Ferris).

Fish out of Water[17]—putting a character in a world they are not familiar with. They don't know the rules, the language, social customs, geography, or expectations. Most *RPG* (*Fallout 4*) in games, *Alice in Wonderland* or *Big* in film. It connects the viewer to their own memories of being insecure as they encountered unknown situations.

Whydunit[18]—a variation on the crime plot with the difference that it's not as much about who committed the crime but *why*. Puts the viewer in the point of view of a detective, sifting through the evidence, and asking in the end "Are we this evil?" (i.e., Film Noir).

A Road Picture—a journey in search of a prize, but main character discovers something more valuable—themselves or love (i.e., *The Wizard of OZ, Back to the Future, Witcher3*). The plot's focus is on the characters met along the way and the trials they encounter. While the outward progress is measured by distance covered, the true measure of success comes from internal growth (*Finding Nemo, North by Northwest, Cars*).

The Underdog—the underrated character who turns out to be the most capable of them all. This genre focuses on those characters who succeed in spite of themselves; whether by luck or sheer perseverance, not giving up (i.e., *Hobbit, Breaking Bad*).

Redemption/Disillusionment—a bad character turns good or a good character turns bad, two sides of the same coin (i.e., Tragedies—*Hamlet, Macbeth, Othello*, etc.) (Figure 5.4).

Institutionalized[19]—stories about groups, families, and institutions… *Who's crazier, me or them?* Stories are about the consequences of putting the group ahead of the individual. Loyalty versus logic, *House of Cards, Star Wars, The Hunger Games*.

Figure 5.4

Tragedies, *Hamlet* by Pedro Américo, 1893.

Only a Few Basic Plots

Brian Prisco asserts there are no new stories, just new ways to tell them.[20] At the same time, Christopher Booker came to the conclusion that there are only seven basic plots.[21] Such plots revolve around a hero or heroine with whom the audience can identify. These plots consist of a character arc at its core, are derived from well-established myths, and integrate well-known symbolism uncovered in Carl Jung's research. Booker's plot structures can be seen in Fantasy and RPG games as well as virtual reality.

1. *Rags to Riches*—a young, poor hero kept down by obnoxious people, the hero perseveres, achieving some success, only to have it all fall apart. As they grow as a person, they find a new strength inside them which is the key to their success that results in a happy ending. *Cinderella, Pretty Woman, A Bug's Life....*

2. *The Quest*—the main character, and his companions (a wide assortment), leave home and set out on a journey seeking a treasure (i.e., an object, a place, or secret information). There are temptations along the way impeding their progress but they persevere and finish with a happy ending. Most stories have some part of this plot structure *The Odyssey, Lord of the Rings, Mass Effect: Andromeda* (Figure 5.5), *Harry Potter....*

3. *Voyage and Return*—the hero enters a magic land where things are a bit crazy (numerous Tricksters). Things are OK for a while and then fall apart quickly. The hero overcomes threats, confronts their inner demons, faces death, matures, and returns home. *Wreck-it-Ralph, Finding Nemo, Guardians of the Galaxy....*

4. *Comedy*—two people (lovers or buddies) are kept apart by misunderstandings. Contributing to their separation are forces trying to keep them apart[22] (i.e., perceptions, their parents, the situation) which must be overcome. Everything is cleared up and they get together by the end—*When Harry met Sally,* any romantic comedy.

5. *Overcoming the Monster*—a hero learns of a great evil and goes on a journey to destroy it. It may be a predator or the guardian of an oppressive way of life. In the end, the hero emerges victorious with a reward, in a new setting, and a new love. *James Bond* to *Super Mario.*

6. *Tragedy*—the main character has a major character flaw, or makes a decision they can't take back, which leads to their downfall. They start off OK but then there is downward spiral and everything they try to do just makes it worse. A morality tale. Shakespeare (i.e., *Macbeth, King Lear), Breaking Bad, House of Cards.*

7. *Rebirth*[22]—similar to tragedy, but the main character changes their ways, becomes a better person, and saves themselves at the last minute. *Star Wars* (Hans Solo*), Kung Fu Panda* (Po), *Sleeping Beauty.*

Figure 5.5

Mass Effect: Andromeda—The Quest Genre. (Copyright 2016, EA.)

Michael Hauge has observed that most stories (95%) have only five visible objectives.[23] This approach is effective for focusing short films as well as keeping scenes on track.

Five Story Goals

1. **To Win**—at love, a battle, sporting events…. This goal would encompass most media (film, video games). The main character is driven to win. Love—*500 days of summer, Love Actually, Kung Fu Panda*. Sports—*Need for Speed, John Madden Football, Tiger Woods Golf*….

2. **To Escape**—death: physical or psychological death, if there is a chase scene then the motivation is to escape—a disaster (volcano, the cold), a monster, the truth. *Toy Story 3*.

3. **To Stop**—something bad from happening… a killer, a secret from being revealed, an asteroid hitting the earth. This is the premise of most James Bond films. If they can't stop it from starting, then they at least can stop it from continuing. Most crime dramas, war films, and games (i.e., *Call of Duty*).

4. **To Retrieve**—a treasure (Arc of the Covenant), person (*Taken, Finding Nemo, Finding Dory*) … something valuable that has been stolen or someone kidnapped (*Italian Job, Oceans 11, 12*…).

5. **To Deliver**—person (*Transporter* [Jason Statham]), thing (a ring in *Lord of the Rings*) (Figure 5.6). Delivery stories take something of value to a well-protected destination, far away.

Figure 5.6

The ring in *Lord of the Rings*: The Fellowship of the Ring. (Copyright 2001, New Line Cinema.)

Short stories will focus on just one goal. Feature films combine several goals. In disaster movies, the character first tries to *stop* the disaster, then spends the second half *escaping* the disaster. Games and VR often incorporate all five goals.

References

1. J. Selbo, *Film Genre for the Screenwriter* (New York, Routledge, 2014), 2.
2. R. McKee, *Story*, 80.
3. J. Selbo, *Film Genre*, 172.
4. Ibid, 72.
5. S. Hall, Encoding/decoding, in: S. Hall, D. Hobson, A. Lowe, and P. Willis (eds), *Culture, Media, Language: Working Papers in Cultural Studies, 1972–79* (London, Hutchinson, 1980), 130.
6. J. Selbo, *Film Genre*, 44.
7. S. Solomon, *Beyond Formula: American Film Genres* (USA, Harcourt Brace Jovanovich Inc., 1976), 36.
8. M. Myers, 'The secret life of Mike Myers'—Interview by Bob Strauss, *The Globe and Mail*, March 13, 2009, http://www.theglobeandmail.com/arts/the-secret-life-of-mike-myers/article18139078/
9. A. Wells, *Writing the Romantic Comedy by Billy Mernit* (New York, Harper Paperbacks, 2001), 24.
10. D. Bordwell, *Film Art: An Introduction* (New York, McGraw-Hill Education, 2012), 220.
11. J. Selbo, *Film Genre for the Screenwriter* (New York, Routledge, 2014), 114–120.
12. B. Snyder, *Save the Cat* (Studio City, California, Michael Weise Productions, 2005), 34. For additional information, see Blake Snyder's Glossary of Genre Terms—http://www.savethecat.com/tools/blake-snyders-glossary-of-genre-terms
13. Ibid, 27.
14. Ibid, 30.
15. Dude with a problem films, *Wikiscreenplay*, last modified March 12, 2014, http://www.wikiscreenplay.ca/index.php?title=Dude_with_a_Problem_Films
16. C. J. Bunce, Coming of age movies and why superbad is super good, *Borg*, March 19, 2012, http://borg.com/2012/03/19/coming-of-age-movies-or-why-superbad-issuper-good/
17. J. Selbo, *Film Genre*, 297.
18. B. Snyder, *Save the Cat*, 34.
19. B. Snyder, Ten movie plots, *TVtropes*, http://tvtropes.org/pmwiki/pmwiki.php/Main/TenMoviePlots
20. B. Prisco, Safe house review: Ultrasuede and wallpaper paste, *Pajiba*, February 10, 2012, http://www.pajiba.com/film_reviews/safe-house-review-ultra-suede-and-wallpaper-paste.php
21. C. Booker, The seven basic plots, *TVtropes*, http://tvtropes.org/pmwiki/pmwiki.php/Main/TheSevenBasicPlots
22. T. Nudd, Basic types of stories: Which one is your brand telling? *Adweek*, October 3, 2012, http://www.adweek.com/news/advertising-branding/7-basic-types-stories-which-one-your-brand-telling-144164
23. M. Hauge, *Writing Screenplays that Sell* (New York, Harper-Collins, 2011), 37.

PART 2
Story Elements

6

Story Elements

Premise: What Is It About?

A story's *premise* is the idea[1]—the who, what, and where. Toy Story's premise is *the secret life of toys*. The young boy's favorite toy perceives that his status as the favorite toy is threatened when the boys' parents give him a space cowboy action figure for his birthday. The *Premise* is chiefly all an audience knows, and uses, to decide whether to see a movie, play a game, or interact with VR. Jeffery Katzenberg made this the crux of his argument, in his frequently quoted, internal memo to Disney executives. According to Katzenberg *"we must not be distracted from one fundamental concept: the idea is king… If a movie begins with a great, original idea, chances are good it will be successful, even if it is executed only marginally well. However, if a film begins with a flawed idea, it will most certainly fail, even if it is made with 'A' talent and marketed to the hilt"*[2] (Figure 6.1).

Figure 6.1

Jeffery Katzenberg, founder and president, DreamWorks Animation.

The premise starts off as a *What if* statement. What would happen if people on Wall Street were so greedy they didn't care what happened? What would happen if a shark starts eating people and seemed to be doing it on purpose? While the premise may kick start the story process, a story is never locked into these ideas during development. Ironically, the very ideas that one is so excited about in the beginning are almost never the ones that are kept in the end. Ed Catmull (President, Pixar) describes the process director Pete Docter went through when first starting the animation *Up*.

The first version of *Up* took place in a castle that was floating in the sky, and in this castle, was a king and two sons… One of the sons inadvertently fell overboard and was down wandering… (when he) came across a large bird. This version didn't work. The only thing kept was the bird and the word *Up*.

The second version was an old man in a house… and after the wife died the house floated up into the sky and landed on a lost Russian dirigible (blimp)… that (version) didn't work. We kept the house and the old man.

The next version landed in Venezuela where the birds laid eggs that gave you eternal life. But you had to keep eating the eggs. And that's why Muntz stayed there for the eggs. But it wasn't working. The path (developing story) is totally unpredictable. There is nothing about starting that which said how it was going to go… Ed Catmull[3] (Figure 6.2).

Figure 6.2

Up. (Copyright 2009, Disney • Pixar.)

Premises are not sacrosanct. View them as starting points that will inevitably (and often radically) change. Katzenberg did concede that though his focus is on the core idea, all animations must also contain *a good story, well executed*. Katzenberg conceded that he only knew of one time where in the field of animation somebody had a bad idea and had perfect execution, *Ratatouille*. "*I assure you this is a bad idea. Let's have a semi-realistic rat in a kitchen cooking... No one in their right mind is going to say, 'Well, that's a good idea.' It's a bad idea, but it's so beautiful in its execution and such a great piece of storytelling.*"[4] Ed Catmull (Pixar, president), Andrew Stanton (director of *Finding Nemo*), and Pete Docter (director, *Inside-Out*) have all emphasized that Pixar's success with story is due to its emphasis on *development* that trumps *idea* every time.

Nonetheless having an idea, the viewer can immediately relate to helps the process immensely. Producer Robert Kosberg believes that story development will not succeed "*if the initial concept is not clear. Find great ideas, keep asking yourself—'Do you have a good idea here?'*"[5] Successful premises—a shark menacing a resort town, a group of misfits set out to stop the destruction of the universe, an unquenchable appetite for money on Wall Street, etc. At its heart, it is still about a character with a problem—a teenager is mistakenly sent into the past, where he must make sure his mother and father meet and fall in love; then he has to get back to the future (*Back to the Future*).[6]

Figure 6.3

John Lasseter, director, *Toy Story*, chief creative officer Walt Disney Studios.

> As we develop a story, the plot (premise) changes dramatically, characters come and go, but... what you can't change later is the heart (theme) of the film—that's like the foundation of the building. You've got to get that right up front, because everything builds off that. You can't add that later. You can't punch up the heart... that's what I look for.
>
> John Lasseter[7] (Figure 6.3)

Theme: What Does It Mean?

The theme is the *why* of the story—"Greed leads to ruin" (*Wolf of Wall Street*), "We are a family" (*Guardians of the Galaxy, Avengers*), "No place like home" (*Wizard of Oz*)... which are universal beliefs (or a variation) about human nature. Theme is what the story *means* (*Titanic* theme—love transcends death) versus the premise (*Titanic* premise—young lovers on a ship doomed to sink). Every memorable dramatic story has a theme, a controlling point of view (Figure 6.4).

Figure 6.4

Meaning—who is an alien depends on your point of view. Planet 51 2009. (Copyright TriStar Pictures. Ilion Animation Studios.)

Traditional themes can show up in vastly different stories. The theme "family comes first" is frequently recycled—it is found in *The Godfather*, *The Sopranos*, as well as comedies, *My Big Fat Greek Wedding*. The theme "What the character wants is not what they need" spans the spectrum of cinematic stories... *Citizen Kane, Batman, Shrek* as well as the ever popular theme "Who am I"—*Wreck-it- Ralph*, Disney's *Tarzan*, the Jason Bourne series, *Blade Runner*.

Should a story start with a theme or discover the theme in the process? If, when starting the story, there is already a theme then the way forward is known—what the point is, where the story is headed, and what needs to be included. The downside of this approach is that the writer can unwittingly find themselves advocating for an idea in the process. Rowe[8] pointed out in 1939 "*The impulse to start from theme is widespread but with so many social issues and political points of view this approach can quickly degenerate into propaganda.*" A story works best when it embodies the theme but does not argue or preach it.

Others advocate that starting with a three-dimensional (3D) character reacting believably to a situation then, more often than not, a solid theme will emerge on its own.[9] This works well when shifting between the positive and negative poles in a story. Charlie Kaufman believes coming up with a compelling story means considering "*opposite, even repulsive ideas.*"[10] The downside is that what comes out of this process may lack cohesion; it will just be random. However, this is not altogether insurmountable if one adheres to the old screenwriting axiom—story writing is in fact story *rewriting*.

6. Story Elements

In finding a theme, think of it in terms of a small sentence: **subject** (*love*), **verb** (*can transcend*), **object** (*death*) (e.g., *Titanic, Romeo and Juliet*). Theme is a point of view. If the love is the subject, then the point of view might be… love is destructive (*Mr. & Mrs. Smith*), love is where you find it (*Love Actually*), love isn't about appearances (*Beauty and the Beast*), love can conquer insanity (*Beautiful Mind*), love doesn't last but it's better than nothing (*Annie Hall*). Pick a generic concept: family, love, revenge, greed… and then expand: love requires sacrifice (*Casablanca*), or the opposite, love isn't enough (*Witness, 500 Days of Summer*).

As the theme emerges it largely reflects what the author believes about the world. Bill Nicholson, writer on *Gladiator*, indicated that the script he inherited read as a revenge theme. He stated that he prefers "*to see a movie about a man who wants to love somebody… Who does he love? …he loves his wife and child.*" The theme changed to become—*he wants to go home to those he loves.* This was emphasized in the opening images, walking through wheat fields at his home supported with dialog "*What we do in this life echoes in eternity*" reinforcing the theme of being together with his family in the afterlife. Bill said "*I rebuilt … (the) scenes, so we could play this theme all the way through.*"[11]

There is a consensus among story theorists that theme is first and foremost communicated through imagery (Show don't Tell). In *Inception*, the first image is kids playing on a beach; in *Guardians of the Galaxy* (Figure 6.5), we see the family at hospital. Linda Seger states "*One of the most important methods for communicating theme focuses on the images chosen.*"[12] The theme can be as basic as good (shown as light) and evil (shown as dark).

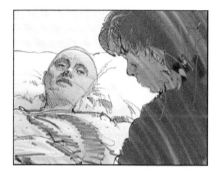

Figure 6.5

Peter and his mother, *Guardians of the Galaxy*. (Copyright 2014 Disney.)

According to Screenwriter Jimmy McGovern "*a good story must be laden with themes, laden with argument… (however) it ought not to intrude upon the story. You shouldn't be aware of the themes or the arguments until after you've watched it.*"[13] Theme is best communicated through the character arc.[14] The main character cannot attain their goal until they learn to live by the values of the theme. The viewer observes this in the character's actions and reactions as they overcome their faults, becoming whole (character arc), and reaching their goal. For additional insights into creating themes, see Karl Iglesias's book, *Writing for Emotional Impact*, pages 42–48.[15]

Emotion

Karl Iglesias states that we are in the *"emotion-delivery business."*[16] Irwin Blacker asserts that *"Plot is more than a pattern of events; it is the ordering of emotions."*[17] Viewers come to a story *curious, anticipating* the journey ahead. However, they stay because of the *tension* raised, until finally they exit with *satisfaction.* Emotion is what makes us feel alive. We seek dramatic stories for many reasons, not least of which is to feel (alive).

In most scenes, someone is in the grip of emotion. However, in keeping a viewer watching, the emotions of the characters are not the most important—it is the emotions the viewer feels. There are three levels of emotion for a viewer.[17]

1. Voyeuristic—curiosity (getting the audience hooked)
2. Vicarious—audiences identify with what the characters are feeling (first emotions in viewer)
3. Visceral—a viewer's emotional reactions in the story (the most prevalent—keeping them hooked)

The range includes excitement, satisfaction, trepidation, shock, surprise, contempt, joy… all the feelings one hopes to experience in VFX, VR, animation, and interactive games.

The most important thing… for all of us, is what emotional story are we telling? Meg Lefauve, writer, Inside-Out.[23]

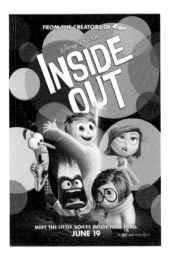

Figure 6.6

Inside-Out. (Copyright 2015 Disney Pixar.)

Charles Darwin, wrote in 1872 that *"expressions of emotion are universal they don't differ by culture."*[18] This was confirmed by Paul Ekman's[19] research in the twentieth century that there are six universal emotions that are easily recognized by others—happy, sad, fear, anger, surprise, disgust, and sometimes contempt (i.e., *Inside-Out*[20]) (Figure 6.6). There are not only numerous variations but also short duration emotions such as amusement, contentment, embarrassment, excitement, guilt, pride, relief, satisfaction, sensory pleasure, and shame.[21] Alex Martinez's recent research found subtle compound emotions: sad/fear, sad/anger, fear/anger, fear/surprise, happy/surprise….[22] Of the myriad emotions possible, the most useful in characters are those that can be readily perceived by viewers. It is important to recognize that a character's emotions are not the same as those the viewer experiences. Often in comedies, we see people who are frustrated or annoyed (*The Big Bang Theory*) in contrast to the viewer who is laughing as they identify with similar experiences—taking pleasure that now it isn't happening to them. In the same vein, in horror stories, characters can be calm but the viewer is experiencing tremendous tension because they have seen what is just around the corner.

There are three conditions that must be met in enabling a viewer to experience emotion. First, the viewer must empathize with the character; second, the viewer must know what the character wants (and want the character to have it); and third, we must understand the values at stake in the character's life. Within these conditions, a change in values moves the viewer's emotions (i.e., a poor character becomes rich).

Generating Emotion[24]

1. *Setting up the viewer* to understand a character's reactions—it isn't sufficient to just show emotion in characters (audience as voyeur). Audiences don't feel empathy for a sad child until they know why the child is sad (i.e., mother is dying [opening, *Guardians of the Galaxy*]).

2. Character is *facing something really bad* (life or death, betrayal...) the worse the better.

3. Character tackling a *life changing situation* (stakes are high). Trying to ensure things work out to their advantage (*Hangover*).

4. A realistic situation that the *viewer can relate* to. Something the character would likely have to face in this particular story world.

5. *Surprises that make sense* in hindsight and that the audience could have figured out if they had all the facts (withholding information).

6. Create anticipation, then *delay the payoff*... string the audience out (*Witness*).

7. *Ticking clock* technique to increase tension.

8. *Force the character to choose* between two terrible choices, from bad to worse.

9. *Change the pacing* of the scenes: in *Burning Safari* there is a long setup followed by short scenes in the chase (Figure 6.7).

10. *Show characters reacting*—show what fear, grief, silliness looks like. Reactions clue in audiences to emotions in the story. See "How Does an Editor Think and Feel?" on Vimeo for excellent examples.[25]

The need to build an *emotional reality* is something Pete Docter says he learned from the late Joe Grant—the longtime Disney artist whose work dates back to 1937s *Snow White and the Seven Dwarfs*. One thing Joe was always saying "*What are you giving the audience to take home?*" Docter recalls. He was talking about the emotional connection ...you have to make the audience feel they're watching themselves in some weird way—even if, as in our films, the characters are bugs and monsters and toys.[26]

Emotion is multifaceted. In portraying grief... is it a single emotion? Elisabeth Kübler-Ross established that there are five stages of grief: denial, anger, bargaining, depression, and acceptance.[27] Robert Plutchik came up with a wheel of eight primary emotions and their variations. It is clear reference of the basic range of human emotions[28] (Figure 6.8).

> *The hardest thing to get is true emotion. I always believe you need to earn that with the audience. You can't just tell them, "Ok, be sad now."* John Lasseter.[29]

Figure 6.7

Burning Safari, change in pacing to generate emotion, http://www. williamtre butien.com

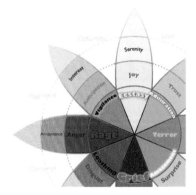

Figure 6.8

Plutchik Wheel of Emotions. For complete wheel see http://www. copypress.com/blog/your-fragile-emotions-illustrated/)

Setting

"The story is about where it takes place as much as anything else. The location becomes the huge, important character... in the story; it can't be separated from the story"[30]—the Coen Brothers talking about their approach to *No Country for Old Men*. Settings, story worlds, are not passive but as significant as any major character (i.e., *Titanic, Gravity, Twister, Perfect Storm*).[31] Character is best understood in terms of an active relationship between the individual and the world in which they move. As soon as character is detached from environment, the setting becomes a nebulous group of qualities—stripping the story of its sense of reality.[32] To make a story world concrete, to make it real, there must be both a sufficient number of details that make sense in relation to the world to generate believability for the viewer.

> From (the) first glimpse of the first image, the audience inspects your fictional universe, sorting the possible from the impossible, the likely from the unlikely... (for) within any world, no matter how imaginary, only certain events are possible or probable."[33]
>
> Robert McKee

A setting is more than just a location, it is a specific time (period), it is a set of rules, and a level of conflict (backstory).

Time period—stories are set in the past, present, or future. Stories take place over the course of a day, year, or even a century (i.e., *Titanic*). Time provides a context for the rules (social expectations of everyone) active in the time period of the story together with the clash between the audience's point of view and the norms of society during that time period (i.e., *Back to the Future, Midnight in Paris*).

Place/Location where the story takes place—geography (*Finding Nemo* versus *Mad Max, Fury Road*), city (*Despicable Me* [Paris] versus *The Secret Life of Pets* [NY]), structures (i.e. *Titanic*, Millennial Falcon [*Star Wars*]), and streets (*Coco* versus *Big Hero 6*). Giving the story not only a sense of authenticity, but also is a symbolic extension of the story's conflict, energizing the action. *"It is a lot of work to create an entire world... I spent an awful lot of time thinking about the details of the world and working it out in depth"*[34]—J. K. Rowling, *Harry Potter* (Figure 6.9).

Figure 6.9

J. K. Rowling, author, *Harry Potter.*

Rules—start by establishing the rules of the world as soon as possible so the viewer doesn't get frustrated due to confusion as to how things work.[35] The rules of the story world span its codes of behavior, political framework, daily cultural interactions, and social patterns. These rules become the jumping off point for the conflict.

Conflict—there are layers of conflict that make up the story shaped by the environmental structures. This can be day-to-day conflicts from confined spaces or social customs that force people together (i.e., soap operas, reality shows). Conflict can also emerge from environmental factors (long-term survival—wilderness to homelessness). Interestingly, the most played games are those with multiple levels defined by geography. These have the ability to pull us into the changing environments (i.e., Portal2, World of Warcraft).[36]

> (Lasseter) what I look for early on is…. setting. Where is this movie taking place? Is it someplace I would love to go, and I would love to spend time in this world? (As the story develops) you can't just pick the story up and move it to a different (location)…[37]

Today in serialized stories, it is the story world itself that becomes the subject: in television (i.e., *Lost, Gotham*), in games (i.e., FPS [*Mass Effect 3*]), and in virtual reality (*Lucky's Tale, Edge of Nowhere*) (Figure 6.10). A change in location is common in signaling the viewer that the character has moved on emotionally. Most stories begin by establishing the setting as a point of departure for the character. This serves as comparison between their old life and new adventure that confronts their inner demons.

Chris Wedge, director *Ice Age and Epic*, describes his process "*I always start with an idea for a place, or a world… a lot of my development process involves reverse engineering, you know, getting to the most important part last, which is character… So, here's a world, what could happen in that world?*"[38] Location is so important that Robert McKee is emphatic that the greatest source of "audience dissatisfaction" is the lack of information about the setting. If the conflict is detached from the setting what's left are the generic stories.[39] See Robert McKee's Story Seminar—*The Setting,* on YouTube.[39] John Truby has an excellent breakdown on story worlds in his book *The Anatomy of Story*, pages 141–189.[40]

Figure 6.10

Lucky's Tale. (Copyright 2014 Playful Corp.)

References

1. L. Egri, *The Art of Dramatic Writing*, 46.
2. J. Katzenberg, "Letters of Note" edited by Shaun Usher, *Variety*, 1991, January 31, http://www.lettersofnote.com/2011/11/some-thoughts-on-our-business.html
3. E. Catmull, Commencement Speaker, University of Utah, 2012, May 2, https://www.youtube.com/watch?v=g2xiHugl98w
4. A. Serwer, Brainstorm Tech video, Katzenberg on the future of movie watching, *Fortune*, 2011, http://fortune.com/2011/07/20/brainstorm-tech-video-katzenberg-on-the-future-of-movie-watching/
5. R. Kosberg, *The Screenwriter's Bible by David Trottier* (Kindle Edition, Silman-James Press, 2014), Kindle Location 771.
6. D. Trottier, *The Screenwriter's Bible* (Kindle Edition, Silman-James Press, 2014), KL 884.
7. J. Lasseter, 'Pixar's John Lasseter Answers Your Questions' interview by Stephanie Goodman, *ArtsBeat*, 2011, http://artsbeat.blogs.nytimes.com/2011/11/01/pixars-john-lasseter-answers-your-questions/?_r=0
8. K. T. Rowe, *Write That Play* (New York, Funk and Wagnalls, 1939), 50.
9. K. T. Rowe, *Write That Play*, 52.
10. C. Kaufman, *Plot & Structure by James Scott Bell* (Cincinnati, Ohio, Writer's Digest Books, 2004), 123.
11. B. Nicholson, *Script* (Gladiator directed by Scott Ridley, 20th Century Fox Distribution, 2008, DVD Supplemental Disc).
12. L. Seger, *Making a Good Script Great*, 17.
13. J. McGovern, *Mark Lawson Talk To... Jimmy McGovern* (London, BBC 4, 2010), http://www.bbc.co.uk/programmes/p00c5vh0
14. M. Hauge, *Screenplays*, 82.
15. K. Iglesias, *Writing for Emotional Impact* (Kindle, WingSpan Press, 2011), 42–48.
16. K. Iglesias, *Writing for Emotional Impact*, 16.
17. I. Blacker, *Elements of Screenwriting* (New York, Pearson, 1996), 23.
18. C. Darwin, The expression of emotions in man and animals, *Wikipedia*, 1872, last modified February 23, 2017, https://en.wikipedia.org/wiki/The_Expression_of_the_Emotions_in_Man_and_Animals
19. P. Ekman, *Emotions in the Human Face* (Los Altos, California, Malor Books, 2013), 40.
20. P. Docter, *Pixar Inside Out—The Story behind the Story* (DVD supplemental video), https://www.youtube.com/watch?v=6nlF557dZXI
21. C. Calistra, The universally recognized facial expressions of emotion, *Kairos*, 2005, https://www.kairos.com/blog/the-universally-recognized-facial-expressions-of-emotion
22. A. Martinez, Happily disgusted? Scientists map facial expressions for 21 emotions, *The Guardian*, 2004, https://www.theguardian.com/science/2014/mar/31/happily-disgusted-scientists-map-facial-expressions
23. M. Lefauve, *The Story behind the Story from Inside-Out* (supplemental DVD disc).
24. B. Hill, Creating emotion in the reader, *The Editor's Blog*, 2011, http://theeditorsblog.net/2011/01/30/creating-emotion-in-the-reader/
25. T. Zhou, How does an editor think and feel? *Vimeo*, 2016, https://vimeo.com/166319350
26. C. McCollum, 'Up' is one of Pixar's most complex, stunning films, *The Mercury News*, 2009, http://www.mercurynews.com/movies/ci_12431229?nclick_check=1
27. E. Kübler-Ross, *On Death and Dying* (New York, Scribner reprint, 2011), 11.
28. R. Plutchik, Wheel of Emotions, *Wikipedia*, last modified February 10, 2017, https://en.wikipedia.org/wiki/Robert_Plutchik
29. J. Lasseter, 'John Lasseter gives the lowdown on Bolt' by Brian Gallagher, *MovieWeb*, 2009, http://movieweb.com/john-lasseter-gives-the-lowdown-on-bolt/
30. Ethan and J. Coen, 8-Minute Coen Brothers Interview on 'No Country for Old Men', *MovieWeb*, 2007, http://movieweb.com/movie/no-country-for-old-men/joel-and-ethan-coen-interview/
31. J. H. Lawson, *Theory and Technique of Playwriting and Screenwriting* (Estate of John Howard Lawson, 2014), 349, http://wwwjohnhowardlawson.com
32. J. H. Lawson, *Theory and Technique*, 120.
33. R. McKee, *Story*, 69–70.
34. J. K. Rowling, interview by Christopher Lydon, The Connection, (WBUR Radio, 12 October, 1999, Part 5), http://www.accio-quote.org/articles/1999/1099-connectiontransc2.htm
35. D. Calvisi, *Story Maps* (Los Angeles, California, Act Four Screenplays, 2012), 132.
36. J. Juul. A clash between game and narrative. A thesis on computer games and interaction fiction (*Master's thesis*, University of Copenhagen, 1999), http://www.jesperjuul.net/thesis/
37. J. Lasseter, 'Pixar's John Lasseter Answers Your Questions' By Stephanie Goodman, *New York Times*, 2011, http://artsbeat.blogs.nytimes.com/2011/11/01/pixars-john-lasseter-answers-your-questions/?_r=0
38. C. Wedge, *Directing for Animation by Tony Bancroft* (Burlington, Mass, Focal Press, 2014), 190.
39. Robert McKee's Story Seminar, *YouTube*, 2008, https://www.youtube.com/watch?v=g-SfvGUmr_A
40. J. Truby, *The Anatomy of Story* (New York, Faber and Faber, Inc., 2007), p. 141–189.

7

Story Mechanics

What Is a Scene?

Scenes make up the units of change in a character's life. That is why they exist, their purpose.

Figure 7.1

Alfred Hitchcock.

Scenes are the smallest *story* unit. Scenes can be thought of as a story in miniature—containing a setup, conflict, and resolution.[1] The resolution of one scene should imply the next scene, for all scenes link with the scene before and the scene after them. Think of a *scene* as a link in a chain that fits together with all the other scenes. These links come in a variety of sizes and purposes (shorter, longer, information, drama, revelation...). No scene is an island unto itself. No matter how great a scene is written, if it doesn't link to other scenes, the story will die from lack of continuity. Without the connection with other scenes, the story stops progressing, the audience becomes confused, then bored, because the story doesn't make sense.

What are scenes made of? Scenes are composed of multiple beats. Beats are the smallest *action* unit.[2] Beats make up the *action-reaction-action exchanges* that together, add up to a scene. *Action*—Policeman informs the terminator he will have to wait to see Sarah Connor, *Reaction*—Terminator says *"I'll be back,"* *Action*—Terminator crashes car into police station (*3 beats*).

Alfred Hitchcock said, *"Drama is life with the dull bits cut out"* (Figure 7.1). If a scene doesn't have a purpose, then get rid of it. At various points in the development process it is important to actively search for scenes to cut that serve little purpose (e.g., cut entrances and exits unless they have a specific narrative purpose to the story).

Purpose of a Scene

1. **Adding information**—that advances the story—a location, the changing mood, or clues that provide insight as the character gets closer to their goal.[3] A scene's information is more than something to be checked off a list. It should be engaging and entertaining—this is fundamental to any dramatic scene.
2. **Change**—through action or revelation change the direction of the story or indicate change in the character.
3. **Reveal character qualities**—advancing the viewer's understanding of who the character is in the scene. Conflict, choices, or behavior reveals character. In *Guardians of the Galaxy*, Peter Quill is willing to take a beating to retrieve the cassette tape given to him by his mother.
4. **Reinforce the theme** by using a combination of image, action, and dialog.

Scene Components

1. Scenes contain multiple beats, *action–reaction–action–reaction*... until it reaches an unforeseen reaction beat.[4]

2. Scenes are mini-stories with a *setup, confrontation, and resolution.*

3. At the end of the scene, there is a switch in *polarity*—a switch from positive (things are going well) to negative (things are going badly) or negative to positive.[5]

4. Scenes have their own mini crisis—What are they going to do next?

5. A scene primarily takes place in one location, within the same time frame.

6. A scene must have a point that is clear to the viewer.

Figure 7.2

A scene is like a box into which everything is put to make it work.

Do a search in YouTube for "scenes" and compare it against this list. Screenwriter William Goldman recommends looking at a scene as a box into which the writer puts whatever will make the scene work. This can include setting, time of day, weather, furniture, food, machines, props, situations, passion, motivation... anything to energize the scene[6] (Figure 7.2).

Every scene contains some level of conflict. Ed Hooks cautions that the term *conflict* can become an obstacle in itself.[7] He advises visualizing a scene as a *negotiation*—one character pressuring another to do something they don't want to do. The writer must ask "Does this cause a minor turning point? Does the scene change anything?" If it doesn't change anything then it isn't needed. To learn more about scenes, go to *Story* by Robert McKee, pages 233–251.[8]

How Do Scenes Work?

Stories are divided into acts, acts into sequences, sequences into scenes, and scenes into beats. Each is differentiated by the degree they turn the story in a different direction.

Figure 7.3

William Goldman, screenwriter.

William Goldman said, "*I never enter scenes until the last possible moment … and as soon as it's done I get the hell out of there*"[9] (Figure 7.3).

Where do scenes start? Open on the action already in progress. In analyzing scenes, it is clear that an entrance and exit are often not necessary. Story continuity dictates that the strongest scenes start where the last one left off. Goldman believes *it's possible for each scene to consist solely of a period of confrontation. Done well, the drama is built around confrontation/crisis in a sequence that never seems to stop moving.*[10]

To determine where scenes start, you need to first know where the last scene ended. Conceive of scenes as links in a chain.[11] The previous scene should provide a direct connection to the start of the next scene by generating questions in the mind of the viewer—has the polarity changed (i.e., negative to positive, positive to negative [good to great, bad to worse]) and where are things headed? The Hollywood axiom for scenes is… start the scene *as late as possible* (in the middle of action already in progress).[12]

Where do scenes end? The flip side where to start a scene is to end the scene *as soon as possible* (you don't need an exit). Scenes move forward action, reaction, action… until they suddenly hit an unexpected reaction.[13]

Types of Scene Endings[14]

1. *Change in direction* of the story; what will happen next?
2. *Change of perception*—either by the viewer (new insight about the character) or from the character (new understanding of their situation [preferably related to the theme]).

The end of scene is apparent when the dynamic in a character's life has changed and the question of "*Now what are they going to do?*" smacks them in the face. The ending of a scene works best when it permits the viewer to infer the next scene.

How to differentiate scenes? This is usually reinforced by a visual change in location or time frame (i.e., first in the bar, then later out on the street). Contrast scenes by look, length, and content: long/short, night/day, image/dialog, interior/exterior, close-ups/full shots. While scenes are most often demarcated by location, there can be scenes at the same location *if* the dynamic between characters changes; one goes up (wins) and one goes down (loses). This can be seen as a change in polarity: a scene starts positive or negative as soon as it changes to the opposite polarity, it is time for a new scene.[15] In *Guardians of the Galaxy*, there are a number of scenes in the prison that change by polarity, time of day, and location within the prison. Due to the regularity of certain scenes, they acquire generic labels: action scene, chase scene, love scene, and climax (the obligatory scene, a scene viewers expect before the end of the story).

Why do scenes fail? They don't make a clear dramatic point—they are left ambiguous. Characters should experience strong emotions (whether expressed or stifled) to affect the viewer. Checklists are an effective method to ensure scenes are working.

Scene Checklist[16]

1. Does this scene provide needed information?
2. Did this scene provide insight into the characters and their actions?
3. Does this scene contribute to the greater story theme?
4. Is there dramatic/entertainment to the scene?
   a. Does it hook the viewer to want to know what happens next?
   b. Does it raise the viewer's expectations?
   c. Is there discovery in the scene?
5. Are the scenes connected?
   a. Is this scene the result of the scene preceding it?
   b. Is the following inevitable?
6. What is the point of the scene? Does it make a needed point?
7. Does this scene start as late as possible? Does is end soon enough?
8. What preceded this scene? What follows this scene?
9. Does anything happen? Does anything change?

What is a beat sheet?—A bulleted list of significant dramatic/comedic… moments, events, or turning points in the story. Beat sheets are a long-established construct in Hollywood for analyzing a story… whether it be a flowchart, index cards, or sticky notes stuck to a wall. It is helpful in scrutinizing a story's continuity. There are two versions of a beat sheet—generic and plot specific.[17] In preproduction, a generic version can be as simple as "main character is introduced"; the specific version can be "Jennifer walks out of her neighborhood bar." A beat sheet (similar to a list of scenes) expands and contracts. It functions as a search tool in constructing a story as well as an outline. See *Zootopia Beat Sheet* by Cory Miles.[18]

Narrative Questions

Figure 7.4

Andrew Stanton, director, *Finding Dory.*[24]

Figure 7.5

What will happen to Po? *Kung Fu Panda.* (Copyright DreamWorks Animation.)

Posing questions automatically creates a mental itch that needs to be scratched.[19] The tried and true way to evoke a viewer's innate curiosity is to set up story questions.[20] Raising questions keeps an audience hooked, wanting to know what happens next. Andrew Stanton, director, *Finding Nemo* (Figure 7.4), and Bob Peterson, screenwriter, *UP*, stress that in good storytelling, two plus two never gives you four, it just gives you two plus two... *Don't give the audience the answer; give the audience the pieces and compel them to conclude the answer...* (audiences) are rewarded with a sense of delight when they find the answers themselves.[21]

For Orson Scott Card (*Ender's Game*), narrative questions are an essential story tool.[22] All stories are technically mysteries... the viewer does not know what will happen next.[23] Questions activate the cause-and-effect detective process in viewers—a question leads to an answer which in turn raises another question and so on. *Kung Fu Panda*—How will Po fulfill his destiny? Can Po get into the tournament? Will Po be acknowledged as a Kung Fu Master by the Furious Five? Will Tai Lung's nerve strikes incapacitate Po? Will Po defeat Tai Lung? (Figure 7.5).

Types of Narrative Questions

1. *Goal question*—will they achieve their goal? This can range from—will they get the last piece of chicken to will they survive? This is the most common question (e.g., *Mad Max: Fury Road*).
2. *Dramatic question*—will I be found out? Will they learn the truth? (e.g., *Mulan*, girl disguised as boy).
3. *Emotional question*—how will they react when they learn that...? (e.g., *The Big Short*).
4. *Thematic question*—what is most important in life? (e.g., *The Wizard of Oz*).

Questions drive a story! What questions are to focus a viewer's attention to specific information that requires an answer. By creating questions, the viewer is motivated to look for answers in the story. The answer may be how a character will react and what subsequent action they will take next. Questions direct a viewer's thoughts about what is happening and subliminally specifying a range of possible answers.

To uncover the answers to the story's narrative questions, the viewer must connect the clues planted earlier in the story. As questions are raised and answered, the story's meaning emerges from the specific questions brought to the viewer's attention. This foreshadowing (hinting at an answer but still withholding information) compels the viewer to fill in the blanks, to guess at possible reasons, and make assumptions. Warning: don't generate too many questions at once, creates confusion, or leave them unanswered for too long. Questions are so powerful that viewers will be resentful if the story does not tie up the major loose ends by the time the story is over. *Star Wars: Episode VII* raises one last question at the end, to be answered in the next movie—(Where [the ....] has Luke been?).

In *Toy Story*, there is a narrative question for… (Figure 7.6)

Figure 7.6

Narrative Questions, *Toy Story*. (Copyright 1994 Disney • Pixar.)

1. *Each story* (Will Woody still be Andy's favorite toy? [central question])
2. *Each act* (Act III—Will Buzz and Woody get home?)
3. *Each sequence* (Will Buzz and Woody work together to get out of Sid's room?)
4. *Each scene* (Will the other toys see that Buzz can't really fly?)
5. And even *each beat* (Woody—Will Buzz listen to me?)

The narrative contains a trail of questions for the viewer to follow. The motion of story is from question to answer—from doubt to certainty.[24] Without *narrative questions*, there is no holding the viewer's interest, and without the *answers*, there is no emotional satisfaction for the viewer.

Surprise

Surprises are one of those fundamental tools of story that keeps the viewer hooked, reorients viewers to new directions, and provides needed insights for story progression. Surprise is the sudden gap between our expectations and what actually happens.[25] Surprises can be a line of dialog, a behavior, or reaction—consistent with a character's personality and situation going forward.[26] If surprises aren't built on consistent behavior, then it isn't a surprise as much as a clever manipulation that doesn't ring true. This results in the viewer thinking it must be a plot hole, which in turn causes them to wonder if there are other plot holes and if this story is worth staying to the end for.

Think of surprise as the art of hiding and revealing. It is a game of hide and seek for the viewer. They realize at the start of the story there is (1) much to be revealed about the characters, (2) circumstances will change, and (3) get ready for surprises ahead.

The great stories are memorable because they have well-constructed surprises in them. But surprises don't just happen; they are planned in a story. This is done through *setups* and *payoffs*. One of the joys in *Oktapodi* are the surprising payoffs to the familiar setups—the octopods escape when they seemingly have no chance.[27] The *surprise* became the way they continued to use the environment to escape (i.e., swimming pools and telephone lines to launch themselves through the air) (Figure 7.7) upending the viewer's expectations. These were pleasant surprises that showed the animator's inventiveness. Be careful of falling into the trap that all surprises are bad in stories—just because most surprises are bad. The most memorable moments in story are good surprises.

It is an *earned* surprise, as opposed to a shock surprise which owes its shock to the "sudden" revelation between expectation and outcome. Surprises most often consist of unexpected obstacles, complications, person, objects, or events that block their way.[28] Remember Samuel Goldwin's truism—*If the story you're telling, is the story you're telling, you're in deep sh*t*. In the end, the biggest surprise in a story, that viewer has been waiting to learn, is what the story is really about.

Figure 7.7

Oktapodi, http://www.oktapodi.com, Courtesy of Emud Mokhberi.

Techniques for Surprise

1. *Break expectations* by letting the viewer expect the obvious (set them up), then switch the outcome.

2. *Secrets revealed* are fundamental to surprise—who knows what, when. Some of the best secrets are revealed at the end (e.g., *The Usual Suspects*, *The Sixth Sense*). Secrets drive scenes—a hidden character flaw, a secret ability (e.g., *X-Men*), their real identity (who they used to be—*John Wick*, a top hitman).

3. *Foreshadowing* (a setup, anticipation) that doesn't pay off in the way expected. *"I'll be back"* in *Terminator*—the surprise, he returns immediately by crashing into the police station and takes on every single cop in the place. Yes, setup can be a cliché but the viewer will overlook this if the payoff is unique and *surprising*.

4. *Misdirection* (i.e., red herrings) divert the viewer's attention from what is actually happening. In *The Sixth Sense*, the viewer is led to believe that Crowe survived his shooting. To mislead the viewer—link this misdirection directly to the logic of the story, and reveal it later.

5. *Events happen offscreen* to be discovered later (i.e., the character knows more than the viewer). Events are hinted at... but remain hidden from the viewer. Thus, information must be controlled as to (1) *when* to reveal, (2) *how much* to reveal, and (3) *how often* the viewer gets new information.

6. *Reversal of fortune*, a 180-degree turn to maximize the surprise; the outcome is a complete opposite of the viewer's expectation. A surprising reversal when the skinny kid outsmarts the massive character (e.g., *David and Goliath*) (Figure 7.8). Or any movie with John McClane (*Die Hard*).

7. *Shock* is a sudden and intense surprise that exploits a viewer's startled response (common in the horror genre). However, audiences now consider such devices a cheap trick. Use it judicially.

8. *Plot holes* can be a surprise but not in a good way. Actions take the viewer by surprise because they don't make sense. The viewer has not been prepared with background information because the writer didn't know how to solve the story problem they created.

Figure 7.8

David and Goliath, Peter Paul Rubens 1660.

Suspense

One of the more powerful tools in a story's arsenal is *suspense*—feelings of mental uncertainty, accompanied by anxiously awaiting an outcome. This condition makes viewers want to know "what happens next"; their brains desperately seeking closure.[29] Scientific research reaffirms the effects of suspense: it sustains focus, increases memory, and compels us to know (we must stay until we learn what happens).[30] There are *three essential elements to suspense.*[31]

1. *Caring about the character*—If the viewer can't identify, or at least sympathize with the character, there won't be suspense. There must be a connection with the viewer, they must care what happens.
2. *Probability of imminent danger*—a bomb under the table (Alfred Hitchcock), running out of air (*Gravity*), a secret to be revealed.
3. *Uncertainty*—how things will turn out. There must be an equal likelihood of succeeding or failing in the scene, in reaching the final goal.

> *Suspense It's a hint of future danger or the promise of things to come through a twist, a clue, or character nuance. This creates anticipation and tension, worry, and intrigue.* Francis Glebas.[32]

These three elements together make for suspense. Iglesias sums it up as "... *suspense is about the potential of bad things happening to a character we care about. We need the viewer to start worrying.*"[31]

Techniques for Suspense

1. *Show success and failure*: Keep the outcome in doubt by making the (1) character's progress incremental, (2) progress that always comes with a price, and (3) complications (injuries, obstructions, people that come along). This adds tension.
2. *Increasing the danger*: This will automatically up the suspense meter. Stock-in-trade of genres such as action/adventure, crime, and horror. The viewer starts bracing themselves for the worst but hoping for the best.
3. *Warnings (foreshadowing)*: To introduce expectations of trouble. We see something, we hear something, or we are setup to expect something—this can range from the Stay Puft Marshmallow man (*Ghostbusters*) to Darth Vader. In our own lives, the anticipation of a confrontation is always worse than the actual event. Foreshadowing works especially well when something appears innocent but menacing events, still to come, are implied.
4. *Serious consequences*: Then remind the viewer of consequences. This can be physical (injury/death) or emotional (i.e., loss of love or respect). Consequences are what a viewer thinks about when the character is forced to make a choice (between two bad options [*Sophie's Choice*]), do dangerous work (bomb diffuser [*Hurt Locker*]), or trapped in a bad situation (*Gravity*) (Figure 7.9).

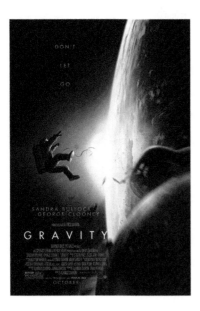

Figure 7.9

Gravity, US poster art, 2013. (Copyright Warner Bros. Pictures/ Courtesy Everett Collection.)

5. *Introduce surprise*: Surprise keeps viewers on notice that a sudden turn of events can occur at any time. Whether it be secrets revealed, unpredictable reactions... always delay the consequences and reactions to increase the tension. It keeps viewers anxious.

6. *Time limit*: Every second counts. This technique is used frequently but is always effective. Ticking clock and parallel action (cross-cutting)—oxygen gauge in *Gravity*, hourglass in *The Wizard of Oz*, rose petals in *Beauty and the Beast*.

7. *Show what they are up against as formidable*: Showing the opposition makes the conflict visible, casting doubt on survival. The viewer needs to see how powerful the enemy (Xerxes—*300*), how immense the earthquake (*San Andreas*), or how cold is the ocean (*Titanic*). It becomes clear the odds are not in the main character's favor.

8. *Viewers knows more than characters*: Important information is first revealed to the viewer—where the bomb is located, where the monster is hiding, where is the kitten? (*Feed the Kitty*, *Looney Tunes*) (Figure 7.10). It is excruciating for the viewer to watch as the characters don't see it coming. The tension and suspense permits *"the audience's experience to become more visceral... almost a primal experience."*[33] Alfonso Cuarón, director, *Gravity*.

Tension is intensified suspense. This is accomplished by delaying the outcome of the conflict. Screenwriter William Goldman said out of all the things you can do to the audience *most of all, make them wait*—who will she chose, will they escape? In *Mad Max: Fury Road*—will Max survive and get free? (Figure 7.11). CineFix has an excellent analysis of tension in *Sicario* on YouTube. Don't forget, no matter how bad things get; tension doesn't work if the viewer can predict the outcome.

> *The secret to storytelling is story-delaying.* Francis Glebas.[32]

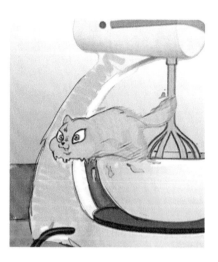

Figure 7.10

In *Feed the Kitty*, the viewer knows more than characters. (Copyright 1952, Warner Brothers.)

Figure 7.11

Mad Max: Fury Road, 2015/Copyright Warner Bros. Pictures/Village Road show/Courtesy Everett Collection.

Comedy

Comedic devices include (1) breaking expectations, (2) looking at the world with a skewed point of view, and (3) absurd but plausible exaggerations.

Figure 7.12

Rocky mitigates the predicament, *Guardians of the Galaxy*, Rocket (voice: Bradley Cooper), 2014. (Copyright Walt Disney Studios Motion Pictures/Courtesy Everett Collection.)

- **Breaking expectations**—*things that don't belong together*—incongruities of people, places, things, words. We operate in a world of expected outcomes, and react (laugh) at clashes between expectations and what actually occurs.[34] Shifts, and unexpected twists; *moving a thing from where it belongs to where it doesn't* (e.g., Albert Einstein entered in a beauty pageant).[35] These mental shifts are not just physical, they include social clashes of logic—*I told my doctor I broke my arm in two places*, the doctor said: *Stop going to those places.*
- **Comic perspective**—an obsessive way of looking at the world, at odds with reality as we know it. The rule is to take this point of view to the extreme: Sheldon (*Big Bang Theory*), the nerd who sees the whole world through a scientific point of view. It is from such flaws that comedic possibilities emerge. In truth, a character without such personality flaws is generic, offering limited options for humor. Sheldon not only sees the world as strictly logical but is also a know-it-all, socially clueless, and an egomaniac. A character's flaws likewise serve to open the emotional distance between the viewer and the comic character—enabling the viewer to laugh at the character. It isn't funny if you know the person that slips on the banana peel too well—the pain is too close to home.
- **Exaggeration** is reframed as the Wildly Inappropriate Response by John Vorhaus.[36] This is the foundation of much comedy—*Monty Python* (i.e., grandmothers spraying graffiti), *Zoolander* (extreme narcissism). A fear of dogs becomes a fear of puppies (playing off an extreme response to a trivial context). Exaggeration isn't just an over the top reaction (e.g., joyful becomes manic, frugal becomes stingy), it can be the understated—*Why would we care about saving the universe?* (Rocky—*Guardians of the Galaxy*) (Figure 7.12).

Comedy techniques include *repetition* (phrases or physical actions out of context when repeated build anticipation), *substitution* (word or gestures that have double meanings [i.e., hot]), *innuendo* (taboo breaking or suggestiveness), *pacing* (speeding up or hesitation in response), *exaggerated stereotypes* (quick communication with emotional distance), and *opposites together*. Determine the complete opposite of a character (e.g., the person they would least want to spend time with), then put them together in a situation. A quiet character is teamed up with a partner that doesn't stop talking; a man who doesn't like children must work in a preschool.

Insightful comedy comes out the gap between real reality and comic reality.[36] Funny lives in this gap—Marty McFly (*Back to the Future*) goes back to the 1950s where a down vest is seen as a life preserver. The 1990s sitcom *Wonder Years* excelled at the gap between what a child knows and what an adult has learned from experience. Comic reality on the other hand does an excellent job of shining a bright light at the absurdities of real life. Comedy is often more truthful than drama. It reveals truths one can't say out loud.

It works best when the character flaws are ones we can relate to (they are like us) as well as they are basically good at their core—the naïve (Charlie Brown, too trusting), the blockhead/know-it-all (Kramer [*Seinfeld*]), the put upon everyday person (Bob Newhart, can't catch a break), the kid who is always up to mischief (Calvin ([and Hobbes]). The viewer can not only relate to their own experiences, fears, and secrets but also knows why it's funny. Charlie Brown may have his flaws but he is vulnerable with a good heart. These have become recurring classic comedic character types—because they are like us.

We must all start with the believable... All drama, all comedy... stems from the believable, which gives us as solid of a rock as anyone could ask from which to seek humor, variations on the believable—that is the essence of all humor. Chuck Jones *(Figure 7.13)*.

Figure 7.13

Chuck Jones, director, *Looney Tunes, Bugs Bunny,* and *Road Runner* cartoons.[37]

Subplot

A story's primary plot is the main character going after what they desire as they confront the obstacles that stand in their way. Subplots are the smaller confrontations/conflicts, usually with family, friends, allies... even themselves. Subplots could be reframed as *sub-conflicts* with other characters. In a sense, each character can be seen as a subplot, with a specific purpose in the story.

Subplots serve a variety of functions—(1) clarify action/theme, (2) solve plot holes with main plot (i.e., initiate the inciting incident), (3) reveal background information or unseen motivations, (4) change the mood (e.g., humor, peril), (5) prompt the viewer to make plot connections, (6) change the direction of the action.... Subplots come in the form of *complications, contrasts*, or *reinforcement* of the direction/theme of the story. Think of subplots as *supporting-plots*. The subplot interactions *reinforce* who the main character might be—supporting the connections viewers are already making in the story.

Subplots bring a sense of realism by interrupting the main story's flow.[38] Why is this? Because *life* doesn't move forward all at once... there are interruptions, distractions, and failures along the way. These complications from subplots *play havoc* (e.g., impede, accelerate) with the main character's quest to get what they want. The subplots increase the drama by making it harder for the main character

to *directly* get what they want. Subconsciously, a viewer knows from their life experience that getting what you want is never straightforward.

Subplots provide *contrast* by bringing in a different point of view. Do things make sense when the viewer sees things through someone else's point of view? The insights make it more meaningful because we are getting a broader view of the situation. In Shakespeare's *Romeo and Juliet*, the viewer sees not only their specific love story but also the subplot of their families' (Capulets and Montagues) hostility toward each other (Figure 7.14). This *contrast* exposes all the complications keeping the lovers apart, making the story all the more traumatic for them.

Subplots need to cross paths with the main plot! Subplots are not just incredibly entertaining sub-stories in their own right but have a distinct story purpose. Save those independent subplots and tangents for the sequel.

Figure 7.14

Frederick Leighton, The Reconciliation of the Montagues and the Capulets over the Dead Bodies of Romeo and Juliet, 1850.

If the question is *how does a character express their inner emotions in their external behavior?*—the subplot is the answer.[39] By showing how a character reacts to other characters, the viewer will learn what is going on internally. Using a close acquaintance to confront the main character is always an effective device. Subplots expose the inner struggles a character seeks to keep hidden (i.e., trouble connecting with others—Sheldon, *The Big Bang Theory*).

This internal conflict within the character can be considered a subplot in its own right. Their internal struggle, this subplot of the main character battling their inner demons, needs to be resolved before the climax (usually just before). To reiterate, Peter's dilemma (*Guardians of the Galaxy*) is that he wants to be rich, but as he begins to care about these strangers he questions that desire. What he gradually realizes is that he needs love more than he wants money... Gamora, the emotional subplot; a choice between want (money) or need (love). If he doesn't sacrifice what he wants by the end, the viewer will conclude he hasn't changed and the story ends as a tragedy (i.e., *Blow*). However, when he rescues Gamora by putting his life on the line and telling his enemies his location, this reveals to the viewer that he has changed (Figure 7.15).

Figure 7.15

Guardians of the Galaxy. (Copyright 2014 Marvel Studio.)

This need versus want subplot is almost always about one's *relationship to others*; love (*Star Wars, Casablanca, Brooklyn*), Friendship (*Lethal Weapon*), Family (*Modern Family, Finding Dory*).[40]

> As human beings, we often lose sight of what's really important. We think it's about getting the prize and having the toys, despite experience telling us that life's great joys are internal rather than external. A great transformative story reminds us of this eternal truth. How do you do that? With a subplot that offers your protagonist what they need—but that requires them to give up on their illusory want.[40]
>
> Allen Palmer

For additional insights into subplot, see pages 160–170, the *Transformation Arc* by Dara Marks.[41]

Foreshadowing: Creating Anticipation

Foreshadowing is the hinting about something that might become important later in the story. It is used to prepare the viewer for reveals later in the story. A story's genre often serves a similar function as the viewer anticipates what's coming based on the structure of specific genres (e.g., horror, detective genres). Foreshadowing can be as subtle as storm clouds on the horizon or as blatant as Romeo and Juliet talking about wanting to die rather than live without each other.[42]

Planting something early prevents the viewer wondering "Where did that come from?" later in the story. In *Toy Story*, Sid puts a match stick in Woody's holster, which is needed later to light the rocket strapped to Buzz's back. If it hadn't been shown earlier either it would need to be explained, interrupting the pacing of the scene, or worse… the audience intuitively knowing the solution was contrived to end the scene (Deus Ex Machina).

Foreshadowing gives credibility to a character's actions and abilities by laying the groundwork for these activities later in the story. In *Avatar*, Jake's disability comes from his earlier combat experience which is needed later to lead the Na'vi later against Quartich's army (Figure 7.16). In *Inside-Out*, it is foreshadowed that Riley is entering that stage of life when emotions swing erratically from one moment to the next. In *Frozen*, the viewer is slowly introduced to Elsa's cryokinetic powers and witness them getting increasingly out of control.

Deaths are often foreshadowed in animation to prepare young audiences. Bambi's mother's death is foreshadowed by her warning to Bambi about the threat of man. Charlotte's death is foreshadowed by her explaining to Wilbur that all living things eventually die. Mufasa's death is foreshadowed by his telling Simba that the great kings of the past look down on us from the stars.

Figure 7.16

Jake's military connection. *Avatar* 2009. (TM & Copyright 20th Century Fox. All Rights Reserved/Courtesy Everett Collection.)

If something has been foreshadowed, there is nothing that your character can't do or that couldn't happen in your story world. In science fiction and fantasy stories, the laws of physics can be altered if the audience has been forewarned.[43] This is possible if either of these two conditions are met:

1. The character has the ability to do something (action or ability) because the viewer has seen a small preview.[44] This lends credibility.
2. The viewer has been told of omens, predictions, warnings, or hints. Thus, when something extraordinary happens… it is accepted. It also is satisfying for the viewer as they think back to the earlier hints and make the connection.[45] A common device in Game of Thrones.

In *The Matrix*, Neo's resurrection from having died would be a bit difficult for the viewer to accept if they hadn't previously been introduced to Nebuchadnezzar, received highly technical explanations, watched increasingly metaphysical feats, and heard dialog loaded with heavy religious and mythical symbolism (*"He is the one."* Figure 7.17). The viewer is predisposed to look for meaning in the story. It is the foreshadowing that provides the cues the viewer seeks. The fun in figuring it out comes from the breadcrumbs the storyteller provides along the way—without being overly obvious.

Don't underestimate the critical role foreshadowing plays in triggering *anticipation* in viewers. Viewers spend a great deal of time in a story anticipating what will happen next. *Anticipation* works by (1) *repetition* (power of three), (2) *delayed gratification*, and (3) *surprise*.

In *The Three Little Pigs*, the first house out of straw is destroyed (foreshadowing), the second house out of sticks is destroyed (repetition), the viewer waits as the wolf goes to the third house (power of three) and antici-

Figure 7.17

Neo as "The One," from *The Matrix*. (Copyright 1999, Warner Bros.)

pates it will come down too but when it doesn't (surprise) … the twist hooks the viewer, wanting to find out what happens next. In *Jaws*, the same thing happened with how many barrels the shark could take down with him as he submerges… *"he can't take down one"* (he does), *"he'll never be able to take down two"* (he does), and *"it's impossible for him to take down three,"* and the shark takes them all down.

Anticipation works in several ways, (1) hoping or dreading something would happen and (2) hoping or dreading something will not happen. To make the anticipation even more excruciating, make the character directly responsible for delaying the anticipated outcome. To build in the delay force the character to choose between two undesirable outcomes—the resultant indecision postpones the inevitable.

Anticipation hooks a viewer's emotions and intensifies or drops those emotions as they wait for the payoff. It is the waiting that amplifies *what could be*. Our imaginations always turn something potentially unpleasant into something worse (the coming shot in the doctor's office). Anticipation makes a scene far more memorable.

References

1. R. McKee, *Story*, 233.
2. D. Trottier, *Screenwriters Bible* (Kindle, Silman-James Press, 2014), KL 4159–4163.
3. L. Seger, *Good Script*, 91.
4. J. Yorke, *Into the Woods* (London, The Overlook Press, 2014), 94.
5. S. Field, *Screenplay*, 44.
6. B. Goldman, Helping Evolve the Script, *The Motion Picture Editors Guild Newsletter*, 1995, 16(5), September/October, http://www.editorsguild.com/v2/magazine/Newsletter/goldman.html
7. E. Hooks, *Acting for Animators* (London, Routledge, 2011), 22.
8. R. McKee, *Story*, 233–251.
9. W. Goldman, *Adventures in the Screen Trade* (USA, Grand Central Publishing, 2012).
10. Ibid, 44.
11. L. Seger, *Good Script*, 75.
12. D. Calvisi, *Story Maps* (Act Four Screenplays, 2012), 127.
13. J. Yorke, *Into the Woods*, 95.
14. S. Field, *Screenplay*, 44.
15. J. Yorke, *Into the Woods*, 95.
16. P. Lucey, *Story Sense* (New York, McGraw-Hill, 1996), 119.
17. L. Brooks, *Story Engineering* (Cincinnati, Ohio, Writer's Digest, 2011), 265.
18. C. Miles, Zootopia Beat Sheet, *Save the Cat*, March 25, 2016, http://www.savethecat.com/beat-sheets-alpha
19. L. Brooks, *Story Engineering*, 265.
20. K. Iglesias, *Writing for Emotional Impact*, 84.
21. A. Stanton, Understanding Story: Or My Journey of Pain, Los Angeles Convention Center, Screenwriting Expo 5, 2006 *Rage Against the Page*, December 19, 2006, http://rageagainstthepage.blogspot.com/2008/12/andrew-stanton-pixar-transcript-keynote.html
22. O. Scott Card, *Storytelling Workshop* (Orem, Utah, Utah Valley University, September 20, 2012).
23. K. Iglesias, *Emotional Impact*, 85.
24. F. Glebas, *Directing the Story*, 111.
25. J. Casti, *Complexification: Explaining a Paradoxical World through the Science of Surprise* (New York, HarperCollins, 1994), 6.
26. K. Iglesias, *Emotional Impact*, 66.
27. Ibid, 106.
28. Ibid, 103.
29. M. Konnikova, On writing, memory, and forgetting: Socrates and Hemingway take on Zeigarnik, *Scientific American*, April 30, 2012, http://blogs.scientificamerican.com/literally-psyched/on-writing-memory-and-forgetting-socrates-and-hemingway-take-on-zeigarnik/
30. T. Mallory Holland, 3 Big reasons why suspense is an effective storytelling technique, *Skyword*, 2016, http://www.skyword.com/contentstandard/art-of-storytelling/3-big-reasons-why-suspense-is-an-effective-storytelling-technique/
31. K. Iglesias, *Writing for Emotional Impact* (USA, WingSpan Press, 2011), 94.
32. F. Glebas, *Directing the Story* (London, Focal Press, 2006), 19.
33. A. Cuarón, *The Making of Gravity* (Blu-Ray Disc, Warner Brothers, 2013).
34. H.-L. Bergson, *Laughter: An Essay on the Meaning of the Comic* (USA, Arc Manor, 2008 [originally 1900]), 44.
35. J. Vorhaus, *The Comic Toolbox* (USA, Silman-James Publisher, 1994), 22.
36. J. Vorhaus, *Comic Toolbox*, 22.
37. C. Jones, *Chuck Amuck*, 33.
38. A. Palmer, The secret to subplots, *Cracking Yarns*, January 26, 2011, http://www.crackingyarns.com.au/2011/01/26/the-secret-to-subplots-half-revealed/
39. D. Marks, *Transformational Arc*, 160.
40. A. Palmer, The one plot you really need, *Cracking Yarns*, January 30, 2011, http://www.crackingyarns.com.au/2011/01/30/the-one-subplot-you-really-need/
41. D. Marks, *Transformational Arc*, 160–170.
42. Foreshadowing examples, http://www.foreshadowingexamples.com
43. M. Gazzaniga, *Human: The Science behind What Makes Your Brain Unique* (New York, Harper Perennial, 2008), 190.
44. M. Hauge, *Screenwriting*, 127.
45. L. Cron, *Wired for Story*, 216.

8

Interactive Narrative

Why Story in Games/VR?

Interactive stories differ dramatically from those in animation. In animation, everyone is on board to realize the story. In games/VR, the primary objective is the immersive experience. Story is an important component but story plays a secondary role to the interactive experience. Story not being primary is a difficult concept to come to terms with from the perspective of film and animation.

The strength of interactive games is its *immersive flow*.[1] This flow, when coupled with story components energizes the experience.[2] Injecting story into a game provides a *context* increasing the feeling of immersion and *believability,* enhancing the suspension of disbelief. The viewer knows who the characters are, their situation, and the relevant artifacts of the story world—all of which imparts meaning to the reactions of the player. In an FPS (e.g., *Titanfall* or *Battlefield),* the experience just isn't as sustaining if the player is killing random people as compared to eradicating international terrorists. The command "move and shoot" becomes "*secure the downed aircraft,*" and "stay here and don't get killed" becomes "*hold the square against enemy troops at all costs*"[3] (Figure 8.1).

While not all games tell stories (i.e., puzzle games—*Tetris*) story's role varies by a game's own distinct genre. Adventure games are significantly narrative driven, FPSs contain strong narrative aspects, and RPGs are heavily influenced by the narrative component. Progress in a game has a close correspondence with the character's arc in a game's narrative.

Figure 8.1

Titanfall. **(Copyright 2016 EA.)**

The player's choices both influence, and are influenced by the game's narrative. The player's actions have a connection to the underlying story. The goal becomes tangible, something the player is motivated to achieve—and willing to work harder to obtain.[3] Story raises the emotional intensity, giving meaning to the obstacles overcome and the rewards attained (i.e., *Portal*). As the player's experience becomes increasingly intense (comparable to progressive conflict), players are further motivated to advance through the game—to find out what happens next. Artifacts, missions, and objectives become something more than cool, connecting the player to a larger narrative. Toiya Kristen Finley states *"Even the items players would collect to create into weapons says something about the state of the world and the character would use them."*[4]

The connection between story and character also enriches immersion through *identification*, as players relate to characters who have similar traits, or qualities they wish they had (e.g., magic powers, superhuman strength). Ironically, identification may even be stronger in games/VR than animation as the player has the ability to replay events. Players get to experiment with *alternative choices* after faltering the first time through. They incorporate what they learned about the strengths and weaknesses of the player–character as well as implement *new knowledge* learned about which obstacles the character can and cannot overcome.

It is the knowledge gained by *experience* in the game which is instrumental in the success of serious games (i.e., health games). Games enable insights to be gained through *experience*, as opposed to *observation* and *instruction* in traditional linear media and learning methodologies.

Figure 8.2

Christopher Nolan.

Games and animation both gauge progress by rewards attained or obstacles overcome. But it is in connection to story, where what the player has been through becomes more than just a sense of completion, but rises to a feeling of satisfaction by the end.

> … if you picture the story as a maze, you don't want to be hanging above the maze watching the characters make the wrong choices because it's frustrating. You actually want to be in the maze with them, making the turns at their side, that keeps it more exciting… I quite like to be in that maze.[5]
>
> Christopher Nolan (Figure 8.2)

The challenge for the narrative designer is anticipating (1) what the player will learn? (2) how they will react? (3) what they will have experienced by the end? Always keeping in mind—how much freedom do the players need to define themselves in the world and find their role in the story?[6]

Story versus Narrative

The concept of narrative is the story "*telling*," not the story. The "basic story elements are the *what* (plot, character, setting), while *storytelling* elements are the *how* (genre, style, composition, pacing, editing…). In food terms, story elements are like the ingredients of a cake, while storytelling elements are how those ingredients are measured, combined, prepared, baked, decorated, and presented."[7]

In animation, the order in which images are perceived changes the meaning. The direction of a story can be grasped from just the first two or three images with the brain conditioned to start making assumptions and constructing scenarios out of the most minimum of information. An interactive narrative foregoes the tight sequence control of a traditional story and in its place puts emphasis on who or what is driving the story. In a game/VR, the narrative may be driven by player, plot, interactive mechanics, or the character.[8] It is essential to clearly establish who or what is driving the interactive narrative.

Narrative driven by player—The choices a player makes triggers narrative events. This occurs whether planned by the designer or not—an emergent narrative. To keep the story heading in the coherent direction, the narrative designer must design the potential choices a player *can* make. Such choices are then limited to *what is possible* based on its game mechanics. Tobias Heussner points out in Massive Multiplayer Online games (MMOs) (i.e., *World of Warcraft, Battlefield 4*) "*players interact with this story through quests and NPCs, but the set-up, events and outcome of the story are determined by the developers*"[9] (Figure 8.3). The player can choose to which factions to belong, their interaction with that faction, and the order of quests they undertake.

According to Heussner, from these choices they create a unique story, in the player's minds, linked to the larger story of the *World of Warcraft*. While players do not necessarily directly influence the larger story (e.g., the fall of a kingdom, *Lich King*), they do influence the local story within the region they are located. This provides the feeling that they have played a part in that larger story. The risk, if it's not well designed, is the player will feel manipulated rather than satisfied.[10] The key is how the events and characters are presented, making the choices feel self-determined. The designer knows that the player's choices have a certain probability, for humans are psychologically hardwired to choose good over bad in the established context[11] (to kill is bad… except if they are trying to kill you or your family, *Call of Duty*).

Narrative driven by plot—In a plot-driven narrative, the focus is on *what happens* over *why it happens*. Plot-driven narratives thrive on creating opportunities for action to maintain interest in the story: *rescue your friends, stop the monster, save the universe*. The plot is made up of a series of ever more difficult challenges, ever-increasing conflict, and more emotionally intense climaxes for each level. The puzzles are harder to solve, the obstacles are harder to overcome, and the conflicts get more dangerous leading to the final climax. In the end, it should feel that both the gameplay, and story, has led up to this point.[12]

Narrative driven by game mechanics—A game's features, simulations, and feedback loops can have narrative events embedded in their mechanisms. At its most basic, narrative information becomes part of the game's reward system—reveals, cut scenes, narrative dialog (e.g., *Portal*) are dispensed when reaching in-game goals. Such rewards coupled with story cliffhangers at the end of levels (i.e., *God of War*) stimulate the player to want to know "*what happens next*," motivating the player to explore further and discover what is possible as they progress in the game.

Story can then serve as a framework for gameplay to be hung on. It can be used by the player to map their way to new rewards. Toiya Kristen Finley stresses that "*championing the story*" is more than being an advocate, it is making "*sure that the story and the world embodies the gameplay and the mechanics.*"[13]

Narrative driven by character—A story develops from *well-defined* characters in familiar situations. The character operates autonomously (i.e., built-in behaviors) with the player influenced to make decisions that sync with the character's logic. Early character-driven games include the *Final Fantasy* and *Tomb Raider* franchises. Character traits affect the game play; if a character has a limp, then that limp must impact the progress of the character. Zombies must move with the expected jerks and pauses (Figure 8.4). The key to player–character narratives are experiences and emotions that players can relate to from their own experiences, *Animal Jam*. Warning: the potential downside is that the player's role shifts—instead of doing, the player observes; instead of interacting, the player listens.

Game narratives are not driven by just one approach; it is a mixture of available approaches—plot, player, and game mechanics. The strength of determining the driver/approach of the game's narrative is that it provides focus for intent and direction in the game.

Figure 8.4

Characters with distinct movements, *Plants vs. Zombies 2*. (Copyright 2013 EA.)

Environmental Storytelling

The scale of the space in VR and MMO games transforms designers from storytellers to narrative architects.[14] It isn't composition as much as Feng Shui, environmental placements with purpose. Spatial games (*Need for Speed, World of Warcraft*) have much in common with traditional stories such as quests and journeys—as well as film genres such as science fiction, war, horror, fantasy, and adventure[15] (Figure 8.5). Henry Jenkins anticipates that with the growth of VR there will be greater representations of narrative worlds with a massive spatial component.[16]

Figure 8.5

Need for Speed. (Copyright 2015 EA.)

Don Carson (Disney Imagineering) has shared how the concept of *environmental storytelling* is crucial to their work. "*It is the physical space* (Disneyland) *that does much of the work*" of connecting story to the theme park experience. Visitors come prepped, with their knowledge of Disney movies and animations, ready for an adventure. "*The trick is to play on those memories and expectations to heighten the thrill of venturing into (this) created universe.*"[17]

To make this leap from *story-as-plot* to *story-as-space* requires a nontrivial shift in thinking. A spatial story is less about a tightly organized plot structure and more about a *body of information.* Henry Jenkins proposes that environmental storytelling contributes to an immersive narrative experience in four distinct ways:[18]

1. *Evocative spaces* draw upon preexisting narrative associations (stories and genre traditions) already familiar to viewers. Such games, with a heavy narrative component, can build upon already predigested stories to enhance both the immersive and story experience (i.e., *World of Warcraft, The Walking Dead*). These spaces are transmedia in nature... it is less about the individual work being self-sufficient, than each work contributing to a larger narrative economy.[19] The key is to exploit the narrative strengths that each media has to offer (i.e., books, games, VR, animation).

2. *Enacting stories*—Jenkins advocates designing the story's geography around the player's movement through the space. The features of the environment (i.e., obstacles, characters) directly inhibit or accelerate the player's progression through the game and to the story's resolution.[20] This is possible because while certain plot points are fixed (i.e., setup, major turning points, resolution), there are a number of other story elements that are a bit more mobile. These other story elements may be encountered in a variable order and still the player can assemble them into a story.

That story is constructed out of *micronarratives* or story blocks (small bursts of story information [dialog with NPCs, reminders, in-game artifact texts, character advancement, and cut scenes]).

3. *Embedded narratives*—the game space becomes a place stuffed with narrative memories to be unlocked by the player. Embedded in the documents, garbled transmissions, and undeciphered code, is a story about the history of what happened, who lived here, the living conditions, the purpose of the place, the mood, and what might happen next.[21] These *staged areas* contribute to the game's immersive flow by engaging the player to reconstruct the action through acts of discovery, supposition, and investigation. As the player sorts through the information looking for cause-and-effect logic they move closer, piece by piece, to a complete story—the *Unravel* theme, love is what holds us together? (Figure 8.6). Game designer, Steve Powers stresses that *"meaningful narrative is inferred by players if you give them cues but leave them the space to imagine."*[21]

Figure 8.6

Unravel—love is what holds us together. (Copyright 2016 EA.)

4. *Emergent narratives*—game spaces are charged with potential for story. It is designed to enable players to construct their own stories from the situation. There isn't a predetermined story line but conflict is inevitable because not everything is possible (e.g., *Sims*). The stories emerge from the player's choices as they set priorities for space and relationships (Figure 8.7: *Sims*). Before interactive games, there was Monopoly, where narratives emerged as we moved around the board. Players went from being elated to devastated, as fortunes were won or lost in the process of landing on real estate. Environmental narratives are becoming ever more impactful in VR.

Figure 8.7

Sim City. (Copyright 2014 EA.)

VR Story (Telling?)

Story is primary in animation, plays, novels… but in VR, story is but one facet of a multifaceted, collaborative endeavor. VR changes the traditional paradigm—story is secondary to the concept of "presence" in the VR world. In animation, breaking the fourth wall is rare (characters looking at the camera, acknowledging its existence). But in VR, the whole point is that the viewer is meant to feel as though they are physically "present." Saschka Unseld, the creative director at Oculus Story Studio, indicated that in the VR Cartoon *Henry* (Figure 8.8) it's weird if Henry doesn't recognize the player sitting on his living room floor with him… "'*It's just like Why don't you look at me? I'm right here*'… but when Henry does recognize you it carries an emotional connection, an empathy."[22]

VR comes in three forms, not all of which are conducive to story:[23]

Figure 8.8

Henry. (Copyright 2016 Oculus Story Studio.)

Figure 8.9

One of the first examples of film, a train coming into the station. *L'Arrivée d'un train en gare de La Ciotat*, 1895, Auguste Lumière.

Figure 8.10

GE 360 VR, a train traveling across the country. Created by ReelFX. (Copyright 2016 General Electric.)

1. *360 VR*—no intent for story. It is about spectacle, similar to the first examples of film (1895) (Figure 8.9). It is a 360-degree look at the environment, with emphasis on proof of technology or documenting reality (Figure 8.10).
2. *Immersive VR*—intentional story, first-person narrative (viewer's point of view). There is still 360-degree perspective on the world but the viewer is in a narrative world.[24] Emphasis is on the immersive experience with tactical (skill) and strategic (game based) interactions. Possible Swayze effect (as in the movie *Ghost*)—the viewer cannot be seen and heard, essentially operating like a ghost.
3. *True VR*—doesn't exist just yet, story to be a significant component. It includes 360 and immersive but requires real user choice and reactive environments.[24] A full body experience where the viewer is not only seen, heard, but also even more significant… can change most anything.

The difference between a story in animation (passive viewer) and VR (active viewer) is that if the viewer is not the most important thing in the story then everything that has been created is for naught. The viewer being centric in VR is analogous to our experience on amusement park rides, in haunted houses, or one's birthday party. Another intriguing difference is that when the viewer initially enters VR, they immediately have an *existential crisis*—where are they? Can they move? Can people hear or see them? Can they change anything? A viewer/character can only do what the designer has implemented. Thus, what they *can do* defines *who that viewer–character is*.[25]

Bernard Haux of Oculus Story Studio, confirms that in the beginning, it is more about getting the viewer ready for the experience.[26] He believes the beginning is critical:

1. *The In*—showing the world before starting the story (similar to film).
2. *Letting Go*—the viewer–character starts to take over.
3. *Call to Story*—allowing the elements of story emerge.

In *True* VR, it is not about storytelling. It isn't about *telling* a story but about anticipating… listening.[26] Andrew Cochrane proposes that it works best to get out of the "telling" mode of story and think about creating an experience. *DayZ* is not so much a game as much as a survival course. *Journey's* emergent narrative comes out of its spaces—where the storyteller becomes more a world builder (*Journey*—Figure 8.11), while *Uncharted* aims for a more tightly focused narrative experience straddling the line between traditional story and experience.

Figure 8.11

Emergent narrative, *Journey*. (Copyright 2012 thatgamecompany.)

References

1. M. Csikszentmihalyi, *Flow* (New York, HarperCollins Publishers, 2009), 9.
2. S. T. Coleridge, Biographia Literaria (1817), Chapter XIV, *Wikipedia*, last modified February 17, 2017, https://en.wikipedia.org/wiki/Suspension_of_disbelief
3. C. Bateman, *Game Writing: Narrative Skills for Videogames* (USA, Cengage Learning, 2006), 4.
4. T. K. Finley, *The Game Narrative Toolbox* (Boston, Massachusetts, Focal Press, 2015), 6.
5. C. Nolan, Christopher Nolan's 'Inception'—Hollywood's first existential heist film by Geoff Boucher, *Los Angeles Times*, April 11, 2010, http://herocomplex.latimes.com/uncategorized/christopher-nolans-inception-hollywoods-first-existential-heist-film/
6. T. Heussner, *The Game Narrative Toolbox* (Boston, Massachusetts, Focal Press, 2015), 121.
7. J. Cantor, *Secrets of CG Short Filmmakers* (Boston, Massachusetts, Cengage Learning PTR, 2014), 19.
8. P. L. Ounekeo, *Driving Forces of Narrative in Videogames, Exploring Videogames: Culture, Design and Identity*, N. Webber and D. Riha (eds) (ebook, Inter-Disciplinary Press, 2013), 52.
9. T. Heussner, *Game Narrative Toolbox*, 122.
10. Ibid, 121.
11. N. Brown, Are we fundamentally good or evil? Neuroscience has an answer, *Skyword*, April 20, 2016, https://www.skyword.com/contentstandard/creativity/are-we-fundamentally-good-or-evil-neuroscience-has-an-answer/
12. T. Heussner, *Game Narrative Toolbox*, 122.
13. T. K. Finley, *Game Narrative Toolbox*, 6.
14. H. Jenkins, Game design as narrative architecture, USC blog, 2004, 3. http://interactive.usc.edu/blog-old/wp-content/uploads/2011/01/Jenkins_Narrative_Architecture.pdf
15. H. LeFebvre, *The Production of Space* (London, Blackwell Publishers, 1991).
16. H. Jenkins, *Game Design*, 5.
17. D. Carson, Environmental storytelling: Creating immersive 3D world using lessons learned from the theme park industry, *Gamasutra*, March 1, 2000, http://www.gamasutra.com/view/feature/131594/environmental_storytelling_.php
18. H. Jenkins, *Game Design*, 6.
19. Ibid, 7.
20. Ibid, 8.
21. H. Smith, M. Worch, What happened here? Environmental storytelling session, gdcvault, Game Developers Conference, San Francisco, California, 2010.
22. S. Unseld, The Most Important Movie of 2015 is a VR Cartoon about a Hedgehog by Angela Watercutter, *Wired*, July 28, 2015, http://www.wired.com/2015/07/oculus-story-studio-making-henry/
23. A. Cochrane, *Creating Narratives for Virtual Reality* (Stuttgart, Germany, FMX16, April 28, 2016).
24. A. Cochrane, How Virtual Reality could Change Storytelling' by Megan Logan, *Inverse*, April 29, 2016, https://www.inverse.com/article/14971-how-virtual-reality-could-change-storytelling.
25. E. Skolnick, *Video Game Storytelling*, 118.
26. B. Haux, *Storytelling in VR* (Stuttgart, Germany, FMX16, April 26, 2016).

PART 3
Character Development

9

Character

Character

What is a dramatic *character*? How do they differ from you and me? Characters in a dramatic story are at a significant turning point in their life and faced with making difficult choices they can no longer avoid. They have been in denial about themselves. Tim Johnson (director—*Over the Hedge, Home*) stressed that in animation "*Often what a character wants is not what they need.*"[1] To create engaging characters, it is best to view them from the inside out; to understand what drives them.

Figure 9.1

Tragic flaw—psychological or physical, *The Theory of Everything*, 2014. (Copyright Focus Features/Courtesy Everett Collection.)

Figure 9.2

Characters need distinct points of view; Andy holds onto his hope, while Red has resigned himself to never being free. *Shawshank Redemption*. (Copyright 1994, Columbia Pictures.)

What Are the Dramatic Qualities of a *Character*?

1. A dramatic character is **obsessed** about something. While all characters are pursuing their desires, it is the main character who is *relentless* in going after what they want. McKee states that the character's obsession must be "*powerful enough to sustain (their) desire through conflict and ultimately take actions that create meaningful and irreversible change.*"[2] There is a zealous commitment to their goal even if the character may outwardly appear passive or weak (e.g., *High Noon, The Equalizer, The Finest Hours*—the everyman archetype has the potential to become a hero).

2. The main character's *unconscious need* is the **opposite** of their *conscious desire*. This works well because it creates an inner conflict that helps move the story forward.

3. The character's unique **capabilities match** the opposing forces they are up against... in hindsight. The viewer roots for the character, because this means the character could, just possibly, get what they want. This keeps the outcome plausible. Frodo Baggins has the right stuff (e.g., heart, determination) to resist the ring and keep it out of the hands of evil.

4. The character is someone the audience can **identify** with, strikes a chord with the viewer. This is someone they can root for and identify. McKee indicates that "*the unconscious logic of the audience runs like this: 'this character is like me. Therefore, I want him to have whatever it is he wants, because if I were he in those circumstances, I'd want the same thing myself.'*"[2]

5. Characters have a **tragic flaw**, a defect, that is holding them back and could eventually doom them. Such flaws are primarily psychological (e.g., narcissism [*Iron Man*], grief [*John Wick*]) but could just as easily be a physical impairment (*Theory of Everything* [Stephen Hawking]) (Figure 9.1).

6. Characters have a **distinct point of view**—how they see and interact with the world around them. Syd Field pointed out that in *Shawshank Redemption*, the juxtaposition of different points of view heightens the tension of how things will progress—Andy believes "*hope is a good thing*," Red believes "*hope is a dangerous thing*" in prison[3] (Figure 9.2).

7. Characters have a **mood** they carry around with them—angry, happy, freewheeling.... This is not their personality but their way of dealing with the world. In *The Heat*, Sarah is arrogant/uptight in contrast to Shannon who is foulmouthed/rebellious, while in *Halo*—Master Chief is stoic.

Story characters fall into two types, stereotypes and archetypes. Viewers are already familiar with these categories, either consciously or subconsciously.

Stereotypes are a simplified version of specific groups of people, by their gender, race, occupation, culture, etc. Stereotypes are the fastest way for our brain to categorize different people. Everyone has a set of mental stereotypes that come into play when meeting someone new.

> *...a story cannot be told about a protagonist who doesn't want anything, who cannot make decisions, whose actions affect no external, visual change.* Robert McKee.[6]

Stereotypes are a useful resource for secondary characters. However, they are deadly for your primary characters in lengthy stories because they possess only the most superficial qualities of people. These might be thought of as stock characters (see a list of stock characters on Wikipedia [e.g., Mama's boy, Village Idiot, Tomboy]).[4] In short stories, we find far more one-dimensional, stereotype characters because of limited time for character development.

Archetypes differ in that they are universal characters that inhabit the collective unconscious of all human beings.[5] These characters are common across cultures—Hero, Mentor, Shadow figure (villain), Everyman, Trickster....[5] Archetypes are the various roles one assumes during life. At one time or another they are us, as we move from being the hero, a father figure, everyman, jester (the funny one), trickster (duplicitous), or villain (betray friends). Knowing how these characters contribute becomes part of your toolset in story.

Character-Driven Story

Character-driven stories focus on the internal change a character goes through—that can be perceived/seen by the viewer. These stories include love stories, coming-of-age, redemption, institutionalized, education, and disillusionment genres. They require difficult choices the main character must make. The key components in a character-driven story include

1. The main character is driven by what they want in life
2. The focus is on the relationship conflicts that result from their character shortcomings
3. The theme is about personal growth (e.g., love, redemption, courage…)
4. The change a character goes through is fundamental to this type of story
5. The longer the story the more complex the character needs to be

Character-driven stories often start with someone stuck in life. Why they are stuck and can't move forward is what grabs the attention of the viewer: what does the character want, why can't they get it, and is this what they really need? The answers lead to the character's needs and what they must overcome or accept in themselves. To reiterate, *frequently what a character wants is not what they really need*, in *Wreck-It-Ralph*—is the solution to Ralph's problems really a medal? It does take time to find the right balance between "want" and "need" during development. The answer is not always obvious.

Many writers feel that the concept of a "character-driven story" is redundant—all stories are character-driven.[7] The purpose of the external events and situations are for revealing what drives the characters, but what really energizes a story are the choices characters make under pressure. Their reaction to what is happening around them—*"When life ends up breathtakingly fu***d, you can generally trace it back to one big bad decision"* (narration in *Deadpool*) (Figure 9.3). While all stories are a combination of character-driven versus plot-driven, by understanding what kind of story it is easier to keep the story's development on track. Sometimes this may get down to 51% character-driven versus 49% action, or the other way around. Knowing your emphasis improves one's focus.

Figure 9.3

Action comes out of the character's choices to their situation. *Deadpool*. (Copyright 2016, 20th Century Fox Film Corporation.).

Character-Driven Categories

1. *The Quest*—the main character goes in search of something and along the way they learn a lesson and experience a significant personal change (e.g., Luke in *Stars Wars,* Frodo in *The Lord of the Rings,* and Jack Cooper in *Titanfall 2*) (Figure 9.4).

2. *The Transformation*—a life changing experience enables the main character to see life differently (e.g., *It's a Wonderful Life, Iron Man, Shawshank Redemption*). What does the character have to learn to conquer their demons…to trust, to love, to be responsible?

A viewer is sustained in a story more by a character's attitudes, choices, and the changes they go through than with the action itself. This requires being clear *who* the story is about—through whose eyes the story is being told. Is it clear who is the hero (protagonist) and villain (antagonist)?

In character-driven stories, the conflict comes out of the fact that they both want the same thing. The conflict is not as simple as the fact that one person is good and the other is bad. This approach avoids a clichéd evil, but has the downside of confusion if the viewer doesn't know who to root for—who to identify with?

How to determine a character-driven story? If the primary storyline is the *change*, the main character goes through in the story (Character Arc) … it is a character-driven story. A *Character Arc* in a story is how the character is transformed. If the character is the same at the end of the story as they were in the beginning there is no character arc, it is not a character-driven story. Some would question that without a transformation is there even a story?

Figure 9.4

Quests—*Titanfall 2.* (Copyright 2016 EA Games.)

Archetypes

Stories share universal character types called archetypes.[8] These recurring characters (i.e., heroes, villains, mentors, etc.) can be found at both the individual level (in our dreams) and within the collective consciousness of society from the myths that have been passed down through generations. The understanding of archetypes is crucial to successfully exploiting the universal roles characters play in stories—hero, everyman, trickster etc.

The most universal archetypes are Hero, Mentor, Guardian [of the Threshold], Herald, Shapeshifter, Shadow [Villain], and Trickster. Archetypes continue to evolve (e.g., everyman, child-like adult, caring mother, the nerd, good girl...) but in any story, there can be only a limited number the audience can relate to at any one time. By definition, archetypes are universally understood characters common across all cultures.

What makes archetypes so fascinating is that they are not rigid character roles but can vary within the same character adding to the complexity of the story.[9] Archetypes are common across cultures and can change within a character. The longer the story... the more likely that a character will take on more than one archetype. A character might enter the story as a shadow/villain archetype only to become the hero by the end of the story. This switching of roles was a central theme in *Megamind* (Figure 9.5). Vogler suggests visualizing a character's archetype as a variety of masks they wear as needed.[10]

> Archetypes are universal, characters, common across all cultures.[10]

Carl Jung first devised the term archetypes in 1919 and later expanded the concept into personality types. Archetypes can be thought of as variations of a complete personality. They represent the various roles (i.e., child, trickster, bad guy) we adopt in life which is why we can easily relate to them. See *The Writer's Journey* by Chris Vogler, pages 33–92, for a detailed explanation of archetypes.[11]

Figure 9.5

Characters swtiching their archetypal roles, *Megamind*. (Copyright 2010, DreamWorks Animation.)

Hero—(classic) brave, self-sacrificing, moral. Heroes are often seen in search of who they really are or can become. They are often the main character (protagonist) that the audience identifies with. The one willing to sacrifice (e.g., their life) for the group. Captain America, Luke Skywalker, Simba (*Lion King*).

Mentor—wise, motivates, teaches. Mentors serve to teach the hero and to give them what they will need (e.g., lightsaber). These gifts have to be earned by learning, sacrifice, or commitment. Mentors motivate the hero to overcome their fear. They serve as their conscience. Obi-Wan Kenobi, Mufasa.

Shadow figure—evil, negative. Shadow characters (antagonist) are the villains. This negative archetype can be another person, emerge from the shapeshifter, or even later emerge in the hero themselves from something repressed. Shadow characters often believe they are doing good. Darth Vader, Scar (*Lion King*) (Figure 9.6), Captain Salazar (*Pirates of the Caribbean*).

That's part of the power of stereotypes—they set up expectations, so you can surprise your reader (viewer/player). Orson Scott Card.[12]

Shapeshifter—selfish, cunning, intelligent... friend or foe? They build tension in the story because the audience is never sure who they are or what they might do. Their ability to change their thinking or appearance can be a catalyst for change in others. Shapeshifters range from literal shape changing (e.g., vampires, zombies, werewolves [*Twilight*]) to changing roles (good girl to temptress [Sandy in *Grease*]).

Tricksters—pranksters to troublemakers. Tricksters can be sidekicks in Disney films (Olaf [*Frozen*]), *Looney Tunes* characters (Bugs Bunny, Daffy Duck), even the main character—Jack Sparrow (*Pirates of the Caribbean*). Tricksters are those characters that urge us to take chances.

Herald—is more a functional role in a story. To provide information (exposition). C-3PO, R2-D2... whoever (or whatever [a storm]) provides the impetus to get the adventure started and keep it going.

Threshold Guardians—Forces that stand in our way. These can range from people in our past that continue to haunt us to Cinderella's stepmother. Often seen in Coming of Age stories as the bully (Biff [*Back to the Future*] to Regina George [*Mean Girls*]).

Figure 9.6

Hero archetypes, mentor archetypes, villain archetypes. (Copyright Walt Disney Pictures.)

Stereotypes

Stereotypes are an *oversimplified concept of a specific group of people* (i.e., gender, race, occupation, etc.). To recognize a stereotype, ask—does the character look and act as expected? If they do and nothing is different, then it is a stereotype. True stereotypical characters don't change who they are (e.g., the Simpsons [Figure 9.7], Sheldon Cooper [*Big Bang Theory*]). If stereotypes do change on episodic television, the change is temporary and they change back by the next episode.

Judging people based on their external characteristics is an evolutionary mechanism, part of a person's survival instinct to differentiate friend from foe. It is the quickest way for the brain to evaluate new people. We all have an inventory of stereotypes that come into play when meeting someone new. This ubiquitous feature of stereotypes makes them useful devices in stories.

When characters are first introduced, they trigger an impression of a stereotype. This familiarity permits a quick entry into the narrative. The viewer draws upon their preconceived expectations for how a stereotypical character is supposed to behave. The flip side is, if the character does look, speak, and act as expected they quickly become predictable and boring; a teacher acts like a teacher, a politician speaks like a politician—clichés.

Figure 9.7

The Simpsons as stereotypes. *The Simpsons*, l-r: Bart Simpson, Marge Simpson, Lisa Simpson, Homer Simpson, Maggie Simpson in "Super Franchise Me" (Season 26, Episode 3, aired October 12, 2014). (TM & Copyright 20th Century Fox Film Corp. All rights reserved/Courtesy Everett Collection.)

Since stereotypes can't be avoided, the writer needs to at least be able to recognize them so they don't weaken the story. The damage comes about when stereotypes are inadvertently substituted for archetypes. This is a recurring problem resulting in superficial characters in contrast to archetypes that resonate across cultural boundaries. Stereotypes are often considered a storyteller's worst dilemma—using stereotypes in a story but being able to see when they are undermining the story.

On the other hand, stereotypes can be used effectively when an author recognizes they are using stereotypes and upends their expected behavior—stereotypes doing something unanticipated (i.e., a politician tells the truth) surprising the viewer. This approach makes stereotypes very useful in comedy. Comedy is populated with stereotypes that break expectations. It is that deviation from the expected that stands out and gets an audience's attention. It piques their curiosity.

Stereotypes not only look but also react as one would expect all characters in this grouping to react. It is a generic, not an individualistic, response. Stereotypes are reinforced daily through advertising—moms stay at home, prepare sit down meals for the family, and wear dresses. Though there is a low percentage of moms who stay home and have time to bake, this caricature has been seen repeatedly on TV, so viewers come to believe it. Commercials create whole scenarios through such connotations: dads working in cubicles, a dog fetching the newspaper—all images that are cliché but are useful for they rapidly establish time, place, and character in less than a second.

When using stereotypes, put them in opposition with each other. This pitting of a clichéd view of the world against a contradictory way of looking at the world creates tension; it exposes their superficiality. These situations are common in family stories where a conservative character lives with a progressive character—*All in the Family* to *Modern Family*. This opposition technique is effective in putting the stereotype in a situation that is out of their comfort zone.

While there are a limited number of archetypes that cultures have in common (8–20), there are an unlimited number of stereotypes specific to cultures. This is because unlike archetypes that are universal across cultures, stereotypes are always distinct to each specific culture. For example, every culture has its stereotype for a taxi and its driver. A taxi driver in London is different from the same person in New York City, Delhi, Beverly Hills….

Ironically, a number of our most beloved characters are stereotypical on the outside but transform into beloved archetypes along the way (e.g., Laura Croft, Chief in *Halo*) (Figure 9.8). Where this gets confusing is that often archetypes come dressed as stereotypes (a hero in the form of a farm boy [*Star Wars*] or as an overweight office worker [*The Incredibles*]). The key is to focus on how characters *act*. Their actions are what differentiate archetype from stereotypes. To make this happen, unique backstories are valuable in providing references to draw upon. The switching of how a character acts is effective in games/VR that are experienced for 20–50 hours or a TV series that spans multiple seasons.

> *Story is about archetypes, not stereotypes.* The archetypal story unearths a universally human experience, then wraps itself inside a unique, culture-specific expression. A stereotypical story reverses this pattern… It confines itself to a narrow, culture-specific experience and dresses in stale, nonspecific generalities. Robert McKee.[13]

Figure 9.8

Halo—Master Chief. (Copyright Microsoft.)

Backstory versus Character Profile

Backstory is comprised of what has happened in a character's life before the story starts. It isn't a biography of everything in their life but one that specifically focuses on the information relevant to a character's flaws and their conflict. Creating complex, interesting characters starts by mining this information for ideas. By understanding what a character brings to the story, it is easier to construct believable reactions and choices.

Viewers want to identify with the character. What the backstory provides is a context to the character, their experiences, and how they got to this point in their life. It is the information in the backstory (exposition) where the viewer begins to identify with the character. What do viewers and characters each have in common?

Figure 9.9

James Cameron, director, *Avatar.*

The process of writing a good script (story) is writing characters that have complete lives, that have complete pasts. Everything that they do... is determined by what went on before that. So it's the art of setting up those characters as quickly but as completely as possible. It is often difficult to predict before the fact exactly which piece of information or given character trait will be necessary. James Cameron[14] (Figure 9.9)

To turn a scene in a different direction, using a *reveal,* requires information from the character's backstory. A reveal comes out of something in a character's past they have kept secret. It is often some event in the character's life that has caused great emotional damage that keeps them from going after what they want. The reveal emerges when the character can't hold back any longer and must go after what they want (e.g., a girl, a job, to move somewhere else [*Brooklyn*]). Director Lee Unkrich indicated that in *Toy Story 3*... *"What was interesting to us was analyzing the reasons why Lotso was the way he was. When we came up with the notion of a toy being lost and then going through all these obstacles to find his way back home only to discover he had callously been replaced.... If you are going to be in this world of toys you don't want to give the toys human problems but toy problems"*[15] (Figure 9.10).

Figure 9.10

Lee Unkrich, director, *Toy Story 3.*

The story's *setting* also has a backstory (e.g., *No Country for Old Men, Big Action Hero 6*). The setting provides pivotal moments that lead up to the predicament that the player finds themselves in. In *No Country for Old Men*, the main character is out hunting in the middle of nowhere and stumbles across a drug deal gone bad. Setting is vital in video games/VR as it orients the player to their situation (e.g., what are they facing? what is possible in this situation?). How they got themselves into this situation may not be seen but it is referenced as the player moves through the environment... game level to game level.

Because most of the backstory is never seen on the screen, its influence is often overlooked. McKee and Egri considered the use of setting one of the most underused tools in the story development process.

Background information comes in two forms: external *backstory* information or internal *character profile* insights. The direction that story development takes determines which of the two are most important. Not all questions are relevant. Compiling a list of questions is useful for development. These lists may be tailored not only to each story but also to an author's sensibilities (e.g., animator, VR/game designer, etc.). It is important to put together your own list that is matched to your viewpoint.

Angus MacLane, *Toy Story Toons: Stir Fry*, said that in creating the characters, John Lasseter (VP Creative, Disney/Pixar) would quiz him on whether he had a backstory for all the characters in the group. *What toy line did they come from... was it a TV show, a movie... so I wrote them all out, also wrote out the others toys in that assortment*[16] (Figure 9.11).

Figure 9.11

Angus MacLane, director, *Toy Story Toons*.

Backstory Questions (External)

- Appearance?
  - Age, gender, locomotion, speech patterns, voice, etc.?
- Role in society?
  - Education, family, upbringing, relationships, lifestyle, hobbies/sports, ethnicity/heritage, livelihood/work, religion, status, rituals?
- Background?
  - Success and failures, diseases, disappointments, successes, embarrassments, threats, talents?

Character Profile Questions (Internal)

- Character's passions? What they love, their dreams, what do they really want more than anything else?
- Character's flaws, quirks/mannerisms, habits?
- Character's point-of-view?
  - Values, attitude, sense of right and wrong, ability to empathize, feel compassion
- Personality—emotional? Logical?
- Strengths and weaknesses (what they are good at doing and not good at doing)?
- How characters see themselves?
- How others see the character?
- Character's deepest secrets?
- Fears, phobias? Why? How did they get that way?
- Intelligence?
- 100% compulsive about what?

Identification/Empathy

Identification is the viewer relating so closely with a character that they vicariously experience the same emotions—joy, sorrow, and pain. Identification (empathy) is the most compelling method for a viewer to enter, and stay, with the story. As the character encounters conflict, the viewer encounters the conflict right alongside them. If the character is in danger, the audience feels frightened; if the character suffers loss, the audience feels sad.[17]

Identification is possible because we have gone through experiences that have resulted in similar emotions. As we empathize, we *become* that character on a psychological and emotional level. Lajos Egri emphasizes that it is through emotion that identification is established.[18] Director Joss Whedon talks about how he viewed it in *Avengers*... "*it is Steve and Bruce, more than anyone else on the team, (who) are identification figures. To experience with them both the magnificence and absurdity of this thing taking off... became a very important part of the emotional journey.*"[19] We relate to not just the positive qualities of the character, but also to the more embarrassing traits that we keep under cover. With negative traits, the key is to give characters' familiar flaws and foibles because we recognize those in ourselves (Hiccup—*How to Train Your Dragon*) (Figure 9.12). Identification originates with similarities between the viewer and characters—attitude, appearances.

Identification can transfer from one character to another.[20] Over the course of the story, the viewer is not limited to identifying with just one character. In Terminator, we identify with Kyle Reese (his determination), Sarah Connor (her vulnerability), and even the Terminator (an invincibility). At the same time, it is not uncommon for viewers to find themselves relating more with the situation the character finds themselves in.[21]

Figure 9.12

Hiccup, *How to Train Your Dragon.* (Copyright 2010 DreamWorks Animation.)

Identification is not passive but an active process in story. It is sustained by presenting circumstances the viewer can relate to throughout the story. How a character psychologically responds to the situation is what holds the viewer's attention. The more prevalent responses include fear to danger, anger to unfairness, and likeability as one does good toward others.

Michael Hauge[22] emphasizes that making your character *likeable* is key to identification. Is the character someone the viewer would like to be around? Someone who is loved by family and friends, outgoing, personable, nice to kids? Likeability includes *funny*, or what happens to the character is funny. If characters make people laugh, then even if they do things that are a bit dodgy (e.g., Will Ferrell characters), they will be forgiven and embraced. Within likeability is also *strong/good*—the character is good at what they do... dedicated, honest, someone who can do things others can't. Likeable traits include kind, daring, enthusiastic, generous, kindhearted, passionate, a good person, etc.

Lagos Egri underscores that great stories are not populated with outlandish characters but characters we recognize as real flesh-and-blood human beings. This is accomplished by making the character similar to someone he/she knows and making the viewer imagine what is happening to the character could happen to him/her.[23]

Identification with a situation is generated when characters are going through times of stress, drama, or crisis.[24] It is a form of catharsis. Two of the most identifiable situations are unfairness and danger. When something *unfair* happens to a character, the viewer immediately relates to the times in their own lives when things were unfair. Michael Arndt, writer for *Toy Story 3*, shares…

> You have got to have something that is going to make the whole world seem a little bit unfair. So not only does Woody get replaced, he gets replace by this total doofus, this total imbecile that doesn't even know he is a toy. They get in this argument on whether Buzz can fly or not, and Buzz jumps and bounces, and flies around the room. And all the other toys, go OMG he can fly. The key thing here is that everyone is impressed for the wrong reasons. In the case of Nemo, we don't need to add insult to injury, we already understand that the world Marlin lives in unfair. But on the other hand, with the Incredibles, the reason, superheroes get banned, is that Mr. Incredible was trying to do the right thing.[25]

The other is *danger*, the character in jeopardy—threatened by *physical loss* (job, house, health, life [*Mad Max: Fury Road, Jurassic World*]) or *emotional loss* (love [friends and family], being exposed, fear, embarrassment). Audiences automatically feel empathy with the character. Once the audience starts to worry about what will happen to the character they have an emotional stake in the outcome, they are hooked (Figure 9.13). For additional information on identification, look into *Writing Screenplays that Sell* by Michael Hauge, pages 49–56.[26]

> *You have to identify with your situation and characters, can't just write "Cool". What would make you act that way?*[27] Pam Coats, Pixar's 22 Rules of Storytelling

Love Your Characters

There is an axiom in story that *you must know your characters*. However, there is an additional piece of the puzzle that isn't mentioned as regularly but is probably even more important—"*If you* (the storyteller) *don't care about the characters then nothing you do matters... no explosion, no special effects, no space ship flying will matter to anyone at all if you do not love and care about the people in the story*"[28] J. J. Abrams (Figure 9.14).

Gabe Newell, President of Valve, said they incorporated this concept of caring about your characters in the game *Half Life*, where the characters play *catch* with their new hulking robot weapon, D0g.[29] Michael Arndt shared that "*If I could give one bit of advice... 'love your characters', that is a mistake I saw over and over again, people writing stories with characters that were either really boring or generic..., or characters they actually didn't like. To me, the number one commandment... is don't condescend to your character. Your character should be as smart as you are if not more so.*"[30]

Figure 9.14

J. J. Abrams, director.

The viewer needs to first know a character before they can identify emotionally with the character. This starts by *revealing the character's motivation* (e.g., *Lives of Others*, *Captain America—Civil War*). As Atticus Finch said in *To Kill a Mocking Bird* "*you never really understand a person until you consider things from his point of view... Until you climb inside of his skin and walk around in it.*"[31]

The story process starts with the storyteller caring about their characters. At the same time, it is crucial to differentiate between caring about your characters and *falling in love* with your characters—where they become precious, and protected, at the expense of the story. This is seen repeatedly in people new to the process where the story development gets derailed as the author becomes protective of their initial concept and first ideas about the characters.

Viewers care about characters that are (1) capable, (2) empathetic, and (3) good people.[32] Using these concepts help to develop characters and situations that engage the viewer. Make a list and just keep adding to it.

1. Characters that are **capable**—knowledgeable, courageous, successful, tough, passionate, charismatic, and strong.
2. Characters that **generate empathy**—characters may have experienced loneliness, danger, injury, rejection, abandonment (Rey—*Star Wars: Episode VII*), betrayal, vulnerability (*Mad Max: Fury Road*), handicaps, misfortune (*Finding Nemo*, Marlin lost his family, wife… and then his son is gone), mistakes, and regret. Warning, this is also a category crammed with clichés repeatedly portrayed in the news media.
3. Characters with **good qualities**—kind (*Save the Cat*), generous, open, loves and loved by others (Tony Soprano), ethical, loyal, responsible, fight for what they believe (*Braveheart*), risk their life (Woody to rescue Buzz), forgive, help others (Riddick).

It can't be stressed enough, if the storyteller doesn't care about the characters, no one else will. The writer has to care about all the characters… even the villains in the story—Did James Cameron, the director, love or hate his *Terminator*? (Figure 9.15). Karl Iglesias has a great section on Techniques for Empathy in his book, *Writing for Emotional Impact*, pages 67–73.[33]

Figure 9.15

The Terminator straightening his hair, revealing that is more than just a machine, he cares about his looks. (Copyright 1984, Orion Pictures Corporation.)

References

1. T. Johnson, *Directing* (Turin, Italy, View Conference, Oct. 27, 2010).
2. R. McKee, *Story*, 137.
3. S. Field, *Screenwriting*, 44.
4. List of stock characters, *Wikipedia*, last modified October 16, 2016, https://en.wikipedia.org/wiki/List_of_stock_characters
5. C. Jung, *The Portable Jung*, J. Campbell (ed.) (New York, NY: Penguin Books, 1976), 178.
6. R. McKee, *Story*, 138.
7. Ibid, 44.
8. C. Jung, *Psychological Types (The Collected Works of C.G. Jung, Vol.6)*, (New Jersey, Princeton University Press, 1976).
9. V. Propp, *Morphology of the Folktale* (Dallas, University of Texas Press, 1968).
10. C. Vogler, *The Writer's Journey*, 34.
11. Ibid, 33–92.
12. O. S. Card, *Characters & Viewpoint* (New York, Writer's Digest Books, 1988), 44.
13. R. McKee, *Story*, 4.
14. J. Cameron, *Terminator 2, Story Segment* (Lions Gate, 2009), DVD supplemental disc.
15. L. Unkrich, *Toy Story 3, Story Segment* (Walt Disney Productions, 2011), DVD supplemental disc.
16. A. MacLane, *Pixar Short Films Collection*, Volume 2 (Walt Disney Studios, 2012), DVD.
17. M. Hauge, *Writing Screenplays*, 49.
18. L. Egri, *Dramatic Writing*, 44.
19. J. Whedon, *The Avengers, The Making of Segment* (Paramount Studios, 2012), DVD.
20. J. Ellis, *Visible Fictions: Cinema, Television, Video* (London: Routledge, 1992), 42.
21. I. Ang, *Watching Dallas: Soap Opera and the Melodramatic Imagination* (London, Methuen Publishing, 1985), 44.
22. M. Hauge, *Writing Screenplays*, 6.
23. L. Egri, *Dramatic Writing*, 44.
24. R. Kilborn, *Television Soaps* (London, Batsford Publishing, 1992). 44.
25. M. Arndt, *What I learned at Pixar about Story, Toy Story 3* (Walt Disney Studios, 2012), Blu-Ray Disc.
26. M. Hauge, *Writing Screenplays*, 6.
27. P. Coats, *Pixar's 22 Rules to Phenomenal Storytelling*, September 23, 2015, https://www.visualnews.com/2015/09/23/22-rules-to-perfect-storytelling-from-a-pixar-storyboard-artist/
28. J. J. Abrams, Storytelling Across Platforms (Dice Conference, 2013), http://www.dicesummit.org/dice_summits/2013-dice-archive.asp
29. Ibid., Newell.
30. M. Arndt, *Little Miss Sunshine: The Shooting Script* (San Francisco, Cody Books, 2007), https://www.youtube.com/watch?v=bsEkf_TYV6s
31. H. Lee, *To Kill a Mockingbird* (New York, Grand Central Publishing, 1988), 44.
32. K. Iglesias, *Writing for Emotional Impact* (Los Angeles, Wingspan Press, 2011), 67.
33. Ibid, 67–73.

10
Character Elements

Story World as Character

A setting is not passive,[1] it is a dramatic force as powerful as any character (e.g., *Oz, Titanic, Gravity, Moana*). It works well to think of the story world (setting) as another character in the story. Story worlds, like characters, have backstories with histories, geography, politics—why things are the way they are today (i.e., Seven Kingdoms of Westeros). A story world's variables center around time, place, and social constructs.

The *Time Period* is set in either the past, present, or future. Society's rules, indicative of the time, provide the context to the inevitable clash between how a viewer sees the world today and the viewpoint from the story's time period (i.e., *Back to the Future, Midnight in Paris*).

The *Location* (where the story takes place) limits what is or is not possible in this world. Place may be a planet (Mars, Ahch-To), specific geography (e.g., desert, mountains), structural configurations (e.g., streets [Boston, Calcutta, Hogsmeade), spatial design (e.g., buildings, rooms), etc. The determining factor is the connection of the location to the story; *Spotlight* and *The Town* are both Boston specific while *Journey*, the video game, is in a vast desert. *Revenant* and *Deepwater Horizon* are both closely tied to their landscape (Figure 10.1).

Social frameworks[1] are society's constructs that individuals struggle against on a daily basis. These are the political, ideological, historical, cultural, and social patterns that define a specific environment. They may be supportive or stressful, inclusive or isolating (i.e., Hunger Games). These make up the layers that shape the story. In a story, this can range from conflict that is personal to individuals battling institutions (e.g., *Evil Empire, First Order, DMV*). Stories emerge out of the myriad of encounters we all experience. Lawson emphasizes that "*from its first glimpse of the first image, the audience inspects your fictional universe, sorting the possible from the impossible, the likely from the unlikely.*"[1] As J. K. Rowling has indicated, it is a lot of work to create an entire world. She spent an awful lot of time constructing the world and working it out.[2]

Figure 10.1

Setting as important a narrative element as character. *Deepwater Horizon*, US Poster, 2016 (Copyright Summit Entertainment/Courtesy Everett Collection.)

Story worlds provide a sense of believability. Only certain events are possible or probable which can drive the action. This sense of place, when it does well, serves double duty as a symbolic extension of the story's conflict. Boston is a favorite location for dramas that use Boston's reputation a place with strong family and community ties (i.e., *The Town, The Fighter, Spotlight*). It is this connection to place that separates these stories from generic conflicts that could be anywhere. These story worlds are part-and-parcel of the enticements that motivate a player to progress through the different levels in a video game. Players will inevitably continue to progress through the environment just to learn what is around the next corner (e.g., *World of Warcraft, CyberHeist* [Figure 10.2]).

Character can only be understood in terms of an active relationship between the individual and the world in which they interact.[3] As soon as character is detached from the setting... the character becomes a general set of character traits. Robert McKee is convinced that the greatest source of *"audience dissatisfaction"* in movies today is a lack of knowledge about the setting.[4] The chief source of story clichés comes from writers not knowing the world of their story. In fact, many writers don't give much thought to the setting until the end. At that point, a setting might be randomly chosen from the fashionable locations being covered in the media. Such stories quickly disintegrate into clichés inside a host of other clichéd worlds.

In the end, when the story is over, it isn't the plot that is remembered—it is the situation and characters ... and occasionally the theme.

Figure 10.2

Cyber Heist, a two-person game, where one is infiltrating the space of the computer while the other is navigating the physical space of the DOE.

...what I look for early on is.... the setting. Where is this movie taking place? Is it someplace I would love to go, and I would love to spend time in this world? (As the story develops) you can't just pick the story up and move it to a different (location).[5]

John Lasseter, Chief Creative Office, Disney/Pixar

The key to getting story worlds right is to never forget that within any world, no matter how fantastic, only particular events are possible or probable.[6] In upper class society, if they wish to affect political change do they turn to fundraisers or street marches? Each story world has its own laws for what could and could not happen within it. In Sci-Fi and Fantasy, once these laws are established, they must be followed to maintain believability. This believability can impact a story to such an extent that the story world evolves into a narrative in its own right. In VR, its narrative and the story world are one and the same.

Goal: What a Character Wants

An essential element of story is *what does the main character want.*

- David Mamet defines story as the essential progression of incidents that occur to the hero in pursuit of one goal.[7]
- Iglesias sees story as someone who wants something badly and is having trouble getting it.[8]
- McKee indicates that the main character must have a clear and conscious desire.[9]
- Cowgill affirms that every story is about the quest to attain a goal and whether the character will achieve it or not.[10]
- Trottier says that in virtually every story, the central character has a conscious goal. The goal is whatever your central character outwardly strives for.[11]

The main character's goal is a clear, visible goal, that the viewer can follow—to be with each other in *Romeo and Juliet,* take out terrorists in *Call of Duty 4.* Once the viewer has been clued in as to what that goal is then everything moves in that direction with the main character taking action to reach that goal (i.e., destroy the Death Star in *Star Wars*). That is when becomes hooked. As Monica, in the sitcom *Friends,* said "*It... just... got... interesting!*" (S5, E24). When a viewer doesn't understand what a character *wants,* then the basic connections between scenes unravel—with no thread to follow.

Along the way, it takes achieving small goals (getting to the location, finding the sword) if the character is going to achieve their goal. At the same time, if not all of the short-term goals are achieved, the viewer's interest will be heightened. In *Guardians of the Galaxy,* Peter (Star Lord) is not successful in selling the orb for money. Such setbacks cast doubt on whether he can get to his final goal and keeps the audience hooked.[12] External short-term goals happen every two to four scenes (~3–7 minutes) and are linked in some way to the final goal. Edson points out that these linked goals maintain continuity in a story.[13] Hauge reinforces this perception by emphasizing that "*Every scene, event, and character contributes to the hero's outer motivation.*"[14] He stresses that this is so important it should become part of everyone's story checklist.

Goal Traits

1. The main character *becomes obsessed* in reaching their goal.
2. The character is eventually *willing to risk everything*, physically and emotionally. The character must reach the goal or else all is lost... survival (*Star Wars*), self-esteem (*Ratatouille*), love (*Shrek*).
3. The goal must be *visible*. When the goal is clear the audience sees a mental picture of what achieving it would look like in the end. Along the way, the character must do things that can be seen, rather than just talking about doing them.
4. The goal must be *achievable but seem unattainable*. The challenge is to make it sufficiently plausible that success is possible while at time the obstacles appear just too insurmontable.[15] It is a delicate balancing act to not make it inevitable or impossible to attain. The goal is sufficiently difficult to achieve so that the character *changes* while moving toward it.
5. The goal must be *matched to the story*. An archaeologist is after an artifact, they are not trying to design women's swimwear (Figure 10.3). The goal needs to make sense for the character.[15] How does the specific goal relate to the events directly leading to the climax?

> Sometimes we have to give up the thing we want the most—even our dreams. *Spider-Man 2 (2004)*.

6. There needs to be *specific endpoint* to the goal. It has to be clear to the audience when the goal has been achieved.
7. A goal that *brings the characters into conflict*.[16] There are obstacles in the way of getting what you want in any story. It often comes in the form of characters who want the same thing.

Goals can change. In the animation WALL-E, his initial goal was keeping things in order. After Eve appeared then she became his desire. In *Avatar*, Jake's external desire was to become whole again, an avatar permanently. However, after falling in love with Neytiri, his goal became to save Na'vi. Shrek initially just wanted to be left alone, that changed after falling in love. By the end, his goal was to stop the wedding because he wanted to be with Princess Fiona.

Figure 10.3

Goal is matched to character. An archeologist seeks a lost ark. Raiders of the Lost Ark. (Copyright 1981, Paramount Pictures.)

Need: What a Character Really, Really Wants

A story starts by showing what a character *wants* but as the story progresses it reveals what a character really *needs*. Both appear to come from the same place but often what we *want* is only the most obvious and easiest thing at hand to fill that *need*. It only works for a short while. Need is some part of a person that is damaged or missing (e.g., unloved, fearful) and serious enough to be derailing their life. In a story, *need* denotes an unconscious, inner force that compels a character to act without understanding the real reasons why.[17]

Figure 10.4

Michael Hauge, screenwriter.

Lagos Egri summarized a character's *need* as "insecurity... *the most central and complex of all human emotions and conflicts.*"[18] For Hauge, need is tied to what he considers the most important story element—the character's motivation (Figure 10.4).[19] A story doesn't really start until the motivation kicks in. *Rocky* accepts the fight *to prove he's not a bum*; Maggie trains to show she is more than *trash (Million Dollar Baby)*; Luke leaves Tatooine to avenge his guardians' death but his real motivation is to prove *he is a man* (*Star Wars*) (Figure 10.5).

Inner needs include overcoming fear, stopping the pain from past wounds, finding love. These get converted into external "wants"—control, power, things, fame, money... in a bid to fill the emptiness. Without a character's *need* driving the story, the *wants* take precedence with the story's *meaning* coming up short at the end.

Getting a viewer *to care* about a character is directly linked to understanding the character's motivation. To keep the motivation real, it is important to ask—*is the character doing what I would do in that situation, knowing what I know*? If a character becomes angry, happy, sad, etc. for no apparent reason, it won't make sense to the viewer. There is no *just because* in a story, where people wake up one day and start doing things differently.[20] If the viewer doesn't have some inkling why a character is doing something, then they stop caring, lose interest... or worse, stop watching.[21] This is where stories become stuck. Problems in story are time and again traced to confusing or even nonexistent motivations.

Figure 10.5

Luke decides to leave Tatooine to prove he is a man. *Star Wars*. (Copyright 1977, 20th Century Fox Film Corp.)

10. Character Elements

What a character says they want is not what they need[22] is almost a cliché in feature animation today. Truism in story—there is no point in having a character consciously want the same thing they subconsciously need. It sabotages the purpose of the inner conflict as an effective story tool.

The *need* and *want* operate differently—a *need* pushes, it drives the character as opposed to a *want* that pulls, drawing a character ever closer. This being pushed often compels a character to act in irrational ways.[23] The viewer relates to this from their own illogical responses to pressures at different times in their own lives.

When a story opens, the character does not know what they really need in life. Viewers relate to this lack of awareness because most of us pursue goals that in the end are not satisfying, don't fulfill our needs. The character becomes aware only near the end of the story, after they have *earned* this awareness, having been put through considerable pain. If a character does know exactly what they need, then there is no character arc, no story, as the solution is straightforward.

Needs are best portrayed by connecting to an event in their backstory. This could be something that has stunted their emotional growth—no parents while growing up (e.g., Luke, Rey, *Star Wars*). It has subsequently shaped how they see themselves and their reactions. As they try to fill this hole, they will often grasp at the closest and easiest solution at hand. This knee-jerk reaction makes it very relatable for the viewer. Unfortunately, for the character, this reaction will invariably result in the wrong choice which leads to inevitable conflict (great for story development). On the other hand, if the character makes the right choice, there is no story.

A character's internal motivation is, by its very nature, invisible. The challenge is to make it visible to the audience (*Show, don't Tell*). The conflicts in animation, VFX, games, and VR all involve characters reacting (i.e., fear, anger, etc.). Which must be shown visually and in turn result in *action*. This is the goal in *Revenant…* going after the killer (Figure 10.6). Story tools such as dialog and flashbacks are best used sparingly as they are most useful for providing story information than creating drama. A downside to flashbacks is that they interrupt the flow of the drama by leaving the story to go to the past.

Figure 10.6

The Goal—going after the killer.

Conflict Reveals Character

Who a character truly is inside is only *revealed in the choices a human being makes under pressure.* The greater the pressure, the deeper the revelation, the truer the choice to the character's essential nature.[24]

Who a person really is down deep, isn't found in what they do, how they look, or how they carry themselves. Only when they are forced to make a difficult choice (i.e., fight, flee, hide…) is their true character uncovered. Only when Peter Quill leaves the safety of his pod to rescue Gamora do we understand he is capable of caring, and sacrificing for someone besides himself (*Guardians of the Galaxy*) (Figure 10.7).

> *Characters are recognizable not only by their personal characteristics, but by how they express these characteristics in response to conflict or love….*[25]
> Chuck Jones (director, Bugs Bunny, Road Runner cartoons etc.)

In a story, appearances can often be deceiving. When the viewer first sees a character, they learn only what can be observed—personality, intelligence, age, values, attitude. From this, they make judgments about the character. But this is not their *true character*, who they really are inside. The challenge is to discover, regardless of what they look like, who is this character really? Are they loving, cruel, generous, selfish….?

Characters are not who they appear to be. This is not only one of life's fundamental lessons we must all learn, but also an integral part of the entertainment in the story—figuring out who is who. It is at the core of many genres (i.e., mysteries, detective stories). In *The Dark Knight Rises*, Selena represents *good* in most of the film, only to discover she has been working for Batman's arch enemy Bane the whole time. In *The Departed*, it was revealed early that Colin Sullivan, who personifies good outwardly… is duplicitous; while Billy Costigan who has a terrible past… is really the good one. In *Brooklyn*, they turned this expectation on its head with the main character being exactly who they appear to be.

Figure 10.7

True character revealed as Peter gives Gamora his oxygen in *Guardians of the Galaxy.* (Copyright 2014, Walt Disney Pictures.)

10. Character Elements

Only in conflict do we reveal our true selves. Will the hero turn out to be a coward or the coward turn out to be a hero? Our defenses keep the world seeing who we want them to think we are.[26] Everyone wears a mask. It is the choices under pressure that strip away that mask for the viewer. This alternative identity, what's behind the mask, is a favorite theme. The Hulk/Bruce Banner, Superman/Clark Kent, Batman/Bruce Wayne, Avatar/Jake Scully (Figure 10.8), Iron Man/Tony Stark, Spiderman/Peter Parker... Who is Darth Vader under the mask? Is James Bond really as superficial as he appears?

Characters who are exactly as they appear to be are not that interesting. It leaves little room for developing the drama. There is an exception—comedy. Two characters may be exactly who they appear but have opposite characteristics. They are then forced to work together. They function as one character with two personalities. This approach is a springboard for visual conflict. The characters will inevitably hit heads because of their different perspectives on life (Unity of Opposites [i.e., *21 Jump Street*, *Toy Story*]).

The artifice of a daily mask we present to others has a psychological basis (the *imposter syndrome*). It is not a disorder as much as adaptation trait in humans. It has been estimated that 40% of successful people consider themselves frauds and 70% of all people feel this at one time or another—the Imposter Syndrome.[27] To maintain these outside perceptions, people will tolerate feelings of being a phony and diligently work to be charming, industrious, and reliable, all in an attempt to prevent the outside world from discovering who they really are.

In story, characters must be forced into more and more difficult situations where they must make increasingly difficult choices, gradually exposing their true character. It is the storyteller's job to continually increase the conflict forcing the character to make these ever more difficult choices.

> *How (characters) respond to a particular incident or event, ... what they do, is what really defines the essence of their character.*[28]

Henry James, 1884 (Figure 10.9)

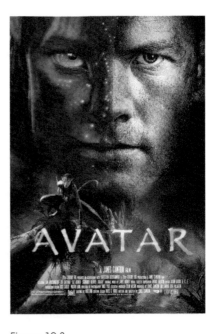

Figure 10.8

Jake and his alternate identity, Twentieth Century Fox Film Corporation/The Kobal Collection.

Figure 10.9

Henry James. As a writer, he emphasized realism in story.

Choices that a Character Must Make

The most memorable stories find characters in situations where they have to make hard choices with real consequences—moral choices work best.[29] In making choices,

> *Rule 1*: Choices must be difficult.
> *Rule 2*: There must be consequences (if personal, even better).

Viewers are intrigued to see how others deal with dilemmas in life. They will follow a character at a crossroads in their life; when change is imminent. Before making *Toy Story*, John Lasseter and Pete Docter came back from Robert McKee's seminar convinced that… *"character emerges most realistically and compellingly from the choices that the protagonist makes in reaction to his problems."*[30] In every story, there is usually one scene where the character, literally, talks about the *choice* they have to make.

- Andy Dufresne to Red (*Shawshank Redemption*) *"It gets down to a simple choice: 'get busy living or get busy dying'."*
- Samwell Tarly (*Game of Thrones*, S5, E7) talking about Jon Snow *"… sometimes a man has to make hard choices; choices that might look wrong to others…."*
- Peter to Gwen (*The Amazing Spiderman 2*) *"I made a choice, this is my path."*
- Remy to his father (*Ratatouille*) *"I don't want you to think I'm choosing this over family… I can't choose between two halves."*
- Oracle to Neo (*Matrix*) *"You are going to have to make a choice."*

This truism about choice under pressure revealing our true selves goes to the heart of story. Michael Arndt (writer, *Toy Story 3*, Figure 10.10) said what he learned about story at Pixar was that your character will come to a fork in the road, and they are going to have to make a choice on how to deal with her new reality.

Figure 10.10

Michael Arndt, writer, *Toy Story 3*.

There's a high road to take, a healthy responsible choice, or a low road to take, and make an unhealthy, irresponsible choice. And remember, if your character chooses to do the right thing, you really don't have a story.

For Woody, he makes the unhealthy choice… Woody tries to push Buzz behind the desk. The key thing here is we are rooting for Woody to do the unhealthy, irresponsible thing because we feel his pain in getting replaced. So… Woody's unhealthy choice… leads to Woody needing to bring Buzz back safe and sound…

With The Incredibles, the responsible choice is for Bob to do what his wife tells him to do… but that would be boring and you would have no story… we are totally rooting for Bob to make the unhealthy choice because we saw how much he loved being a superhero, we saw how good he was at it, and how unfairly it was taken away from him. And that unhealthy choice sneaking around, leads to a crisis. Mirage tracking him down. Syndrome coming out of retirement and you are off into your second act.[31]

Michael Arndt

Making difficult choices shifts to the player in video games and VR. However, it is the responsibility of the designer to create *meaningful choices* if they are to have a narrative impact. Whether it be film, animation, or games, the options for choice include

1. It has to be a *real choice*—the choice between good and evil or between right and wrong is no choice at all.[32] Everyone, with few exceptions, will always choose good as they know it.

2. Choices must have *consequences*, a *moral dilemma*. In *Call of Duty: Black Ops 2, Mission Eight*—if Harper is saved, then Farid will die, which in turn results in Farid not being there later to save Chloe, which results in her not being there to stop the virus by the end of the game. The choice is whether to save a life or all the lives of the world.

3. Viewers need to be *aware that a choice is being made*. One that the character has to agonize over before making the choice. In FPS and RPG games, players are often faced with the choice of who to save and who to sacrifice. *Far Cry 3* emphasizes this in their mission *Hard Choices*.

4. The viewer needs *reminders* of the choice after it has been made. Reminding players can trigger regret in the player when companions are sacrificed, as well as pride when companions were saved. Reminders reinforce the emotional aftermath of the player's choices which in turn infuses more meaning into the experience. Reminders serve to strengthen motivation in films (*Hunger Games*).

5. *The choice must be permanent*. Replay of action changes the narrative. If the player has the option of *do over*, then they engage with narrative at a deeper level (i.e., sports, horror games). This is integrated in *The Walking Dead* game with its *Autosave* feature.

6. *Choice between two undesirable outcomes is effective*. In *Romeo and Juliet*; the choice they face is life-without-love versus death-with-love (Figure 10.11).

Figure 10.11

Romeo and Juliet, 1884 Frank Dicksee—it is the choice they make that has made the story so memorable.

A choice isn't just a mental decision. It needs an action that reveals what the character is thinking and what they may do. Showing these decisions permits the viewer to process what's happening, to take in what the characters are feeling and identify with the emotions.[33]

Change

... as I look at other films that I love... you watch these characters grow and change and affect each other in deep ways, and that's meaningful to me. (*Inside-Out*, Pete Docter, Director)[34]

Types of Change

1. **Physical** change can be ugly to beautiful (*Pretty Woman*), dumb to smart (*Legally Blonde*), weak to strong (*How to Train Your Dragon*), incomplete to whole (*Pinocchio, Avatar*).
2. **Psychological** change includes crazy to sane (Pat, Tiffany [*Silver Linings Playbook*]), sane to crazy (Charles Muntz [*Up*]), innocent to knowing (Giselle [*Enchanted*]), scared to brave (Bilbo [*The Hobbit*]) (Figure 10.12).
3. **Value/belief** changes are just as dramatic: bad to good (*Terminator, Megamind*), stingy to generous (*A Christmas Carol*), Nasty to Nice (Gru [*Despicables*]).
4. **Emotional** change is an effective dramatic technique throughout the story that clues in the audience: Joy to Anger (*Tangled*), Sad to Happy (*Cinderella*).
5. **Motivational** change is whether the goal at the beginning of the story remains the same at the end (money to love [*Guardians of the Galaxy*]). If the goal doesn't change, then the story might be a tragedy—*be careful what you wish for (Westworld)*.[35]

Change must be seen. An audience cannot comprehend what it does not see. Fortunately, change can manifest itself in a character's reactions to conflict. This is often perceived in a character's reaction to the Call to Adventure (Hero's Journey)—their protesting.[36] This is followed by a significant change in their behavior. Seeing the dramatic change in the character reinforced at the end is satisfying for a viewer because it is seen as validation that life can get better.

> *No matter what kind of animal you are... change starts with you.* Zootopia.[39]

Figure 10.12

Psychological change in Bilbo Baggins, The Hobbit: An Unexpected Journey. (Copyright 2012, New Line Cinema.)

- Syd Field states that an important quality for a good character is that they change during the course of the story.
- Robert McKee sees change as an essential part of the main character. Change is revealed over the course of the (story) telling.
- Christopher Vogler states that heroes don't just visit death and come home. They return changed, transformed. "*No one can go through an experience at the edge of death without being changed in some way.*"[37]
- Truby emphasizes that in the vast majority of stories, a character with weaknesses struggles to achieve something and ends up changed (positively or negatively) as a result.[38]

10. Character Elements

Do all characters' change? No, but there are specific criteria that must be met if a character is not to change over the course of the story.

1. Secondary characters don't change (much). Their role is often to advance the plot with their point-of-view. Olaf in *Frozen,* Master Shifu in *Kung Fu Panda*—they are the same at the beginning and at the end.
2. Villains generally get more intense but don't change. They may get nastier, escalate the body count, increase the threats, etc… all contributing to their demise.
3. The main character doesn't change if they are established as having almost no flaws. Their role is to change the world around them. There is still change in the story but the emphasis is how the world is transformed. In *Happy Feet*, Mumble doesn't change, the penguin colony changes. In *Forest Gump*, Forest doesn't change but changes the people around him. In *Gladiator*, Maximus doesn't change but changes the Roman Empire.

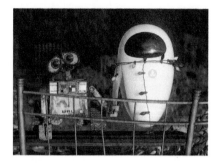

Figure 10.13

WALL-E, 2008. (Copyright Walt Disney Studios Motion Pictures/Courtesy Everett Collection.)

Characters such as James Bond don't change, except in *Casino Royale*, but take note… by the end of the movie he has changed back. Director Andrew Stanton indicated that *"In a way WALL-E doesn't change that much in the movie. He learns a little bit more about the intricateness of love… but the biggest change is really EVE. She is the one that goes through the huge change in the movie. Of being cold and robotic… and then slowly realizing that that directive isn't the most important in life and going over to WALL-E*[40] (Figure 10.13).

The greater the conflict in the character's life, the greater their change. Dramatic change can often be 180 degrees—going from caring only about yourself to caring completely about others (e.g., *Clueless, The Emperor's New Groove*). Change doesn't come easy; it must be earned to be satisfying for the viewer. Change is cumulative, an instant transformation rings hollow because the viewer knows from personal experience that change takes time. We grow in stages. In 1939, Kenneth Rowe stressed that change in a story must always be progressing to a higher intensity[41] (Figure 10.14).

In a television series, the growth pattern may be protracted to keep the series going. While a television's character's change may be dramatic in a single episode, it is common for the characters (and viewer) to forget much of what was learned by the next episode (e.g., Sheldon [*The Big Bang Theory*]). Yes, there is a character change in television/online series… but the progression is glacial.

Figure 10.14

Kenneth Rowe.

Character Arc

A *Character Arc* is a character's change/growth over the course of the story. Traditionally, a character starts at the beginning of the story as someone a bit quirky (even dysfunctional) with flaws. The conflict they encounter forces them to confront their faults and shortcomings. In the end, they have become a *different* person. What changes is their behavior, what they believe, and how they look at the world. The viewer must visually see and hear these differences in the character's reactions.

Figure 10.15

Jake Scully in *Avatar*. Matching fears with obstacles. MCDAVAT FE039.

If there is no character arc, then there is no *dramatic story*. If the character is the same at the end of the story, as they were in the beginning, then it wasn't a drama but simply quantitative information. It is the *change*, the character arc, that grabs a viewer's interest. In *The Hobbit, An Unexpected Journey*: Bilbo (asks)—"*Do you promise I will come back?*", Gandalf—"*No, and if you do... you will not be the same.*"[42]

Types of Character Arcs

1. There is a *significant change* in the character. The classic scenario consists of an improbable hero, who goes through major changes as they confront their fears. Tony Stark (*Iron Man*) is far less narcissist at the end for he thinks more of others before himself.
2. They *fix themselves* by overcoming their internal flaws. They become whole instead of carrying around emotional wounds from their past or have never completed the process of fully growing up into adulthood. To understand character arc, it is necessary to look at the flaws (and fears) that the main character needs to overcome. The flaws provide material to externalize the conflict. Once the character's inner fears are known this can be matched to the conflicts and obstacles that lie ahead. Jake Scully (*Avatar*) (Figure 10.15).
3. They *become a better version* of themselves. The growth involves gaining a new perspective, acquiring new skills, and even assuming a new role in life. They don't repair themselves as much as become an enhanced version of themselves, discovering hidden talents along the way.
4. The character *falls from grace* (a negative arc). Comparable to the cliché of a *fallen angel*. This character's change is "tragic" as they fall into insanity, cruelty, or die in the end. Something goes wrong and they lose complete control—Hobgoblin, Doctor Octopus in *Spiderman*.[43]

In most stories, the main character doesn't happily choose to change themselves. Confronting one's flaws and then undergoing change is not something most people do willingly, it's too painful. Growth comes through failure.

Characters come to the process of change differently.

1. They *don't see the need to change* (Bilbo Baggins, Tony Stark).
2. They are *open to change* but don't know how (*Easy A, Goodwill Hunting*).
3. They want to change but *others don't want them to change* (Cinderella, Rose [*Titanic*], Riley [*Inside-Out*]).

A character arc is directly linked to dramatic desire; if a character wants something, they are going to have to change to get it.[44] The story must create a situation where the character cannot just give up and walk away, then there is no story. Situations that force the character to stay the course:

1. *Others are depending on them* (e.g., *Captain America, Harry Potter*).
2. The *alternative is worse*—their current life (e.g., Po in his noodle shop [*Kung Fu Panda*] Neo in his cubicle [*Matrix*]) (Figure 10.16).
3. *Physically trapped* (e.g., Pi Patel [*Life of Pi*], Cage [*Edge of Tomorrow*]).
4. *In love* (e.g., Finn [*Star Wars: Episode VII*], Rick [*Casablanca*]).
5. *Their obsessions* (tragic flaw) won't let them stop (e.g., Scarlet O'Hara [*Gone with the Wind*], Chris Kyle [*American Sniper*]).

In the Hero's Journey, the character arc follows the traditional track of some unlikely character (Po, *Kung Fu Panda*) overcoming tremendous odds to become the hero. Everything about the main character dramatically changes by the end of the story... except that innermost strength they had to begin with.

A *tragic* character arc is usually found in fairy tales and morality plays (e.g., *West Side Story, Romeo and Juliet, Scarface, Anna Karenina*). Today, the tragic arc is typically reserved for the villain. This can be seen in the Spiderman series (Hobgoblin, Doctor Octopus, etc.) or animation (Gaston [*Beauty and the Beast*], Muntz [*Up*]).

The character arc is so fundamental that it is not uncommon for it to become the theme of the story. Some of the more familiar movies that have change at the heart of the story—*Up, Inside-Out, Breaking Bad*. The central narrative question becomes... *Will the character face their fears, overcome their flaws, and change enough to get what they really need?*

Figure 10.16

Kung Fu Panda, Po the Panda, 2008. (Copyright DreamWorks Animation/Courtesy Everett Collection.)

Character Flaws

Character flaws are the impetus behind the character arc—something needs to change. Without character flaws, there is no reason to change, there are no voids the character is looking to fill in their lives. Flaws also serve to make the main character more relatable. Last but not least, it provides the provocation for conflict. Character flaws are qualities such as Simba's impulsiveness (*Lion King*), Hamlet's indecisiveness, Giselle's naiveté (*Enchanted*), Elsa's lack of control (*Frozen*). Knowing a character's flaws becomes a driving force in the story's development. Superman wasn't as interesting in the first few comics until they came up with Kryptonite.

Not all flaws are bad things. Flaws can also be a good thing taken too far—too trusting (Charlie Brown [*Peanuts*]) or logic (Spock [*Star Trek*]). Michael Arndt emphasizes that *"…your character needs one more thing. He needs a flaw. Now what's key here is that the character's flaw actually comes out of her grand passion. It's a good thing that's just been taken too far."*[45]

Where do flaws originate? Often something from the character's past has emotionally stunted their growth and keeps them vulnerable. It is an emotional wound, though it could be physical, that they carry around with them. These flaws can't be healed until they face the fears that come out of this wound. Character flaws should be obvious. The viewer can see the character is hurting. The trauma can range from abuse, ridicule, and bullying… which in turn triggers defensiveness, self-pity, self-destructiveness, isolation, grudges, anger, etc. Trottier conceives of flaws as almost always triggering some form of self-centeredness, greed, or pride.[46]

Types of Flaws

- **Past emotional trauma/wound**—*Guardians of the Galaxy* opens with the loss of Peter's mother. We learn Rey [*Star Wars: Episode VII*] has been abandoned by her parents. Finn has been institutionalized. These wounds become trigger mechanisms. Marty McFly is called *chicken* in *Back to the Future III* which causes him to react irrationally.
- **Physical deficiency**—Amnesia (Jason Bourne, *Bourne* movies), physical disability (Steven Hawking, *Theory of Everything*), Kryptonite (*Superman*), etc.
- **Psychological challenges**—Never grown up (*Step Brothers, Peter Pan*), Greed (*Wolf of Wall Street*). The director of *Gravity* indicates that main character's flaw is *"she's carrying her grief."*[47] Charlie Brown is perpetually naïve and too trusting (Figure 10.17).
- **Obsession**—something the character can't control. This often starts off as a positive quality that goes too far: loyalty, love, protectiveness (Marlin in *Finding Nemo*). The most common obsession is *fear* that paralyses a character. *Anger* comes up a close second, which then morphs into *vengeance* (i.e., *John Wick, Gladiator*). In *Avengers*, Loki is envious of Thor which turns Loki evil, as he seeks validity.

Figure 10.17

10. Character Elements

Flaws are not randomly selected. If love is the theme, then the flaw is the opposite—they don't feel they deserve love, they lost someone they loved, or they try too hard to be loved.[48] This disparity between the flaw and the theme inherently generates conflict. Flaws come in various intensities:

No flaws are reserved for characters that change their world instead of being changed by the story—Obi Wan Kenobi (*Star Wars*), Maximus (*Gladiator*). The emphasis in the story shifts from a character arc to a story arc.

Minor flaws help make characters more memorable. These are useful for defining secondary characters who are more annoying than anything else: GlaDOS is taunting (*Portal*), Dory is scatter brained, can't stop talking (*Finding Dory*) (Figure 10.18). J. K. Rowling confessed that Harry Potter does have faults. They would be a bit of anger and occasional arrogance.[49]

Major flaws define who they are... narcissistic, weak, ego-manic. The flaw colors their judgment and drives their actions—arrogant (Sheldon Cooper, *Big Bang*) or can't talk to women (Raj Koothrappali, *Big Bang*). These come in very handy during the story's development.

Fatal flaws keep the character stuck in life, not able to go after what they want. Fatal flaws come out during the conflict as the character can only do so much before the flaw stops them. The Cowardly Lion can only do so much until his fear takes over.

A *Tragic flaw* is frequently reserved for villains and responsible for their inevitable downfall. Though if found in a hero, this flaw is depicted as having too much pride (hubris). Such tragic characters ignore the warnings. They defy moral codes of conduct believing they are above society's constraints. Tragic flaws are revealed early in a redemptive story.

> To humanize a hero... give her a wound, a visible, physical injury or a deep emotional wound.[52] (e.g., Luke and Rey, both orphaned by their parents, *Star Wars*.)

Flaws are best when they are familiar to the viewer—such as being awkward around the opposite sex or in high-pressure social situations. They help the audience to relate.[50] There is a great list of character flaws at the site Dark World RPG.[51]

Figure 10.18

Dory who has minor flaws. *Finding Dory.* (Copyright 2016, Disney · Pixar.)

References

1. J. H. Lawson, *Playwriting and Screenwriting*, 348.
2. C. Lydon, J.K. Rowling Interview Transcript, *The Connection* [WBUR Radio], October 12, 1999, Part 5, {8:12}, *Accio Quote!*, http://www.accio-quote.org/articles/1999/1099-connectiontransc2.htm#p5
3. R. McKee, *Story*, 70.
4. R. McKee, Robert McKee's Story Seminar—The Setting, YouTube, October 14, 2008, https://www.youtube.com/watch?v=g-SfvGUmr_A
5. J. Lasseter, Pixar's John Lasseter Answers Your Questions—Interview Stephanie Goodman, *New York Times*, November 1, 2011, http://artsbeat.blogs.nytimes.com/2011/11/01/pixars-john-lasseter-answers-your-questions/?_r=0
6. J. H. Lawson, *Playwriting and Screenwriting*, 120.
7. D. Mamet, *On Directing Film* (USA, Penguin Books, 1992), Preface XV.
8. K. Iglesias, *Writing for Emotional Impact*, 44.
9. R. McKee, *Story*, 138.
10. L. J. Cowgill, *Writing Short Films*, 5.
11. D. Trottier, *Screenwriting Bible*, 11.
12. J. S. Bell, *Write Great Fiction—Plot & Structure* (eBook, F + W Media, Inc., 2004), KL 1508–1510.
13. E. Edson, *The Story Solution* (USA, Michael Wiese Productions, 2012), 156.
14. M. Hauge, *Screenplays that Sell*, 211.
15. J. H. Lawson, *Playwriting*, 163.
16. L. Seger, *Making Good Script*, 156.
17. L. J. Cowgill, *Short Story*, 39.
18. L. Egri, *Dramatic Writing*, 88.
19. M. Hauge, *Screenplays*, 44.
20. L. Cron, *Wired for Story*, 65.
21. L. Seger, *Making a Good Script Great* (Hollywood, California, Samuel French Trade, 1994), 154.
22. T. Johnson, *DreamWorks Animation*, Viewpoint Conference (Turin, Italy, 2011).
23. L. J. Cowgill, *Short Story*, 39.
24. L. Egri, *The Art of Dramatic Writing* (New York, Simon & Schuster, 1960), 181.
25. C. Jones, *Chuck Amuck* (USA, Farrar, Straus and Giroux, 1999), 44.
26. L. Cowgill, *The Art of Plotting* (New York, Back Stage Books, 2008), 77.
27. Imposter Syndrome, *Wikipedia*, last modified February 15, 2017, https://en.wikipedia.org/wiki/Impostor_syndrome
28. H. James, *The Art of Fiction* (Boston, Nabu Press [first published 1884], 2010), 44.
29. L. Cowgill, *Art of Plotting*, 79.
30. D. Price, *The Pixar Touch* (Los Angeles, California, Vintage, 2009), 127.
31. M. Arndt, *What I learned at Pixar* (Blue Ray Supplemental Disc, Toy Story 3, 2012).
32. R. McKee, *Story*, 104.
33. L. Cowgill, *Art of Plotting*, 81.
34. P. Docter, Pete Docter on making 'Inside Out' work: 'How do I make this resonate?', Interview by Drew McWeeny, *Hitflix*, May 27, 2015, http://www.hitfix.com/motion-captured/pete-docter-on-making-inside-out-work-how-do-i-make-this-resonate
35. N. Kress, 4 Ways to Motivate Characters and Plot, *The Writer's Digest*, March 19, 2013, http://www.writersdigest.com/online-editor/4-ways-to-motivate-characters-and-plot
36. T. Culleton, Character Arc, *Fiction Writer's Mentor*, 2016, http://www.fiction-writers-mentor.com/character-arc/.
37. C. Vogler, *The Writer's Journey*, 160.
38. J. Truby, *Anatomy of Story*, 30.
39. C. Zootopia, *YouTube*, January 6, 2016, https://www.youtube.com/watch?v=WWFB-zrxn7o
40. A. Stanton, Director's commentary, *WALL-E* (Disney-Pixar Distribution, 2008, DVD).
41. K. Rowe, *The Play*, 34.
42. The Hobbit Trailer—An Unexpected Journey, *YouTube*, January 30, 2012, https://www.youtube.com/watch?v=nOGsB9dORBg
43. List of Spider-Man enemies, *Wikipedia*, last modified June 1, 2016, https://en.wikipedia.org/wiki/List_of_Spider-Man_enemies
44. K. Rowe, *The Play*, 34.
45. M. Arndt, Story, *Toy Story 3* (2010, Walt Disney Studios, 2011), Blue Ray Supplemental Disc.
46. D. Trottier, *Screenwriter's Bible*, Kindle Location 902.
47. Story, *Gravity Directed Alfonso Cuarón* (Warner Brothers Distribution, 2013), DVD Supplemental Disc.
48. D. Marks, *Inside Story*, 117.
49. Bloomsbury Live Chat with J. K. Rowling, *wikia*, July 30, 2007, http://harrypotter.wikia.com/wiki/Bloomsbury_Live_Chat
50. M. Hauge, *Writing Screenplays*, 44.
51. Character flaws, *Dark World RPG*, http://www.darkworldrpg.com/lore/flaws.php
52. C. Vogler, *Writer's Journey*, 108.

11

Character Values/
Motivation

The Role of Conflict

Conflict generates a story's *action*. Nothing moves forward in a story except through conflict. There can be no change in the characters without unavoidable conflict.[1] Conflict has a tendency to be physical because it makes for great visual drama. However, physical action can only sustain a viewer's attention for a short while. Thus, conflict is not exclusively comprised of fights. To keep a viewer's interest, conflict needs inner turmoil to keep things interesting. This ranges from psychological problems to a clash of personalities (see Unity of Opposites).

Opposing characters can often be seen as the embodiment of disparate ideas which *cannot coexist*. It isn't enough to understand the conflict as strong opposions.[2] It is the opposing beliefs the characters hold that produce the conflict. Effective conflict requires the viewer to grasp the origins of the conflict. Ironically, conflict's motivation is not inherently good or bad. People always believe they are doing good, no matter how dreadful their actions.

Viewers respond to conflict between characters because it reminds them of the friction inherent in their own personal lives.

What generates conflict is emotion. The most powerful emotion in story is *fear*. Fear can either *start the action* (i.e., fear of dying, of being ordinary, of being alone) or stop *an action* from being taken (i.e., fear of rejection, of injury). Dramatic emotions in story include *pride* (ego and power), *greed* (theft), *envy* (jealousy), *anger* (rage, revenge), *sloth* (apathy, not taking care of things), *lust* (obsessive desire), and *gluttony* (too much of anything)—frequently referred to as the Seven Deadly Sins.[3] Without an emotional motivation behind conflict, it can feel repetitive, or worse—gratuitous (superhero fights).

Mulan contained both internal conflict, what is the right thing to do, as well as the physical conflict of defending China against the barbarians. There had to be enough internal conflict (desperation) to drive her to leave home and it had to feel right that Mulan would take this action under such pressure (Figure 11.1).

Conflict itself is not always a negative interaction between characters, though that is generally the case. Conflict can result in positive outcomes—characters grow closer. Ed Hooks advises that to subvert the negative perception of the word conflict we can think of conflict as a *negotiation*.[4] We generally perceive of a negotiation as having any number of conclusions—good and bad.

Figure 11.1

Mulan, having cut her hair, dressed as a man, and leaving home. *Mulan*, Khan (horse, voice: Frank Welker), Mulan (voice: Ming-Na), 1998. (Copyright Buena Vista Pictures/ Courtesy Everett Collection.).

The challenge for any storyteller is how to make conflict meaningful. The key is to tie the conflict to what it represents. Luke and Darth Vader were not just fighting for individual rights versus a well-ordered society—their conflict represented good and evil. How big the stakes are in a conflict depends directly on what the conflict means to the character.[5] Is it about (1) love, family, themselves, (2) how did they get themselves in this situation, (3) how do they react—will they fight or run, or (4) what are the consequences if they lose? The answers to these questions, good or bad, enable the viewer to gain a deeper insight into not only the story, but also how it connects to their own lives. The viewer *wants to see* the impact the conflict has on the characters. Significance emerges from not only where the character has succeeded but also where the character has failed.

No conflict or *gratuitous* conflict undermines a story's success.

1. *No conflict?* Behavioral scientists know that is not how humans have evolved. Society may reward cooperation between people but it hasn't extinguished conflict. Something as innocuous as unintentional interactions, such as rudeness or misunderstandings, can easily fester into something much larger. Stories without conflict tend to have a social message but come up short in connecting to life as we know it. There needs to be some conflict for a viewer to care what happens to the characters.

2. *Gratuitous conflict.* Conflict for conflict's sake can short circuit an animation or VFX film quickly. How many traditional fist fights does it take before boredom sets in? Conflict must be *meaningful* or the viewer's engagement is sabotaged. Whether it be obstacles to be overcome, challenges to be confronted, or goals to be reached, the viewer can't connect if they don't know the *why*. In *Grand Theft Auto*—when characters die gratuitously, the experience of the game isn't as strong as when the player knows why characters are being killed off.

Conflict is a *hook* that grabs a viewer's attention and takes them through a story. It generates tension, demarcates the boundaries of the story, and generates a desire for resolution. Conflict works best when it is linked to the theme. In Shakespeare's *Macbeth,* his unbridled ambition brings him into conflict with anyone in his way which in turn leads to his self-destruction (Figure 11.2).

Whether it be animation, games, or VR...even if the imagery is fantasy, not real, the conflict must still feel real to keep the viewer's interest. The old 1933 *King Kong* movie looks fake but feels real, while the more recent 2005 King Kong movie looked real but felt fake.

Figure 11.2

Shakespeare's Macbeth, who is in conflict with anyone who stands in his way.

Fear: The Inner Journey

The core motivation for any character is fear. Everything a character does is to mask their fear. A character's wants, needs, goals, hopes, and dreams all revolve around an unspoken dread they carry around inside themselves. The journey that viewers really want to see is how characters overcome their fears.[6] Lajos Egri stressed this basic idea of *self-importance* as the prime motivator for character. Wanting to be important in life can be traced to a desire that others not see their fear, the mother of all emotions.[7] Fear is always humiliating, for it shows naked insecurity.

Figure 11.3

Shrek staying protected in swamp. (Copyright 2001, Dreamworks Animation.)

Figure 11.4

Shrek staying protected in armor. (Copyright 2001, Dreamworks Animation.).

Fear is often masked by *declaring loudly* what they really want, but it is all talk. In *Titanic*, Rose talks about her desire for passion and excitement in life but is too afraid to go against her mother and fiancé to break free. Similarly, Shrek is afraid of rejection. He says he loves his solitude but secretly desires to connect with others (Figure 11.3).

Fear grows out of *emotional wounds*. These wounds include *Injustice*—afraid of crime, having been a victim or witness, *Failure*—afraid of making a mistake or being perceived as a failure, guilt, *Betrayal*—afraid to trust, *Isolation*—afraid of being left out, cut off from opportunities (Cinderella), *Abandonment/Rejection*—deserted by family, friends, *Disillusionment*—afraid to hear the truth, and *Rejection* because of physical aliment—a defect, scar, or disease.[8]

Fear results in *an elaborate facade* designed to prevent others from uncovering the truth about characters. This can range from responsible positions (e.g., Doctor, Police) to characters who wear an actual mask—Batman. In Shrek, we see him wearing armor and a helmet to protect himself from… the princess (Figure 11.4).

Fear causes a desire for *control and power* to hide their vulnerability. This can be seen when characters seek to dominate others or accumulate money. This is most obvious in fights over something small. Viewers can relate as everyone has encountered a similar situation with a bureaucracy (e.g., DMV).

Hauge and Vogler[9] propose that it is this *inner* journey of overcoming fear, as opposed to the more visible outer Hero's Journey, that connects most with viewers. Viewers consciously or unconsciously come to see a character make this journey from fear to courage. This inner journey has several key components:[10]

	Outer Hero's Journey	Inner Hero's Journey
1	Ordinary World	Their life has stagnated; they are set in their ways
2	Call to Adventure	*Loss* of the way things were, future is scary
3	Refuse the Call	In *denial*, fear of unknown
4	Meet Mentor	Talking through their fears, unsure of new direction
5	Cross the first threshold	Confronting their fears, though there is backsliding
6	Tests, Allies, and Enemies	*Anger*, afraid of who to trust
7	Approach to Inner Cave	*Bargaining*, afraid he/she is not up to task
8	Ordeal facing life and death	*Depressed*, fear of finally letting go off old self
9	Reward for facing crisis	Agree to consequences of change, they are reborn
10	Road home, work is unfinished	Doubts, must recommit to course of action
11	Climax, resurrection	*Accept* fate, confront biggest feat, no going back
12	Elixir, benefit for all	New, unafraid identity

This inner journey is at the heart of the movie *Gravity*. Director Alfonso Cuarón said "*I never thought I was doing a science fiction movie. I thought I was doing a drama of a woman in space.*"[11] It is evident from the beginning that the main character Ryan (Sandra Bullock) is afraid, while Matt (George Clooney) is not. Her overwhelming fear comes from holding on to the past (loss of her daughter) while Matt lives in the present. As the story progresses, she must face her biggest fear—reengaging with life and feeling emotion again. Cuarón knew that Ryan had to become *fearless*, to regain her desire to engage with life[12] (Figure 11.5).

Trottier states that to get to the heart of the inner journey, one must ask what does my character want most and what does he/she fear the most? Then, the opposition must force him/her to face his/her fear.[13] In the end, story is more about the internal journey, than the external journey.[14]

Figure 11.5

The image symbolizes facing the future unafraid. *Gravity.* (Copyright 2013, Warner Brothers.)

Unity of Opposites

Unity of Opposites is two opposite characters who are caught in a struggle and can't get away from each other. There are three components to the concept of Unity of Opposites—(1) characters who are the opposite of each other, (2) the circumstances that force them together, and (3) why they can't get away from each other.[15] In Unity of Opposites, the characters are forced to confront not just each other but also confront their own problems along the way. Opposite characters pitted against each other are Buzz (delusional) against Woody (rational); Carl in *Up* (grumpy) versus Russell (naïve); Wreck-It-Ralph (Tough/Big) versus Vanellope (Sweet/Small) (Figure 11.6); and Luke (good son) against Darth Vader (evil father).

It gives the story more depth when the character's opposing points-of-view are also the opposite sides of the story's theme. If the theme is family, then one character might be a deadbeat father versus a devoted mother. To find opposites, the question to ask is… who would these characters least want to be with in the whole world?

The key to making Unity of Opposites work is to insure that neither character can walk away but must stay and battle it out—the unity. This was an early problem in the development of *A Bug's Life*. In the first draft, the main character was a circus performer who had no ties to the ant colony and could just walk away when things got tough. When they switched the main character to Flik, he couldn't walk away because the ant colony was his family.[16] What binds opposites together can be

Figure 11.6

Vanellope and Wreck-It-Ralph, *Wreck-It-Ralph*. (Copyright 2012 Disney.)

Figure 11.7

Jinxy Jenkins, Lucky Lou, see http://jinxylucky.tumblr.com/

1. Immaturity (*Ted, Step Brothers*)
2. Work (*The Heat* [Sandra Bullock & Mellissa McCarthy], *Lethal Weapon*)
3. Being chased (*Guardians of the Galaxy, Mad Max: Fury Road*)
4. Wanting the same thing (*National Treasure, Pirates of the Caribbean*)
5. Physical space (together in Andy's room, Carl's floating house [*Up*])

It is this unity, where characters can't get away from each other, that pushes the story to a final breaking point.[17] We see it repeatedly in animation (i.e., *Finding Dory, UP, Monsters*) and in television, (i.e., *Odd Couple, The Big Bang*). When two radically different characters are stuck together it is almost formulaic, but when tweaked, it pays off over and over again. This approach worked well in the student animation *Jinxy Jenkins, Lucky Lou* (Figure 11.7). The unluckiest guy, Jinxy Jenkins, runs into luckiest girl, Lucky Lou and wind up together in a cart that is careening down a hill. The unity, being trapped together in a runaway cart, generates increasing complications.

Unity of Opposites extends beyond just two people:

1. *Multiple opposites*—a large group of people that operate like one personality against someone. This was the case in *Cinderella* with her wicked step mother and sisters.
2. *Changeable opposites*—conflict with a variety of individuals in different ways. This is the case in *The Big Bang Theory* with Sheldon versus everyone else as his opposite. In *How to Train Your Dragon*, Hiccup faces (1) his father's expectations, (2) Toothless, the most powerful dragon, and (3) Astrid, the more capable girl. They all represent some level of capability he does not possess.
3. *Nature as opposite.* Nature is objectified as an opposing force. In *Wild*, the character's urban dependency is in contrast to the self-reliance needed to survive in the woods. Contrasting a character's qualities to the disaster confronting them is key—earthquake, flood, pestilence.
4. *Against themselves.* Conflict between who we really are versus our façade. This underlying theme frequently plays out in television comedies such as *The Office* and *Modern Family*. Internal dichotomy becomes the central theme in dramas such as *Breaking Bad* (Walter White) (Figure 11.8), *The Sopranos* (Tony Soprano), and *Mad Men* (Don Draper). It is seen in the alter egos a character assumes—Iron Man/Tony Stark, Batman/Bruce Wayne.

Figure 11.8

Walter White has more than one identity. *Breaking Bad.* (Copyright AMC.)

Creating Interesting Characters

One of the secrets to interesting characters is *contradiction*. The values, thoughts, or ideas a character hold that are in opposition. Such characters don't fit our first impressions: a sophisticated cannibal (Hannibal Lecter [*The Silence of the Lambs*]); the bad guy who wants to be liked (*Wreck-It-Ralph*); a superhero who is both egotistical and disfigured (*Deadpool*). A character's contradictions help the viewer relate to them. No matter how superior these characters appear they are flawed like us. Building in contradictions prevents characters from being reduced to clichés. For instance, a Mafioso that has unresolved mommy issues (Tony Soprano). Characters become more memorable and unique when characteristics are merged in unpredicted ways. Pete Docter (director, *Up*) has referred to this as the "Clark Kent Syndrome"—one person with two personalities.

The challenge is that your main character must be likeable. Unfortunately, this can lead to bland one-dimensional main characters. Likeable characters with contradictory qualities can result in characters "the audience is still drawn to but are unique."[18] Docter (Figure 11.9) reasoned that because the viewer knows why Carl is hurting in *Up* (lost his wife), the viewer sympathizes when Carl first meets Russell, even though Carl slams the door in Russell's face.

Figure 11.9

Pete Docter, Pixar director.

Syd Field states interesting characters comes out of knowing these four points about them:[19]

- Dramatic need—what does the main character want to gain, get, or achieve?
- Strong point of view—how does the main character see the world?
- Attitude—what are main character's mannerisms or mood?
- Change—does the main character change during the course of the story?

Allen Palmer (Story Analyst) asserts that it gets down to four basic questions that must be answered about a character.[20]

1. Who is the hero?
2. What do they want?
3. What's stopping them from getting it?
4. What's at stake?

For others, no matter how well constructed the characters are—they don't exist in a vacuum. *Looney Tunes* Director Friz Freleng's (Figure 11.10) philosophy of story was "*it is about a character in a situation.*"

Figure 11.10

Friz Freleng.

11. Character Values/Motivation

Character Traits

1. What are they like? Their personality—this gives the viewer an idea of who they are, what makes them interesting. Why we like about them.[21]

2. What is it they want? What are their motives that a viewer will care about?

3. How do they speak? Dialog that is distinct to that character. How do they speak about others? What does this reveal?

4. Who do they know and spend time with—both good and bad? Family, friends, blow up dolls, neighbors, teachers, kids, old people, races?

5. Are they proactive? They react, they take action which moves the story forward.

6. What do they fear? Once known then characters can be put in situations they hate the most (i.e., Raiders of the Lost Arc, snakes).

7. What are their wounds and fears? What is their internal conflict? What are they torturing themselves about?

8. What do their idiosyncrasies reveal? Not just what has happened to them but the things they have done. These quirks are linked with symbolism in the story.

9. How are they like us? Interesting characters have some part of the viewer in them.

10. What are they the best and worst at doing? Contradiction—Sherlock Holmes is the best detective but the worst at relating to other people (i.e., *Elementary, House, Big Bang*—this is a recurring TV premise).

11. What do they look like? The features and behavior which is the opposite of who they really are (i.e., *Colombo*—grumpy but brilliant).

12. What makes them jump for joy and what makes them cry? Their emotions.

13. What are their secrets. What do they keep hidden?

14. Are they likeable? In the sense that the viewer is willing to spend time with them, to live with them for the duration of the story.

When studios ask for three-dimensional characters, they are looking for those internal contradictions that exist within all of us to one degree or another.

The true test of a memorable character is that they cannot be replaced in the story with someone else. It must be their story. Could you replace Wreck-It-Ralph with any other character? No, it's his existential crisis that the story is about, no one else's (Figure 11.11).

Figure 11.11

Wreck-It-Ralph's existential crisis *Wreck-It-Ralph*, Ralph (center, voice: John C. Reilly), 2012. (Copyright Walt Disney Pictures/Courtesy Everett Collection.)

References

1. L. Cron, *Wired for Story* (New York, Ten Speed Press, 2012), 174–83.
2. L. Cowgill, *The Art of Plotting* (New York, Back Stage Books, 2008), 29.
3. A. Shannon, *Seven Deadly Sins*, http://www.deadly-sins.com
4. E. Hooks, *Acting for Animators* (London, Routledge, 2011), 12.
5. E. Skolnick, *Video Game Storytelling* (New York, Watson-Guptill, 2014), 10.
6. A. Ackerman, How to Uncover Your Character's Emotional Wound, *Wordherders*, May 2015, http://www.wordherders.com/uncover-your-characters-emotional-wound/
7. L. Egri, *The Art of Dramatic Writing* (New York, Wildside Press, 2007), 44.
8. A. Ackerman, Understanding Character Wounds: A List of Common Themes, *Writers Helping Writers*, February 27, 2014, http://writershelpingwriters.net/2014/02/help-character-wounds-list-common-themes/#sthash.RCr1TeAF.dpuf
9. M. Hauge, C. Vogler, *The Hero's 2 Journeys* (Audio CD, 2003)
10. A. Palmer, A New Character-Driven Hero's Journey, *Cracking Yarns*, April 4, 2011, http://www.crackingyarns.com.au/2011/04/04/a-new-character-driven-heros-journey-2/
11. A. Cuarón, Gravity "not sci-fi", interview by Tim Masters, *BBC News*, February, 27, 2014, http://www.bbc.com/news/entertainment-arts-26381335
12. A. Cuarón, *Making of Gravity* (Warner Brothers, 2014), Blue Ray Disc 5:09.
13. D. Trottier, *Screenwriter's Bible*, KL 1374.
14. L. Cron, *Wired for Story*, 11.
15. L. J. Cowgill, *Writing Short Films*, 44.
16. J. Lasseter, A. Stanton, K. Reher and D. Anderson, *A Bug's Life—Story Process* (DVD Disc 2, Pixar/Walt Disney Editions, 1999).
17. L. Egri, *Art of Dramatic Writing*, 44.
18. P. Docter, Quint Chats with Pixar's Pete Docter and Jonas Rivera about UP!, *Aint it Cool News*, March 28, 2009, http://www.aintitcool.com/node/40578
19. S. Field, *Screenplay*, 35.
20. A. Palmer, 4 Basic Questions 90% of Screenplays Don't Answer, *Cracking Yarns*, May 18, 2010, http://www.crackingyarns.com.au/2010/05/18/4-basic-storytelling-questions/
21. C. Wendig, 25 Things a Great Character Needs, *Terribleminds*, January 13, 2014, http://terribleminds.com/ramble/2014/01/13/25-things-a-great-character-needs/

Part 4
Idea Development

12

Generating Ideas

Ideas

A story idea includes a character, a situation, and a conflict.

> *Character*—a hungry coyote, a taunting roadrunner, a singing frog
> *Situation*—surrounded by religious fanatics, ignoring their children's advice
> *Conflict*—married to two men, protecting a town from a shark[1]

A story idea/concept in Hollywood is called a logline. It is described in 25 words or less with a strong hook and not an overly complex plot.

- A popular teenager and his two friends ditch school, for the best day ever, as they are pursued by the principal.
- A mischievous boy gets left behind by his family at Christmas and must defend his house from two burglars.

The strongest loglines don't require an explanation, the title explains it all (e.g., *London is Burning, Earthquake*). George Lucas believes that "*A movie is a success or failure from the moment you settle on your concept. It is the primal attachment to the concept that makes the movie work or not.*"[2] This philosophy is reinforced by Jeffrey Katzenberg, founder of DreamWorks animation, who asserts that *the idea is king.* "*Stars, directors, writers, hardware, special effects, new sound systems… all of these can have a role to play in the success of a film, but they must all serve as humble subjects to the supremacy of the idea… a good story, well executed*"[3] (Figure 12.1).

Generating Story Ideas

Personal Experience—draw from personal experiences, especially the ones most people would like to forget—embarrassment, secrets revealed, the first time…, etc. Story ideas are best grounded in the shared experiences of the viewer and story creator. *Write about what you know* is time-honored advice in creating stories. However, personal experiences work best when transplanted into something else, completely different. In the *Sopranos*, the creator David Chase, did not set out to write a mob drama but a drama about his troubled relationship with his mother. He made Tony Soprano a mobster because he wanted to find a way to make the stakes high enough that viewers would care.[4]

Personal experience stories are not autobiographical; it isn't about you—it's about connecting experiences of *ordinary* existence to the story. *Life of Pi* was at its core about the interdependence of life and this point of view. Externally, the story emphasized survival and overcoming fear. William Gordon sums it up by saying stories are about making "*the strange familiar* and *the familiar strange.*"[5]

News—the media (TV, online, comic books) is full of stories which can be used as catalysts to generate ideas. Scenarios can be constructed from random events of what happened previously and what will transpire afterwards. Chris Lockhart uses obituaries to stimulate his thinking. No matter how dreadful, improbable, or ridiculous the ideas that emerge may be, they stimulate one's thinking.

Figure 12.1

Jeffery Katzenberg.

Combine unlike things—cultures, concepts, and genres that are completely different can be combined to see where it leads. Ideas will combine in ways that the logical mind would normally dismiss—mental self-censorship at work. *Lion King* was nicknamed *Bamlet* for the longest time during its development inside the studio. It was a combination of Bambi and Hamlet set in Africa. The series *Deadwood* combined Shakespearian plots set in the old American west. Combinations grab a viewer's attention because the brain senses a familiarity but something is different. Bruner explains that the unexpected outcomes are the result "*of combinatorial activity—a placing of things in new perspectives.*"[6] For additional insights on this approach, the book *Comic Toolbox* is a good resource.

Brainstorming—bouncing off ideas in a group setting introduces different points of view. Within acting, there is an improvisation technique called a "*yes, and...*" exercise. Everyone must say yes to the idea and build upon it. Jason Katz indicated that at Pixar they call it a Gag session, a "*shotgun approach to problem solving... where ideas fly fast and furious... the only rule is to try to make the person next to you laugh.*"[7] Brainstorming produces surprising twists, unpredictable turns, funny situations, and intriguing dilemmas.

Change One Element—a familiar story but just one element is changed... age, gender, occupation, or archetype. *Megamind* continually switched the roles of villain and hero (Figure 12.2). A drama becomes a comedy, the ending and beginning switched, the title gets changed. Most of the results will be ridiculous but a few will become new tangents for further development.

Never trust your first idea—That first idea is most likely similar to the ideas that everyone else has, which is why the initial feedback is wildly positive. The more a first idea is developed the further it becomes ever more clichéd. Idea creation is tough work. One must push past the clichés, those familiar ideas that already exist in our *collective unconscious*.[8] There are a number of techniques for story development. It can start with writing down one's stream of consciousness, letting it lead to something else, and then something else as the ideas emerge. John Vorhaus has a number of suggestions in his book *Creativity Rules*, pages 13–48.[9]

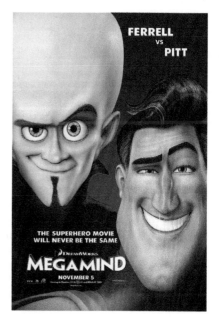

Figure 12.2

Who is the Hero and who is the Villain? *Megamind*, from left: Megamind, (voice: Will Ferrell), Metro Man (voice: Brad Pitt), 2010. (Copyright Paramount Pictures/Courtesy Everett Collection.)

Research

McKee believes the first step toward a well-told story is to create a *"small,"* knowable world. By the end, there won't be anything the writer couldn't answer instantly.[10]

Figure 12.3

John Lasseter, director, *Toy Story*.

The first step in development is research comes in the form of informational, observational, and participatory research.[11] Research generates new points of view and stimulates fresh ideas. It imparts realistic details into the story world. It gives the characters a sense of coming from real life.

Informational Research seeks to know everything about the subject; biological, historical, psychological, and physical. In *A Bug's Life,* Pixar explored how fast an ant could run, how grasshoppers are constructed, and where insects sleep. Bill Cone, Production Designer said we *"studied books on insects and nature photography, watched documentaries."*[12] These specific facts and details gave the story a distinct point of view that didn't exist previously. Specific facts on how creatures interact can provide new options for conflict. This verisimilitude gives credibility to the work, whether it be animation, games, VFX, or VR.

John Lasseter reflected back on *Toy Story*.

To me it was so exciting at this time. I remember... (saying) we are going to go do a little research. So we all climbed into my car and we went down to Toys-R-US and borrowed a company credit card. We would just go through the store, filling the cart up... that's where we started dying laughing because that's where we found the green army men. They came in a bucket... 'Bucket-o-army-men,' we started howling with laughter. That's where we came up with the perspective that these guys are all alive.[13] (Figure 12.3)

Observational Research—Cone, Production Designer for *A Bug's Life,* "Early on I went out looking around in 'nature,' just crawling around on my belly with a camera… took (tons) of pictures… I tried to get down as low as I could get into that scale, thinking about what objects are down there. My biggest discovery was that the world is much messier and more complex than you'd ever imagine."[14] How do people behave—what are the gestures, poses, and choices they make? Visit locations to learn the rhythms of the environment—where do kids play? Where do lovers hang out? Where do people fight? If a specific environment isn't available (i.e., outer space), find something similar and observe the pace (slow/hurried), the sounds, and patterns at different times of day. Observe how other stories answered these questions.

> When we decided we were going to do a prison escape (*Toy Story 3*), we watched a lot of prison movies. There a lot of prison movies out there, I think we watched every single one of them. That totally inspired us.
>
> Director Lee Unkrich.[15] (Figure 12.4)

Participatory Research—before making *Finding Nemo*, the animators went scuba diving. They experienced the resistance of the water, observed the actual diffusion of the light, and swam with the fishes.[16] It isn't enough to observe from a distance or read about a place. One needs to experience it in person, to get a sense of how things really work beyond appearances. It changes things if one actually interacts and connects with the environment and local people. Walk in their shoes—scrutinize how they move, how it is different than what you would do. This can be seen in the "making of" segments from movies and animations.

Assuming people are the same worldwide often leads to generic characters and stories. For example, people around the world have an instinctive sense when one feels their "space has been invaded." The differences are more evident between city residents versus country folks, as well as when people from different cultures are thrown together. The title, *Fish Can't See Water,* by Kai Hammerich, reflects this challenge of staying aware.

> *Research is key to avoiding a derivative/generic story.*

Figure 12.4

Lee Unkrich, director, *Toy Story 3*.

What If?

A *premise* asks the question "What if…?" *What would happen if …* Dinosaurs escaped into a theme park? (*Jurassic World*), The bad guy won? (*Megamind*), A princess has an uncontrollable power to create snow and cold (*Frozen*)? The *What if* question is critical in story development. *What if* toys have feelings? (*Toy Story*), bugs have feelings? (*A Bug's Life*), fish have feelings? (*Finding Nemo*), a little girl's feelings have feelings? (*Inside-Out*) (Figure 12.5).[17]

Lasseter said, "Our films ask 'What if?' questions. What if monsters really did live in your closet? What if a rat wanted to be the finest chef in the most beautiful city in the world? I think our next movie asks the biggest 'What if?' of all. What if the asteroid that wiped out dinosaurs actually missed Earth?"[18]

Figure 12.5

Inside-Out. (Copyright 2015 Disney * Pixar.)

Figure 12.6

Phil Johnston, writer, *Wreck-It-Ralph.*

The terminology can get confusing in the beginning. The terms *idea, concept,* and *premise* have all become interchangeable for *"what the story is about."* The idea, concept, and premise are different steps in the story development process. The differences are

- An *idea* can be as simple as a situation (a fox in a hen house) or a thought… *a long time ago, in a galaxy, far, far away.*
- A *concept* combines the idea with a problem. Often this is equivalent to a story's logline … *a daring archaeologist must stop the Nazis from getting hold of a supernatural artifact. (Raiders of the Lost Ark)* Larry Brooks emphasizes that an idea that asks no question… will not become a dramatic story.[19]
- A *premise* is the idea combined with a "What if…?" question. The responses to "What if?" changes frequently during story development.

Brooks has stressed that a premise may inspire the story but it should not dictate direction.[20] *What if* is a starting point for discovery. In *Wreck-It-Ralph*, its writer Phil Johnston (Figure 12.6), indicated that they came up with a full movie with Felix as the main character. *"The Ralph character was this grubby dude…. then one day, I was like, why are we talking about this guy (Felix) so much, when this guy (Ralph) should be the lead of our movie."*[21] Director Rich Moore said the story changed to *"'What if' we told the story from Donkey Kong's point of view? What is it like to be Donkey Kong?"*[22] Johnston went on to share that the story evolved to embody the *"idea of an 8-bit villain having this existential crisis on what is the meaning of life?…'I do my job every day and I get no appreciation for it.' We redid the entire movie."*[23]

12. Generating Ideas

"What if" establishes from whose point of view the story is to be told. When a story stops progressing, the first question to ask is—*what if we change the point of view*? What if the three little pigs were told from the wolf's point of view? What if it was the three horrid little pigs? What if it was the three little wolves and the big bad pig? The Guardian created an elaborate commercial that revolved around an investigation which revealed that the three pigs had conspired to commit insurance fraud and framed the wolf in an attempt to cover their tracks.[24] To reiterate, *A Bug's Life* story process had just such a problem (Figure 12.7)

Figure 12.7

Development, *A Bug's Life*.

> *Lasseter*: Do you remember the first version of the story? The main character was named Red—he was a red ant. He was not part of the colony… he was part of the circus troop. He was the ring master and we just kept running into problems with the main character… because he could just leave at any time and it was okay.
>
> *Andrew Stanton*: A couple of months earlier I started to sense it wasn't working, but I was afraid to say what I was thinking… But I had started thinking what if the guys that got the circus bugs, one of those ants, it was his movie… because then it's their family. They can't leave the problem they created. What if… Flick was the person that went and got the wrong people?
>
> *Lasseter*: You are the one (looking at Stanton) that taught me that, that taught all of us that… that you do, What If and you throw out this crazy idea.
>
> *Andrew Stanton*: What if… Toy Story started where they fall out of the van at the gas station? It throws your thinking into a place you can't get at any other way…
>
> *Lasseter*: And often times you don't go with that idea but it has changed your thinking and breaks you through that.[25]

James Cameron indicated that he saw something similar in *Termination Salvation*. That they went "*from the first film with the Terminator being the worst bad a** in history. In the second film, he became almost a father figure. The idea of taking John Connor and flipping him to the bad guy is pretty cool because you have to riff against expectations.*"[26]

Cliché

A cliché is an idea that has been seen too many times—predictable plots, retreaded situations, expected endings, and generic characters. Viewers have been satiated by them. Clichéd ideas have been heard or seen so often that they have lost their meaning.

McKee emphasizes that not knowing the world of your story is responsible for creating more clichés.[29] *(Figure 12.8)*

Figure 12.8

Robert McKee.

Overused plots—Love solves everything, it was all a dream, imaginary monster friend and lonely child team up, two animals team up, a child learns something to make them grow up, technology is bad, girl falls in love with boy who is not who what he appears to be, forced to go it alone because parents died, everyone lives happily ever after… except the villain, hero feels guilty for hurting the villain, city dwellers leave for country. *Green Acres, Beverly Hillbillies, City Slickers*…), and country folks go to the big city.

Overused situations—Places with guns (i.e. war zones, police stations, drug deals, dangerous streets), fist fights between superheroes, emergency rooms, violence as solution, law offices, insane asylums, isolated and alone (e.g. *Home Alone*).

Overused symbols—unicorns, butterflies, open windows with curtains blowing, swords, chess boards, sunsets, mountain scenes, gravestones[27]

Overused characters—superheroes, guitar players, robots, big eyed kittens, princesses, mimes, dragons, anybody medieval, aliens (invented new creature), mythological (i.e. fairies, dragons, gnomes), pirates, insane people, bullies, ponies, animals with wings, big-breasted women holding guns.

Peter Selgin believes the key to avoiding clichés is to focus on smaller story worlds. It provides the in-depth details for the understanding of the story world, as well as more opportunities for creating a story that feels authentic. The result will be more original stories and less clichés.[28] Stories wind up with generic settings because the setting has been appropriated from whatever is at hand in film, TV, games, etc. Thus, with the setting being a cliché, it in turn impacts the story, nudging it into a predictable situation.

The tricky part with clichés is they have burrowed into our collective unconsciousness—making them both ubiquitous as well as familiar.[30] This makes them very attractive since they are so convenient and accessible. When we generate story ideas, clichés often appear as the first ideas that come to mind. The familiarity of that first idea translates into conventional plots, stock characters, contrived coincidences, unoriginal situations, and anticipated dialog (which the viewer can finish before the character does). It is not easy to let go of these ideas because they are so familiar—they simply feel right. The first step is to recognize clichés for what they are and move past the well-worn content, no matter how right it feels initially.

Cliché Problems

1. Any story with clichés is *immediately compared* with all other similar movies, games, and animations that have previously done well.
2. The drama in clichés comes *preassembled,* ready to use. This inherent structure is substituted in place of real development.
3. Clichés reinforce the insecurity that *one's* stories aren't interesting enough.
4. Clichés are generalities that lack the details which make a story real.
5. Clichés contain sensational subject matter with little personal knowledge or emotional connection. These clichés are more about melodrama, than drama.

Clichés are vilified because of their negative impact on story, but they can also be an efficient and easy way to get across ideas quickly. They can be regularly seen in commercials, advertisements, blockbuster movies/games, and independent films.

Nicholas Kazan stresses that to stay vigilant "*I'm always on the watch for clichés: I nourish them until they're in full flower, then turn them on their heads.*"[31] It is possible to use clichés if they are recognized and then turned on their head before they undermine the work. Sometimes clichés can be used when over time they have lost that familiarity that made them so destructive in the past. This occurred with *Frozen* (Figure 12.9), which built upon tried and true structures that had become clichéd in the past. Think of clichés as working with dynamite. It can be used effectively, but one must be really, really careful or it can blow up. Mark Sachs has a great compilation of clichés in his *The Grand List of Console Role Playing Game Clichés.*[32]

Figure 12.9

Frozen, (aka FROZEN, UNA AVENTURA CONGELADA), Spanish language advance poster, from left: Elsa (voice: Idina Menzel), Olaf (voice: Josh Gad), Sven (bottom), Kristoff (top, voice: Jonathan Groff), Anna (voice: Kristen Bell), Hans (voice: Santino Fontana), 2013. (Copyright Walt Disney Pictures/ Courtesy Everett Collection.)

Point of View

In *Star Wars,* Obi Wan Kenobi's death devastated Luke who lost his mentor, but Darth Vader was relieved he had vanquished his nemesis. A viewer can't tell if something is good or bad except from whose point of view we are seeing the story. While there may be multiple points-of-view, it is important for the viewer to know from who's point of view the story is told.

- The *omniscient*—an all knowing point of view from a God-like, omnipotent viewpoint. Referred to as third person in writing. More often than not this reflects the writer's point of view who imparts his/her thoughts and opinions into the story.
- The *main character's* point of view is through whose perspective we see the story unfold. This often times includes the main character's adversary; the antagonist.
- Each *secondary character* has a point of view which brings a different perspective on what is happening (C-3P0 was always giving his observations on the situation).

The omniscient (writer's) point of view gives the viewer information, feelings, and thought that no single character would know. It offers a wider, more objective point of view of everything in the story world.[33] This lends itself to more plot-driven stories such as *Star Wars, The Dark Knight,* as well as heavily narrative stories (e.g., *Portal2, Shawshank Redemption*). In game, the omniscient is often used for cut scenes.

The main character's point of view is utilized for strong character identification in character-driven stories.[34] The viewer experiences the story through Peter's eyes in *Guardians of the Galaxy,* WALL-E in *WALL-E,* or Woody in *Toy Story.* The story is skewed by how the main character sees themselves and the world around them—a winner (Zoolander) or a failure (Hiccup). In Star Trek, Spock sees the world logically which frequently puts him in conflict with Kirk who experiences it emotionally. The differences come from their backgrounds, their value systems, what they believe, and do not believe.

For secondary characters, Sol Stein stresses that it is important to "*... give each character a separate set of facts. Don't give them the same view of the story.*"[35] This solves a recurring but deadly problem of secondary characters that act and sound the same. No two people see the world in the same way. It is this individuality that broadens the story world. Give each character individual points of view, beliefs, attitudes, and values, to be revealed through their behaviors and dialog.[36]

To reiterate, changing your point of view is a fundamental technique when the story stops progressing. Bryon Howard, *Zootopia* producer, pointed out that they had spent weeks with Nick, the fox, as the main character but his point of view was too cynical. They started to look at the world from Judy's optimistic point of view, which gave the story more possibilities. They realized immediately that Judy should be the protagonist of their movie[37] (Figure 12.10). Viewers have an expectation that by the end of the story a point of view will have changed; in *Zootopia* it was Nick's.

It is not unusual for the point of view to become the story's theme. In *How to Train Your Dragon*, the message is *how does one look at the world?* It determines how dragons are viewed. Are dragons your feared enemy or the ally needed for survival? (Figure 12.11). Once Hiccup sees them in a different light, our perception is changed along with Hiccup's point of view. This message parallels the theme in *To Kill a Mockingbird—you never really understand a person until you consider things from his point of view.* In the *Looney Tunes Road Runner* Cartoons is Wily-E Coyote an inept carnivore or a hapless stooge being taunted by the Road Runner? What makes it interesting is that the point of view flips back and forth as the director played with these perceptions.

Figure 12.10

Zootopia, (aka ZOOTOPIE), poster, from left: Judy Hopps (voice: Ginnifer Goodwin), Nick Wilde (voice: Jason Bateman), 2016. (Copyright Walt Disney Studios Motion Pictures/Courtesy Everett Collection.)

Figure 12.11

How to Train Your Dragon, Hiccup (voice: Jay Baruchel), 2010. (Copyright Paramount Pictures/Courtesy Everett Collection.)

References

1. J. Sacher, *Amazing Story Generator* (San Francisco, California, Chronicle Books, 2012).
2. K. Iglesias, *Writing for Emotional Impact*, 24.
3. J. Katzenberg, Some Thoughts on Our Business, *Variety*, January 31, 1991: 1+, http://www.lettersof-note.com/2011/11/some-thoughts-on-our-business.html?m=1
4. A. Sepinwall, *The Revolution was Televised* (New York, Touchstone, 2013), 33.
5. W. J. J. Gordon, *Synectics: The Development of Creative Capacity* (New York: Harper & Row Publishers, 1961), 3.
6. J. Bruner, *On Knowing: Essays for the Left Hand* (Boston, Massachusetts, Belknap Press, 1979), 44.
7. J. Katz, *Funny!* (San Francisco, Disney Enterprises, 2015), 8.
8. C. Jung, *Man and His Symbols* (USA, Dell, 1968).
9. J. Vorhaus, *The Comic Toolbox*, (USA, Silman-James Publisher, 1994), 13–48.
10. R. McKee, *Story*, 71.
11. K. Sullivan, *Ideas for the Animated Short*, 54.
12. B. Cone, *A Bug's Life: The Art and Making of an Epic of Miniature Proportions by Jeff Kurtti* (Los Angeles, California, Disney Editions, 1998), 62.
13. J. Lasseter, Filmmakers Reflect, *Toy Story, directed by John Lasseter* (Disney Editions, 2005), 10-year edition DVD.
14. B. Cone, *A Bug's Life*, 62.
15. L. Unkrich, How it's Made, *Toy Story 3, directed by Lee Unkrich* (Walt Disney Editions, 2013), Blue Ray Disc.
16. Making Nemo, *Finding Nemo, directed by Andrew Stanton* (Pixar, released by Walt Disney Video, 2003), Collector's Edition DVD.
17. N. Panda Too, Evolution of Feelings in Pixar Films | from Toy Story to Inside Out, *YouTube*, July 31, 2015, https://www.youtube.com/watch?v=sjvpUs0ywQI
18. J. Lasseter, Disney/Pixar Spotlight On 'Finding Dory', 'Good Dinosaur' & More Charms Cannes, interview by Nancy Tartaglione, *Deadline Hollywood*, May 20, 2015, http://deadline.com/2015/05/pixar-presentation-good-dinosaur-finding-dory-zootopia-moana-cannes-1201430240/
19. L. Brooks, *Story Engineering* (Cincinnati, OH, F + W Media, 2011), 31.
20. R. McKee, *Story*, 112.
21. P. Johnston, *The Making of… Wreck-It-Ralph* (DVD—Supplemental Disc, Walt Disney Editions, 2012).
22. R. Moore, *Wreck-It Ralph' Director Shares Storytelling and Video Games* (San Diego Comic Con, Forbes, YouTube, July 14, 2012, https://www.youtube.com/watch?v=X7eouNi3LRU
23. P. Johnston, *The Making of*, 2012.
24. Guardian open journalism: Three Little Pigs advert—Video (online, the Guardian, 2012), http://www.theguardian.com/media/video/2012/feb/29/open-journalism-three-little-pigs-advert
25. J. Lasseter, A. Stanton, K. Reher and D. Anderson, *A Bug's Life—Story Process* (DVD Disc 2, Pixar/Walt Disney Editions, 1999).
26. J. Cameron, Terminator Genisys "James Cameron" Featurette, *YouTube*, https://www.youtube.com/watch?v=DamFOZpDwm8
27. K. Sullivan, *Ideas for the Animated Short*, 34.
28. P. Selgin, 10 Tips to Avoid Clichés in Writing, *Writer's Digest*, January 31, 2012, http://www.writersdigest.com/whats-new/10-tips-to-bypass-cliche-and-melodrama.
29. R. McKee, *Story*, 72.
30. C. Jung, *Man and his Symbols*, 233.
31. N. Kazan, *Plots and Characters*, 60.
32. M. Sachs, *The Grand List of Console Role Playing Game Clichés* (online, Project Apollo, 2004), http://project-apollo.net/text/rpg.html
33. I. Karl, *Emotional Impact*, 51.
34. D. Trottier, *The Screenwriter's Bible* (Kindle Edition, Silman-James Press, 2013), KL1557–1559.
35. S. Stein, *Solutions for Writers* (London, Souvenir Press Ltd., 1999), 166.
36. L. Seger, *Making a Good Script Great* (Hollywood, California, Samuel French Trade, 1994), 90.
37. B. Howard, The Making of …, *Zootopia, Directed by Rich Moore and Bryon Howard* (Walt Disney Editions, 2016), DVD, Supplemental Disc.

13

Story Development

Development and Checklists

Development is about generating ideas and keeping track of those thoughts. It is important to get the ideas down on paper and into categories—gags, set-ups/payoffs, characters traits, etc. To keep these organized, there are various approaches: notebooks, software (with prompts for specifics), outlines, flow-charts, beat sheets…. Linda Seger suggests using index cards or an updated version—sticky notes in different colors.[1] Each color represents different story components (i.e., storylines, characters, images, dialogue…). The cards/notes can go onto a board or visually accessible on a digital screen, but there needs to be some way to move them around to show the new connections being made between ideas.

Figure 13.1

Chuck Jones, director, *Looney Tunes*.

For Joss Whedon, structure means knowing where you're going… *"I'm a structure nut. I actually make charts. Where are the jokes? The thrills? The romance? Who knows what, and when? You need these things to happen at the right times, and that's what you build your structure around: the way you want your audience to feel. Charts, graphs, coloured pens, anything that means you don't go in blind is useful."*[2]

Development takes place in stages. It starts with brainstorming, then moves on to fleshing out ideas, refining ideas, which stimulates other ideas—it's an iterative process. Chuck Jones (director, *"Looney Tunes"*) generated ideas with what he called *"no"* sessions—no one was allowed to say no to any idea[3] (Figure 13.1). Larry Brooks uses a different process. He writes down the most logical things that could happen next in the story during this development process, lays it all out, is able to see it… "Then—*whatever you do—DON'T do that.* Never accept the obvious, easy, plot."[4]

Development Techniques

1. *Keeping the problem simple and specific:* Begin with the hero already in trouble, but not knowing how to solve it.[5] Focus on one idea, instead of several in the same story. It focuses the viewer, allowing them to more clearly make connections with their own lives.
2. *Everything that can go wrong "must" go wrong* (Murphy's other law):[6] The main character must suffer a lot (not just a little).
3. *Explore all points of view:* during development—not just the opposite ideas, but even the really offensive ideas.
4. *A character has one point of view:* The viewer can't determine what information matters without knowing how the character is looking at the world.[7]
5. *The story reflects a writer's unique point of view:* Connecting this view with something similar that the viewer has gone through in life is key to originality in the material.[8]
6. *Exaggerate:* This isn't realism. Subtlety will not hook the viewer.
7. *The main character must face their biggest fear:* If the goals don't connect to what the character is most afraid of, then it isn't the right goal. Indiana Jones biggest fear was snakes in *Raiders of the Lost Ark.*[9]

These considerations begin to look like a checklist. Screenwriting software programs often have their own broad checklists built in. Many writers keep a running checklist to help them stay focused on what matters most in the story. The key is to compile a list that matches a storyteller's sensibilities. Lagos Egri's list includes—forge an unbreakable bond between protagonist and antagonist, have a clear goal, the character is compulsive about achieving that goal, their compulsion will generate conflict in the story, the character must have 100% of a particular trait (Figure 13.2).[10]

Adam Elliot (director, *Harvie Krumpett [Oscar winner]*) started a list because he wanted to avoid the problem he had seen too frequently of technically good animation but poor story.[11] His list includes (1) compiling a catalog of idiosyncratic or quirky events to go in a draft, (2) constructing vignettes of personal experiences as story events before putting a plot together, and (3) concentrating on character details, which ultimately become the key links between character and relationships. There are a number of development checklists to draw from when making a personal list. The book, *Wired for Story* by Lisa Cron, has checkpoint lists at the end of every chapter. There is the *Pixar's 22 Rules of Storytelling* by Emma Coats.[12] *Writing Screenplays that Sell* by Michael Hauge has lists on pages 34–40.[13]

Figure 13.2

Lagos Egri, playwriting theorist.

Opposition: Antagonism

All heroes are potential antiheros. If pushed far enough, our self-preservation system kicks in and we are capable of terrible villainy.[14] Don't fall for the cliché of the villain/antagonist, who must look and sound evil. Evil comes in many forms.

> In the old days' villains had moustaches and kicked the dog. Audiences are smarter today. They don't want their villain to be thrown at them with green limelight on their face. They want an ordinary human being with failings.[15]
>
> Alfred Hitchcock

The main character's opponent does not have to be evil. It can be that two characters both just want the same thing. Writer Anton Chekhov indicated—"*I did not portray a single villain or a single angel ... (I) do not blame nor exculpate anyone*"[16] making it difficult to tell hero from villain. All characters are essentially both.[17]

Drama works well when it exposes both sides—hero and villain (*Captain America—Civil War*). All of (Shakespeare's) major characters have a point of view they can justify. A story is said to be only as strong as its counterargument. Writer Phil Pullman takes this to heart with his point of view that characters are only shades of evil and less evil.

A narrative becomes stronger when the conflict is about more than characters fighting, but symbolizes ideas in opposition. *Hunger Games* and *Star Wars* used political systems maintaining order at the expense of individuality. Cowgill emphasized that when we truly grasp that our protagonist and antagonists are people who are shaped by their values and beliefs, we can begin to visualize how they represent these ideas in the story.[18]

Ollie Johnston (Disney animator) stressed that "*... in every case, the audience needs to know what the villain wants, why he wants it and something about how he plans to get it. How the villain views what he is doing, his ultimate goals, how he reacts to the others in the story (which) will be the heart of the film*"[19] (Figure 13.3). What makes a character a villain often comes down to not just what they want but how they go after it. In *Snow White*, the Queen wants to be the most beautiful woman. In *Aladdin*, Jafar wants, well, *everything*—sultan's daughter, the throne, the ultimate magic genie.

> The protagonist and antagonist are like finely balanced scales. This balance must arouse the feeling, that no matter how recognizable the story appears, this time the villain could win.[20]

Figure 13.3

Ollie Johnston, Disney animator.

Some villains become as memorable, if not more so, than the hero—Lord Voldemort, The Wicked Witch of the West, The Grinch, and Captain Hook (Figure 13.4). "*A story is only as good as its villain.*" Hitchcock.

Bring the villain in at the earliest possible moment. The audience cannot feel the tension or understand the stakes until the conflict starts.

Memorable Villain Traits

1. A *villain acts:* This differs from a *hero who reacts;* Bugs Bunny never started a fight.
2. A *villain is compensating for an internal deficiency:* The external, physical goal is to make up for the holes in their life.
3. A *villain embodies the hero's problem:* If the hero feels out of control, the villain is in complete control—Hannibal Lecter.
4. A *villain uses deception:* What form of disguise best embodies what they are up to (e.g., temptress, best friend)? Hans assumes the role of noble savior (*Frozen*).
5. *Villains are entertaining:* They personify some outlandishness. Jack Sparrow in *Pirates of the Caribbean.* Get rid of repulsive or cliché villains— those not even the writer can care about.
6. *Villains are not generic:* The details are important. Where they come from and why are they evil—the Joker, Nurse Ratched, Norman Bates, Darth Vader. Evil is more than *that's just the way they are.*

Figure 13.4

Captain Hook, *Peter Pan.* (Copyright 1953, Disney.)

7. *Villains can switch:* A movie length story often starts with the one villain—in *Jaws* it is first the shark, then it is the mayor; in *The Dark Knight* it was the Joker, then it became Harvey Dent.
8. *Villains embody negative emotions all viewers have felt:* greed, selfishness, revenge, desire for power, control, or an irrational mind. When we see characters who are giving in to such feelings, we not only empathize, but we are also intrigued to see the outcome.
9. A *villain can be abstract:* Some unknown danger that is hinted at (more common in horror and war genres). A villain is not confined to just one person, system, or supreme entity. Hitchcock found it in a flock of birds, behind a shower curtain, or out on a country road.[21]

On top of everything confronting the main character externally, there is also some internal opposition. In comedies and coming-of-age genres it isn't the adversary that generates the most conflict, it is the conflict inside themselves (i.e., *The Dark Knight, Westworld*). "*The more powerful and complex the forces of antagonism opposing the character, the more completely realized the character and story become.*"[22] It's the *total of all forces* in opposition that make the story so engaging. Out of all the opponents in a story sometimes the more formidable one is themselves (e.g., self-destructiveness, *The Hurt Locker*). See McKee, *Story,* Forces of Antagonism, pages 317–333.[23]

Problems at the Beginning

Michael Arndt revealed that when working on *Toy Story 3*, they had a hard time getting the story set up in the right way. *"A lot of times when a film doesn't work it seems like the problem is with the ending but actually the seeds of failure have been planted at the beginning."*[24] His solution was to go back and look at how others have set up their characters, their worlds, and their stories. James Cameron did the same thing by going back to take a look at dozens of his favorites openings in film. This resulted in him completely revamping his opening of *Titanic*.

Planting action or dialogue in the beginning can pay off later.[25] In *Guardians of the Galaxy*, the director used a cassette tape with the music's message reinforcing the connection to family. This was planted early and reintroduced often. It was a bit more obvious in *Forrest Gump—Life is like a box of chocolates*.

Planting information works by taking an idea from the end of the story and planting the opposite idea at the beginning. It works because viewer sees the idea has transformed by the end of the story. If the theme is finding true love, the character finds themselves alone in the beginning. If the theme is freedom, the character would be seen trapped before breaking free by the end (*Hunger Games*). Give the viewers something to connect Act I to Act III. Dara Marks stresses that *"A story doesn't begin at the beginning; it begins in opposition to the ending."*[26]

To reiterate the axiom *In Media Res—* the story starts in the middle. *Jurassic World* doesn't begin with the cloning of dinosaurs but with a fully functioning Theme Park of full grown dinosaurs and a hybrid escapes (Figure 13.5). *The Three Little Pigs* doesn't begin when they are born but when they take off on their own and choose building materials for their houses. Many stories begin by showing the viewer that the world can be a scary and dangerous place before anything else. The point of a beginning is to set the conflict in motion.

Figure 13.5

Jurassic World, Chris Pratt, 2015. (Copyright Universal Pictures/Courtesy Everett Collection.)

Where to begin? Screenwriter Nicholas Kazan emphasizes that he begins *"by writing notes, character sketches, lines of dialogue, whole scenes… 'not knowing who is speaking or what is happening, or where it fits into the story.' The last line or image, a dozen different openings, sustained arguments with myself, attempts to find the mythic underpinnings of the narrative, harsh analyses of pitfalls and how to avoid them, outlines, more outlines, detailed outlines…"*[27] (Figure 13.6).

The key to developing story is iteration… doing it over, again, and again, and again. *Writing is rewriting* is a fundamental truism in development. Stories must be repeatedly edited until all the clichés and preciousness are out. Whedon uses this technique. *"Here's one trick that I learned early on. If something isn't working, if you have a story that you've built and it's blocked and you can't figure it out, take your favorite scene, or your very best idea or set-piece, and cut it. It's brutal, but sometimes inevitable. That thing may find its way back in, but cutting it is usually an enormously freeing exercise."*[28]

Arthur Quiller-Couch's often repeated advice *"Murder your darlings"* is as true today as when first given in 1913. When a writer finds themselves protecting rather than creating they are in real trouble. Award winning screenwriter Nicholas Kazan advises new writers, *"The process of creating scenes, scenes that one loves, has led me in the wrong direction far too frequently. What's worse is that one powerful but misguided scene can prompt me to create a series of scenes with considerable entertainment value but no narrative purpose. If I even wonder whether something is wrong, I change it… In making the necessary changes, I ignore the beauty of my scenes, the endearing character touches and I cut them quickly, before I become too attached."*[29]

> *Lisa Cron suggests that one way to determine if what the protagonist wants is their genuine goal is to ask yourself: will she have to face her biggest fear, and so resolve her inner issue, to achieve said goal? If the answer is no, then guess what— it's a false goal.*

Figure 13.6

Nicholas Kazan.[30]

Know Your Ending

Think of an ending as an emotional destination—how will the viewer feel afterward; satisfied, haunted, uplifted?[31] The purpose of endings is not only to resolve the conflict but to also satisfy the viewer emotionally and answer the central dramatic question that was introduced at the beginning. It is always a plus if the ending is entertaining with a surprise. Aristotle advised *"The ending must be both inevitable and unexpected."*[32] Endings fall in several types:

> *The flow of life travels forward, moving from cause to effect, but the flow of story moves from effect to cause... end to beginning.*[36] John Lawson.

1. *Strong endings*—has the central question answered with a twist to drive home the theme. The main character doesn't necessarily get what they want but they do learn what's important in life (e.g., relationships are paramount—*Guardians of the Galaxy*)[33] (Figure 13.7).

2. *Open/ambiguous endings*—leaves things unresolved and open to interpretation. More often than not this leaves the viewer unsatisfied. Frequently found in independent and art films. Check out "ambiguous endings" on *YouTube*.

3. *Closed endings*—wrap up all the loose ends. The viewer is given (or hinted at) the answer to all narrative questions that were raised earlier. The moral of story is clear.

4. *Weak/bad endings*—are made of clichés. An ending that has been seen too many times—it was all a *dream*, death is the solution, a coincidence solves everything, or an ending that needs to be explained.

Figure 13.7

Guardians of the Galaxy, from left: Zoe Saldana, Chris Pratt, 2014. (Copyright Walt Disney Studios Motion Pictures/Courtesy Everett Collection.)

There are a large number of writers who recommend coming up with an ending before jumping into the story. *"If I didn't know the ending of a story, I wouldn't begin,"* K. A. Porter[34] *"Begin at the End and go back till you come to the Beginning, then Start,"* Percival Wilde Andrew Stanton (director, *WALL-E, Finding Dory*) advises, "One of the lessons I'm always saying is... know your ending. Know the punch line to your joke, and then design your joke around the punch line. It's much easier to figure out your story that way or else you are really going to be spinning your wheels going front to back."[35]

Ingredients to a Good Ending[37]

1. **Character must make a difficult choice:** Viewers relate to this ending because life is hard. The main character can't be let off easy, because that's not how life is. Viewers want to know what the character is made of—will the character do the selfish thing or the right thing?

2. **Character sacrifices what they want:** This sacrifice reveals the level of commitment on the part of the character. When things get too difficult will they just give up and go back home? Sacrifice is best made voluntarily than forced on the character.

3. **Character does something they weren't capable of doing at the beginning:** The main character has developed new capabilities (emotional or physical). For this to work, the viewer is given a good idea of the main character's shortcomings in the beginning and overcoming their flaws has an impact at the end.

4. **Character is transformed by the end:** The character overcomes their flaws—inability to love (*Despicable Me*, Figure 13.8). Just before the climax they are transformed. A transformation requires a personal realization that enables the character to regain their moral compass. Marks indicates it requires the character *"to go to those places inside ourselves that have been hidden… where we send our hurt, our shame, our ugliness, our sorrow, our loneliness."*[38] This transformation is most evident when the character exposes those parts of themselves they don't want others to see; facing the potential shame and isolation.

5. **Viewer is emotionally moved:** Often done by having something bad happen before something good. This something *good* does not mean an over the top cliché, bags of money, or immense fame. The viewer is moved because the reward makes sense in relation to the story's theme.

6. **Viewer's tension is released quickly:** Climaxes cannot be fragmented, not if the objective is to move the audience. If the audience is going to experience an emotional rush, the dramatic tension is released in one swift action—*Thelma and Louise* (drive into the Grand Canyon), *Toy Story* (rocket back to rejoin the toys).

7. **Viewer is surprised:** Screenwriter William Goldman: *"The key to all story endings is to give the audience what it wants, but not in the way it expects."*[39]

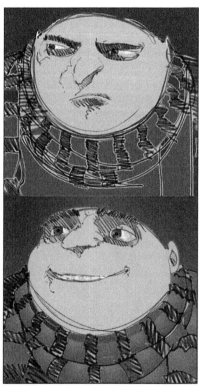

Figure 13.8

Gru is transformed from who they were in the beginning to who they have become at the end. *Despicable Me*. (Copyright 2010, Illumination Entertainment.)

Dialogue: Its Functions

Dialogue is not "real" conversation. Dialogue maintains the illusion of conversation but is far more focused, edited, and lean—using the fewest amount of words needed.

Scientific research has revealed that normal day-to-day conversation has a different purpose than dialogue. Normal day-to-day conversation serves to maintain our relationships with others.[40] As people speak, we start with pleasantries (weather, health) and along the way we settle into ramblings, sentence fragments, awkward word choices, abrupt transitions, sounds... ahs, uhs. Dialogue's purpose has three dramatic functions:

Advance the Conflict—Noted film director, David Mamet *"I've said it before and I'll say it again. One of the easiest ways to create good dialogue is through conflict... one character wants something while the other character wants something else."*[41] Dialogue can quickly switch the direction of the scene—positive to negative, or negative to positive. PRISCILLA: "You are going to save us, aren't you?" RANGO: "Count on it little sister" (*Rango*, Figure 13.9).

Reveal the Individual Character—Who a character really is can be revealed through the words used—vocabulary, sentence length, slang, and even the jargon can indicate the level of education. A character's speech patterns—rhythm, accent, sarcasm—all reveal thoughts and feelings.[42] Dialogue also reveals what one character thinks of another. *"We have been on a lot of adventures together and it seems to me you haven't learned anythin'... anythin'"* (Hangover III).

> For David Mamet, dialogue isn't about revealing character, dialogue is about its purpose—*The only reason people speak is to get what they want.*[41]

Can the viewer recognize the individual character who is speaking? *"Everybody in your scene, including the thug flanking your bad guy... has their own voice, their own identity, their own history... if you don't know who everybody is and why they're there, why they're feeling what they're feeling and why they're doing what they're doing, then you're in trouble."*[43] Joss Whedon

Exposition—Dialogue provides information and clarification for the viewer. *Toy Story 3*—HAMM: *"Aah negatory, it's a Fensler Schneler 380, the finest child proof lock in the world,"* MISS POTATO HEAD: *"We're trapped."* Dialogue is used in VR and games to provide clues for progressing through the levels. In comedy, the dialogue selected sets the tone and mood for the viewer to anticipate funny lines, quips, and jokes.

Figure 13.9

Rango, from left: Priscilla (voice: Abigail Breslin), Rango (voice: Johnny Depp), 2011. (Copyright Paramount Pictures/Courtesy Everett Collection.)[44]

David Mamet is adamant that *"without question, one of the biggest mistakes I see from amateurs are characters who are only talking because they're in a scene. If characters are only talking because a writer's making them, the scene will be maddeningly boring"*[45] (Figure 13.10). The truism *Less is More* means characters only speak when the conflict reaches a point that they have to speak.

What kills Dialogue[46]

1. *More words than needed* is the #1 mistake starting out.
2. *Predictable dialogue* includes pleasantries/everyday phrases (*Hello, Goodbye, How are you?*); as well as derivative lines from other movies (*Live long and prosper, Make my day…*).
3. *Generic dialogue* that is not specific to the individual character is deadly.
4. Characters *saying exactly* what they are clearly thinking, doing, and feeling… no subtext.
5. *Repetitive dialogue* where characters repeat one another; *"Can you get me a drink"* response, *"What kind of drink?"*
6. *Exaggerated emotions* in the dialogue feels amateurish. It results in overacting.
7. *Obvious exposition* through dialogue sounds manufactured.
8. *Weak visuals are explained* through dialogue. This is dialogue used in place of better visuals. A close-up, a cut in, or reaction shot would better serve the story.

Plays, TV, 2D animation, and RPG games all put increased emphasis on dialogue. This can be ascribed to the lower screen detail or in the case of a play, distance from stage. In VR and FPS, the viewer is taking in the whole scene, they aren't tied to a specific piece of camera image presented in a certain order. Dialogue provides narrative information to keep the viewer aware of their situation.

Theater, VR, and interactive games also accept a more expansive approach to dialogue, whereas animation looks to compress and condense dialogue. Characters going off on verbal tangents from the main point of the narrative are tolerated due the extended timeframe of a console game. Such media has its own distinct pacing.

In games, it isn't literal dialogue but sound effects, music, and ambient dialogue that plays a greater role in reinforcing the action and keeping the game progressing. *Ambient Dialogue*[47] conversation in the background (i.e., singing, yelling), can be generated by triggers when entering new areas (*Call of Duty, Portal 2*). It sets up the mood of the environment. At the same time, never underestimate the importance of music—it tells the viewer what to feel. Creepy music increases the tension, playful music sets up humor. Excellent dialogue examples—*"Writing for Emotional Impact,"* Chapter 10, pages 170–223.[48] The *Game Narrative Toolbox* has an excellent section on dialogue in games; Chapter 7, pages 159–181.[49]

Figure 13.10

David Mamet, director.

Subtext

Subtext is the underlying meaning behind the words. At the end of a date, someone says *"Would you like to come in for drink?"* it isn't about being thirsty. The meaning isn't in the literal words. Subtext is what's being implied or can be inferred. It is similar to the function of idioms—*high as a kite, raining cats and dogs, pay the piper, jump the gun.* Subtext is often context dependent, *who is saying it—"I'll be back"* (Terminator, Figure 13.11) or Norman Bates in *Psycho*: *"Mother... isn't quite herself today."*[50]

Subtext Techniques[51]

1. *Contrast action with dialogue*—At the end of *When Harry Met Sally*, Sally says *"I hate you,"* and then kisses him. The physical response to a question or request contrasts with the dialogue. Syd Field pointed out *"What a person does, is what he is, not what he says."*[52] When dialogue is juxtaposed with contradictory action, these gaps pique a viewer's curiosity.

2. *Evading the question*—Changing the subject often reveals more about what the character is *trying not to say* than what they are saying. Every interrogation scene in a detective show (Law & Order, Criminal Minds, CSI) is packed with a character's hesitation, looking away, and thinking about talking. A character can swear up and down they are telling the truth, but it's their actions that define them.

3. *Hide their real emotions*—In real life, people are hesitant to express their thoughts or emotions directly, so they talk around their feelings. When angry at a friend or dealing with the boss, people speak indirectly to avoid confrontation. Emotions are held back to avoid confrontation or appearing vulnerable.

4. *Sarcasm*—Delivery of dialogue to mean the opposite of its literal meaning. Primarily revealed by vocal inflection and expression. Sarcasm might be used to mask vulnerability as they mock others. Characters downplay their beliefs, ideas, even their hopes, and dreams to avoid being mocked themselves. This denying who they are, has produced countless characters who deny their true nature—Wade in *Deadpool*, Wesley in *Wanted*, Katniss in *Hunger Games*.

Figure 13.11

The context—who is saying it—changes its meaning. "I'll be back," from *The Terminator*. (Copyright 1984, Universal.)

Viewers enjoy subtext. It stimulates them to actively make story connections and make them feel smart in figuring it out. When the viewer is being told what is already obvious, it's dull and unsatisfying. Through subtext, the writer hints at the conflicts in the scene without actually identifying them[53]—"*We're going to need a bigger boat.*" (*Jaws*)

To identify subtext, a scene's dialogue can be broken down into three categories:

1. What must be said
2. What can be left implied
3. What doesn't need to be said

To understand what is going on beneath the surface, one must determine the key emotions and then how the emotions might get expressed. If angry, would the character suppress or vent it? If there is tension where is it coming from?[54]

Subtext is the answer to the question of why characters are acting in ways that don't immediately make sense. Subtext works best when implying what a character needs (it's in the theme) rather than what they want.

Subtext is one of the more difficult, but critical aspects to grasp of a story. The balcony scene in *Annie Hall* uses subtitles to reveal the subtext[55] (Figure 13.12). Robert McKee goes into depth on subtext in *Story*, pages 252–257[56] or see Karl Iglesias's book, *Writing for Emotional Impact*, pages 211–217.[57]

> *If a character's true nature is closely guarded and only hinted at in subtext, it carries more weight.* Linda Cowgill.[58]

God, I hope he doesn't turn out to be a shmuck like the others

Figure 13.12

Literal subtext in the *Annie Hall* balcony.[53] (Copyright 1976, Rollins-Joffe Productions.)

Metaphors and Symbols

Story metaphors have double meanings—the literal meaning and the more significant figurative meaning. *Aliens'* figurative meaning is about the Vietnam war—soldiers sent to a far off land, with incompetent leaders, to face an unknown enemy. The *Revenant* uses religious metaphors throughout—rise from the dead, baptism by water, the spiral symbolism (in place of the cross). The purpose of a metaphor is to help the viewer make connections and insights that might normally be blocked by a viewer's preconceptions about the world. Portraying things literally wouldn't get the job done. Metaphors are not new—*"metaphor consists in giving the thing a name that belongs to something else,"* Aristotle, 352 BC.[59]

Metaphors work only when the audience knows what they reference. Does everyone know what is meant by—*the elephant in the room, my heart is broken, or he swims with the fishes*? Each metaphor alludes to something else.[60] In Situation Comedies, a familiar metaphor is to use phrases more indicative of sex, *"was that good for you?"* while watching *Star Wars* (*The Big Bang Theory*). Problems arise if the metaphors are either too culturally specific, *"Bob's your uncle,"* or known only to a specific set of viewers.

Visual metaphors are just as pervasive as verbal metaphors. Alfonso Cuarón, director of *Gravity,* said that he wanted "To play with the themes, not in a rhetoric way, where people talk about them, but in visual metaphors... It started to become clear the metaphorical possibilities that space can bring"[61] (Figure 13.13).

1. Ryan (Sandra Bullock) drifting in space became a metaphor of her life back on earth—drifting without purpose due to the death of her son.
2. Space and the debris became a metaphor for the adversity in life. The debris speeding by every 90 minutes represented the cyclical nature of adversties in life.
3. The ship protecting Ryan in space symbolized the emotional isolation humans use to protect themselves.

Gravity was shot to emphasize life (earth) and death (blackness of space).[62] The movie continually used earth as backdrop representing the astronaut's connection to life. Sandra Bullock saw the earth as *a character* in this movie—the storms, land masses, sunrises were shot to show it as a living being.[63] To reinforce that connection with life, the director purposefully shot the airlock to resemble a womb with Ryan assuming a fetal position in the shot. As the capsule started to sink in the water, her struggle to reach the surface was a rebirth, with the water representing embryotic liquid.[64] This metaphor of evolution continued as Ryan climbed out of the water on all fours, then rising to two legs before taking the first steps of her new life (Figure 13.14).

Figure 13.14

Symbolism of human evolution in *Gravity.* (Copyright 2013, Warner Brothers.)

Are metaphors really that important to a good story? To reiterate the axiom *"If the story you're telling, is the story you're telling, you're in deep sh*t."*[65] In the animation *UP*, Carl's house is a metaphor of himself—it has outlived its purpose, it's old fashioned, it's in the way. The house flying up in the air is a metaphor for Carl striking out for a new life.

Is the movie *Inception* about dreams? Yes, but it also about moviemaking. Each member of the team has a role that corresponds with a role on a movie set (Figure 13.15). In *Inception* Arthur assumes the role of the producer, Yusuf handles special effects, Ariadne takes on the role of screenwriter, and Cobb is the director. The characters scout the dream location, similar to location scouts for movie sets. Their purpose is to change the way someone looks at the world. Such metaphors embed a story with meaning that viewers connect to as well, even if at the subconscious level.

Some of the more effective metaphors incorporate primordial, universal symbols that storytellers use, consciously or unconsciously.[66] Carl Jung believed such symbols are a primary source of material for the underlying meaning in our lives. *"Many... archetypal patterns are bipolar and embody the basic concepts of religion, art, and society: god-devil, light-dark, active-passive, male-female, static-dynamic...."*[67] These symbols might be considered ingrained, tracing back to primitive times. Metaphors resonate because they have been handed down over generations.

Finally, the celebrated science fiction writer, Ray Bradbury, contends that the best stories are metaphors. He describes himself as a *metaphor machine* and that the best way to incorporate them into your work is to first start collecting metaphors for reference.[68]

Figure 13.15

Metaphor for film set, *Inception*, Leonardo DiCaprio (center), 2010. (Copyright Warner Bros./Courtesy Everett Collection.)

Making the Story... Short

Feature movies/animations have 45–60 scenes, 10–12 sequences, and 3–8 acts. Shorts, in contrast, have one to three scenes, one sequence, one act. *Looney Tunes*, director Friz Freleng believes that a short succeeds not because it is the first act of a feature film but because it is direct and simple. It has an economy of structure, plot, and assets not found in feature films.[69] Warning, all too frequently a short jumps out of the gate with *feature movie* aspirations resulting in feature ideas getting squeezed into the short format.

> *Every character should want something, even if it is only a glass of water.* Kurt Vonnegut.

So how many characters, locations, conflicts, and themes should a short have?

A short will have one or two characters, one or two locations, one conflict, and one theme. Only a few essential details are needed—let the viewer's brain fill in the rest. Most shorts fall into three categories:

1. *Situations*—what has or is about to happen. Again, as Friz Freleng (*Looney Tunes*, director) indicated, it isn't about a plot but *a situation*.
2. *Attributes*—how two characters or groups are relating to each other.
3. *Individuals*—are made evident by their clothes, age, manner, etc.

Figure 13.16

Jinxy Jenkins, Lucky Lou, http://jinxylucky. tumblr.com/.[73]

Figure 13.17

Mobile (animation) by Verena Fels.

A short is still about someone who wants something and is having trouble getting it.[70] Karen Sullivan summed it up well: "*The short story has ONE character that wants something badly and is having trouble getting it. That 'trouble' is, at most, ONE other character or the environment that causes conflict. The resolution to the conflict communicates ONE specific idea, theme, or concept*"[71] (Figure 13.16). As Chuck Jones has recounted... they were fortunate there was little budget and only 6 weeks to make a cartoon. They could only have two characters' maximum on the screen at any one time.

The animated short can be summed up as a character spurred to action (10–15 seconds in), gets pushback, things get worse, everything comes apart, has to make a difficult choice with success finally coming at the end. A character's beliefs will likely not change much, but there will be a turn in the values—positive to negative, or negative to positive in the story. Often in a short, it is enough to—retrieve an object, get from point A to point B (*Mobile*, Figure 13.17), uncover a secret, discover something hidden, or solve a problem. It can be as small as a one-liner or a single gag.[72]

Andrew Jimenez (Figure 13.18), director of Pixar's *One Man Band*, advises "*don't over complicate it. Just find one idea that you want to tell… If it's not working, ask yourself why. Don't think you have to pile a bunch of other stuff on top of it to make it work and make it longer.*"[74] A short story is like a good joke. It has a great setup, gets to the point, and pays off right away. Even if it takes you somewhere different from what you expected, it gets to the point in short order. It's just very simple. It is about one idea that has to be very clear. There just isn't enough time to develop subplots in a short.[75]

Timothy Cooper likewise advises that the short should be one or two characters—no more. Emphasis on the flaws of the main character is the fastest and funniest way for an audience to identify. Limit the story to a *single* dilemma that is resolved in some way by the end.[76] Jimenez emphasizes introducing one memorable character that the viewer can empathize with or the story film will quickly be forgotten. Keep the viewer on their toes. Put in twist at the beginning and a twist at the end. Keep the outlook positive in even the darkest story, it's much easier to be cynical. On that same thought, end with a positive spin, if at all possible.[77]

Ideas for the Animated Short by Karen Sullivan is an excellent text. Sources for shorts include TropFest, Pixar, Ringling College of Art and Design, Filmakademie, Gobelins, etc.

> *Professionals have collected their resources for years before their story begins. Folders containing cut scenes, game clips, short films, and the strongest scenes from features that have resonated for them. Traditional artists have done this for centuries with their sketches and source material.*

Figure 13.18

Andrew Jimenez, director, *One Man Band*.

References

1. L. Seger, *Making a Good Script Great*, 5.
2. C. Bray, Joss Whedon's Top 10 Writing Tips, *Aerogramme Writers' Studio*, March 13, 2012, http://www.aerogrammestudio.com/2013/03/13/joss-whedons-top-10-writing-tips/
3. J. Katz, *Funny!, Art of the Gag* (San Francisco, California, Chronicle Books, 2015), 7.
4. L. Brooks, *Story Engineering*, 32.
5. J. Truby, *Anatomy of Story*, 40.
6. L. Brooks, *Story Engineering*, 33.
7. L. Cron, *Wired for Story*, 133.
8. T. Cooper, 7 Simple Secrets for Making an Outstanding Short Film, *Script Magazine*, 2013, http://www.scriptmag.com/features/7-simple-secrets-making-a-short-film
9. L. Cron, *Wired for Story*, 133.
10. L. Egri, *The Art of Dramatic Writing*, 44.
11. P. Wells, *Scriptwriting* (London, AVA Publishing, 2007), 139.
12. E. Coats, "Pixar's 22 Rules of Storytelling," *Aerogramme Writers' Studio*, March 7, 2013, http://www.aerogrammestudio.com/2013/03/07/pixars-22-rules-of-storytelling
13. M. Hauge, *Writing Screenplays*, 34–40.
14. O. Johnston and F. Thomas, *The Disney Villain* (New York, Hyperion, 1993), 15.
15. J. Gunz, Why Hitchcock's Villains Don't Dwell in the Shadows, but in Your Mirror, *Alfred Hitchcock Geek*, 2005, http://www.alfredhitchcockgeek.com/2005/05/why-hitchcocks-villains-dont-dwell-in.html
16. A. Chekhov, *Plays Translated by Richard Gilman* (New York, Penguin, 2002), 44.
17. J. Yorke, *Into the Woods*, 195.
18. L. Cowgill, *The Art of Plotting* (New York, Back Stage Books, 2008), 28.
19. O. Johnston and F. Thomas, *The Disney Villain*, 19.
20. J. Yorke, *Into the Woods*, 194.
21. J. Gunz, *Why Hitchcock's Villains Don't Dwell*, 2005.
22. R. McKee, *Story*, 317.
23. R. McKee, *Story*, 317–333.
24. M. Arndt, What I learned at Pixar, Toy Story 3 Disc.
25. M. Kaufmann, *Plots and Characters: A Screenwriter on Screenwriting* (Los Angeles, California, Really Great Books Publisher, 1999), 209.
26. D. Marks, *Inside Story*, 181.
27. N. Kazan, *Plots and Characters: A Screenwriter on Screenwriting by Millard Kaufmann* (Los Angeles, California, Really Great Books Publisher, 1999), 60.
28. Joss Whedon's Top 10 Writing Tips, *Aerogramme Writers' Studio*, 2012.
29. N. Kazan, *Plots and Characters*, 61.
30. L. Cron, *Wired for Story*, 133.
31. M. Palladino, R. Brown, and P. Bernstein, *Short Story Endings: A Writing Show Interview*, May 2008, http://www.writingshow.com/articles/transcripts/2008/05252008.html
32. A. K. Aristotle, *Video Game Storytelling by Evan Skolnick* (New York, Watson-Guptill, 2014), 89.
33. M. Palladino, *Short Story Endings*, May 2008.
34. K. A. Porter, K. A. Porter Interview by B. T. Davis (The Paris Review, 29 Winter-Spring, 1963).
35. A. Stanton, *WALL-E, DVD, Director's Commentary* (USA, Disney-Pixar, 2009). @56 minutes.
36. J. Lawson, *Technique of Playwriting*, 177.
37. A. Palmer, Great Endings, *Cracking Yarns*, 2013, http://www.crackingyarns.com.au/?s=great+endings
38. D. Marks, *Transformational Arc*, 287.
39. W. Goldman, *Video Game Storytelling by Evan Skolnick* (New York, Watson-Guptill, 2014), 89.
40. J. Yorke, *Into the Woods*, 150.
41. D. Mamet, What Can You Learn from David Mamet about Adding Subtext to Your Script? By Justin Morrow, *No Film School*, 2015, http://nofilmschool.com/2015/12/what-can-you-learn-david-mamet-adding-subtext-script
42. D. Trottier, dialogue
43. Joss Whedon's Top 10 Writing Tips, *Aerogramme Writers' Studio*, 2012.
44. D. Mamet, *On Directing Film* (New York, Penguin Books, 1992), 71.
45. D. Mamet, What Can You Learn from David Mamet, 2015.
46. C. Mortiz, *Scriptwriting for the Screen* (London, Routledge, 2000), 44.
47. T. Heussner, *The Game Narrative Toolbox*, 160.
48. K. Iglesias, *Emotional Impact*, 170–223.
49. T. Heussner, *Game Narrative Toolbox* (Burlington, MA, Focal Press, 2015), 159–181.
50. K. Iglesias, *Writing for Emotional Impact*, 184.
51. Ibid, 211.
52. S. Field, *Screenplay*, 44.
53. K. Iglesias, *Writing for Emotional Impact*, 212.
54. L. Cowgill, *Writing for the Short Film*, 180.
55. Balcony Scene, with all the subtitles, *Annie Hall*, October 22, 2011, https://www.youtube.com/watch?v=7ra7baVjrGA
56. R. McKee, *Story*, 252–257.
57. K. Iglesias, *Emotional Impact*, 211–217.
58. L. Cowgill, *Writing for the Short Film*, 180.
59. A. K. Aristotle, *Poetics* (USA, Witch Books, 2011), 53.
60. English language metaphors, *Wikipedia*, last modified on June 2, 2016, https://en.wikipedia.org/wiki/List_of_English-language_metaphors
61. A. Cuarón, *Making of Gravity* (Blue Ray Supplemental Disc, Warner Brothers, 2013), Time location 2:09.
62. J. Cuarón, *Making of Gravity* (Blue Ray Supplemental Disc, Warner Brothers, 2013), Time location 1:06.
63. A. Cuarón, *Making of Gravity*, 2:09.
64. S. Bullock, *Making of Gravity* (Blue Ray Supplemental Disc, Warner Brothers, 2013), Time location 4:09.
65. J. Cuarón, *Making of Gravity*, 1:06.

66. C. Jones, Top 16 quotes from Robert McKee for screenwriters, storytellers and filmmakers, *Chrisjonesblog*, 2014, http://www.chrisjonesblog.com/2014/07/screenwriters-storytellers-filmmakers.html

67. C. Jung, *Understanding Movies*, 5th edition by Louis Giannetti (New York, Prentice-Hall, 1990), 332.

68. R. Bradbury, Ray Bradbury's Writing Tips by Jim Denny, *Unearthly Fiction*, 2012, https://unearthlyfiction.wordpress.com/2012/09/17/ray-bradbury-writing-tips/

69. F. Freleng, *Funny!, Art of the Gag* by Jason Katz (San Francisco, California, Chronicle Books, 2015), 8.

70. K. Sullivan, *Ideas for the Animated Short*, 22.

71. F. Daniel, *Emotional Impact by Iglesias*, 78.

72. M. Popova, Kurt Vonnegut's 8 Tips on How to Write a Great Story, *Brainpickings*, https://www.brainpickings.org/2012/04/03/kurt-vonnegut-on-writing-stories/

73. K. Sullivan, *Animated Short*, 23.

74. A. Jimenez, *Ideas for the Animated Short by Karen Sullivan*, 64.

75. K. Sullivan, *Animated Short*, 23.

76. T. Cooper, *7 Simple Secrets*, 2013.

77. A. Jimenez, *Ideas for the Animated Short*, 67.

14

Viewer
(the Audience)

The Viewer's Expectations

There is an unspoken covenant between viewer and storyteller. A viewer brings their expectations and the storyteller is to fulfill these expectations. These expectations are contextual. At the beginning of a story, the viewer will learn what is at stake. Before the story ends, the viewer will see the big confrontation (climax). The viewer wants to know the consequences of the choices made by the characters. Last but not least, there is an expectation that the story should have a point.

There are also expectations of structure—cause and effect events enabling the viewer to draw inferences. A viewer makes sense of the story by recognizing the specific story elements and putting them together within a recognized genre. Each genre has its own set of conventions that must be accounted for, so the audience can follow along.

> *Let the audience put two and two together, they'll thank you for it.*
> Billy Wilder, director.

... And by doing that the audience will fill in the blanks... embed their own emotional experience into the journey of the characters.[1]

Alfonso Cuarón

You have one goal: to connect with your audience. Therefore, you must track what your audience is feeling at all times. One of the biggest problems I face when watching other people's movies is I'll say, "This part confuses me." They'll go on about their intentions. None of this has anything to do with my experience as an audience member. Think in terms of what audiences think.[2]

Joss Whedon (Figure 14.1)

Figure 14.1

Joss Whedon, director, *The Avengers*.

The viewer constructs the story in their head, assigning meaning to what they see. As they are watching, the viewer is continually sorting, sifting, weighing new evidence, inferring motives, and explanations, ever suspicious of being taken off guard. They are constantly asking questions—Why did the character do that? Why did he react that way? What will she do now? The viewer is always monitoring the narrative for reversals. The viewer is never passive; they are actively guessing *what will happen next*.[3]

The constant challenge for the storyteller is to put yourself in the place of the viewer. Viewers only know what is in front of them, they have no access to the writer's thoughts and intentions. If the story isn't working, it can't be stated strongly enough that *it is not the viewer's fault.* When a story isn't working, it is likely because of motives other than to entertain and move the viewer emotionally. Such sidetracking motives include (1) to prove something

> When you think about the audience you will be able to take control of the story. As a storyteller, we know where the treasure is hidden (story payoffs), and we are giving the audience clues to find it. Joe Lambert.[7]

(2) to express oneself, or (3) to impress the audience. Warning: once these motives become evident the viewer will feel that they are being manipulated. A story's continuity starts to fracture when either the viewer can anticipate what is going to happen next, or they become confused as to the direction of the story.

As a general rule of thumb, a viewer's IQ collectively jumps 25 points as they pick up cues from other viewers around them in a theater. It is not unusual for the viewer to feel smarter than the storyteller in these situations. There is no story, game, or animation that is going to succeed unless the storyteller has imagined and taken into account a viewer's expectations and reactions. The audience's expectations must be satisfied or there will be an ever dwindling audience.

Peter Docter was mentored by Joe Grant. Grant served as head of Disney's story department in the 1940s (i.e., *Dumbo, Lady and the Tramp*, etc.). He recalled that "*one thing that he (Walt Disney) always asked us was 'What are you giving the audience to take home?' 'What's the audience going to remember from this film?' 'Not only today, but tomorrow, the next year, their entire life?' Usually, it's those great emotional moments that lodge in their memory.*"[4]

Finally, Jim Cummings, independent filmmaker and Sundance Grand Jury winner insists that filmmakers need to make stories for audiences. Even if a filmmaker does not make conventional stories, audiences aren't going to be persuaded to watch until the story links with at least some of their expectations. Too often rejecting conventional structures results in rejecting audiences as well. It is important to understand that one must first succeed in the established market before one can shift paradigms.[4] As Emma Coats emphasized in her *Pixar's 22 Rules of Storytelling*—"*You gotta keep in mind what is interesting to you as an audience, not what's fun to do as a writer. They can be very different.*"[5] Francis Glebas has a wonderful section on audiences in his book, *Directing the Story*, pages 15–18 (Figure 14.2).[6]

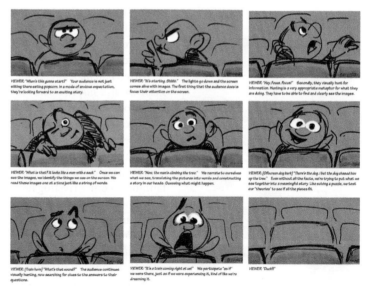

Figure 14.2

What is the audience doing? Francis Glebas's depiction of audience reactions. *Directing the Story*, page 17.

Who Knows What? When?
(Directing a Viewer's Attention)

A viewer will stay hooked when story information is revealed at anticipated points in the story. How information is released to the viewer determines the specific emotional response—curiosity, surprise, suspense, or tension. These are fundamental tools in the story's toolbox. Whether it be animation, VR, or games, each medium's narrative progressively releases information to maintain continuity and keep the viewer engaged.

Who *knows what, when,* and *how* options:

1. Viewer *know less* than the character (mystery, surprise, comedy)
2. Viewer *knows more* than the character (tension, empathy)
3. Viewer *learns at the same time* as the character (suspense, surprise)
4. Viewer *thinks they know more* than the character, but they don't (irony)

This continually switching of who knows what when, keeps the relationships between characters shifting; a stock 'n trade technique in soap operas. It also keeps the relationship between the story and viewer in flux.

At any given moment, the story's creator needs to appreciate when the viewer knows (1) more than, (2) less than, or (3) as much as the characters do. The basic question to ask is who knows what, when, including the viewer, and then to keep track of this information as the story progresses. This is one of the early fundamentals of Pixar Shorts (e.g., *Luxo Jr., Knick Knack* [Figure 14.3]).

> *There is no terror in the bang, only in the anticipation of it.* Alfred Hitchcock.[8]

In the beginning, as the viewer is introduced to the story, the drama revolves around what the main character does and doesn't know.[9] In the classic film *Casablanca*, Rick doesn't know Elsa was married when they met in Paris, he doesn't know Casablanca is becoming increasingly dangerous, and he doesn't know that he needs people more than he is willing to admit. In *Star Wars: Episode VII*, Rey doesn't know who her parents are, why she was left behind, or that she can use the Force.

Alfred Hitchcock's classic example of the difference between *suspense* and *surprise* bears repeating.[10] The difference is predicated on *who knows what, when*. If a bomb suddenly goes off, it results in a surprise of limited duration for the viewer. However, when the viewer is shown the bomb ahead of time, set to explode in 15 minutes, the tension takes a gigantic leap. Under these conditions, an innocuous conversation in a restaurant becomes riveting because the viewer is actively anticipating what is going to happen. The viewer sits in anguish as they want to warn the characters on the screen: "*You shouldn't be talking about such trivial matters. There is a bomb beneath you and it is about to explode!*"[10] A surprise provides a viewer only 15 seconds of surprise, however, by informing the viewer ahead of time, there are 15 minutes of suspense. Hitchcock believed that *suspense* provides a superior impact on the viewer, except "*when the surprise is a twist, that is, when the unexpected ending is, in itself, the highlight of the story.*"[10]

Figure 14.3

Knick Knack. (Copyright 1988, Pixar.)

A Story Trick

A viewer's grasp of a story's continuity hinges on the timing of when they receive the information. An effective technique in story is when the audience gets the information *slightly ahead* or *slightly behind* when the character gets the same information.[11] This technique utilizes the experience of the viewer, who is actively trying to anticipate where the story is headed. The timing becomes key. Firstly, the viewer will lose interest waiting for the character to make the connection of what is happening if the information is revealed too far ahead. While on the other hand, the viewer will become confused if they are clued in too long after the action as to what is going on and why.

Lasseter recommends that *"action timed to be slightly ahead of the audience adds an element of suspense, as well as surprise, in that it keeps the viewer guessing about what will happen next. An example of this is at the beginning of Luxo Jr. Dad is on-screen, alone and still; the audience believes they are looking at a plain inanimate lamp. Unexpectedly, a ball comes rolling in from off-screen. At this point, both Dad and the audience are confused. The audience's interest is in what is to come next."*[11] Remember that a viewer is analyzing every moment in your story. A storyteller must keep track of and anticipate what the audience is thinking and feeling. This allows one to pinpoint where you want them to be in the story. The story can then be constructed and edited to guide the audience[12] (Figure 14.4).

Figure 14.4

Luxo Jr. (Copyright 1986, Pixar.)

Gaps

Gaps open up when the viewer expects a specific action and instead something unexpected happens. Gaps range from furniture that is alive and talks (*Beauty and the Beast*) to actions, superheroes battling one another (*Captain America: Civil War, Batman v Superman: Dawn of Justice*). In dramatic stories, the unexpected doesn't just happen... it needs to happen. In story, there must be gaps between expectation and outcome to keep the viewer's interest—*things are never as they appear*. This is a fundamental in every dramatic story.

Planting gaps are an indispensable skill for any storyteller. It is in these gaps, between reality and a character's skewed point of view, where interesting stories emerge (i.e., a toy thinks he is a "real" space ranger [*Toy Story*], a teenager sees the world as his playground [*Ferris Bueller*]). These gaps motivate the viewer to question why things are the way they are. Could one's point of view be the key to success? Do the normal rules of society still apply? Can we trust what we see? The detective/mystery genre exploits gap upon gap; things are not what they seem (*Law & Order*).

At the very least, *gaps* keep a viewer's attention by keeping them on their toes. To reiterate film producer Samuel Goldwyn's familiar axiom, "*If the story is what the story is about, you are in deep sh*t*" (Figure 14.5). Viewers don't come to see what they already know about this world, they come to see what they don't know or sense—and this is found in the gaps.

Figure 14.5

Samuel Goldwyn, film producer.

Gaps become (1) openings for surprise, (2) opportunities for tension (withholding information), and (3) useful for switching the status of characters. The series *Pirates of the Caribbean* exploits gaps continually as who has the upper hand, only to have the tables turned with one gap after another. This keeps the viewer off-balance, never sure what will happen next, and creates a growing sense of foreboding that "*all is not as it seems*."[13]

When a gap opens, the viewer wants to know *Why*. This opening immediately propels them back through the story as they make connections. It's these contradictions that give the viewer insights that enable them to put together the clues completing the story. Viewers enjoy the rush when they see the big picture come into focus.

Internal Gaps

- Men who.................haven't grown up (*Stepbrothers*).
- Characters who think they are smart.................but aren't (Kramer [*Seinfeld*], Daffy Duck).
- A toy who believes.................he is a "real" space ranger (Buzz Lightyear).

External Gaps

- A video game antihero.................in a young girl's world (*Wreck-It-Ralph*).
- Cowboys who herd.................cats (*Cat Herders*[14]) (Figure 14.6).

Gaps are a tried-and-true method for creating memorable characters. It is their internal contradictions that viewers relate to and make them compelling. TV shows thrive on these characters—Sheldon (*Big Bang*), Holmes (*Elementary*), House (*House*). In *Calvin and Hobbes*, Calvin's whole personality is defined by his *gaps* with reality. He has (1) *inner gaps*, uncontrollable flights of fantasy into other worlds, (2) *external gaps*, Hobbes, his toy tiger, is not real, and (3) *global gaps*, teachers and parents have all, as one time or another, become creatures or space aliens.

Gaps are not in "*What action the character should take,*" this leads to *predictability*. Gaps are also not readily found in "*What action the character could take,*" this leads to *cleverness* which is adequate in the short term but is not satisfying for the viewer in the long haul. Gaps emerge in the *play* between a character's point of view and their situation, "*What action the character would take?*"[15]

Brian McDonald refers to this as "telling the truth" which is much harder than it sounds.[16] In *Raiders of the Lost Ark*, when Indy is confronted by an intimidating character holding an even more menacing sword, he does the logical thing—pulls out a gun and shoots the guy. It is one of the most memorable scenes because it isn't what Hollywood has set the viewer to expect from our heroes. Heroes are not supposed to take the easy way out, they are to confront their enemies, man to man. The gap opens up between the viewer's conditioning, of expected behavior but instead gets pure logic in response to the situation.[17]

One strategy in creating gaps is determining what the "*opposite*" reaction would be. In *Rise of Planet of the Apes*, Will (human) opens the cell door freeing Caesar (ape) but instead of Caesar leaping out of his cage, Caesar pulls the cell door closed, staying inside. This gap shocks the audience into realizing that there has a fundamental change in Caesar and the balance of power has shifted. Caesar's transformation has been withheld from the viewer, forcing them to fill in the gap.[18] In *Toy Story*, when Buzz ricochets around Andy's room in an attempt to fly, Woody expects Buzz's delusion to be exposed. That doesn't happen. Instead, Buzz not only still thinks he can fly, but also now the other Toys think he can fly too (Figure 14.7). More about gaps can be found in McKee's *Story*, pages 147–149[19] or *Comic Toolbox* by John Vorhaus—Comic Characters, pages 30–46.[20]

Figure 14.6

Herding Cats. See commercial at https://vimeo.com/59098832

Figure 14.7

Toy Story. (Copyright 1995, Disney • Pixar.)

Believability

Viewers enter a story wanting to believe everything they hear and see. They willingly *suspend their disbelief*, knowing it isn't real, for the promise of an exciting and meaningful experience. This is only possible due to the implicit understanding between viewer and storyteller.[21]

There is an expectation of a plausible world where cause and effect operate with a certain set of rules.

1. The *action is consistent* with a system of physics whether it be in our world or a fantasy world (e.g., animation, VR, VFX).
2. There are just enough *significant details* so the viewer's imagination can fill in what is needed to believe. At the same time, not too many that they start comparing against what is known about the world.
3. The *actions are causal* and intentional, helping to reinforce the viewer's suspension of disbelief.

Figure 14.8

Horus, falcon-headed male god with a white and red crown.

Figure 14.9

VFX characters, *Avatar*, from left: Zoe Saldana, Sam Worthington, 2009. (TM & Copyright 20th Century Fox. All rights reserved/Courtesy Everett Collection.)

Drama operates in this realm of what is *believable*, not necessarily what is *real*. The irony is there are events that have actually happened in real life, but are not believable in a story—parachute not opening and surviving. The key is that viewers will believe just about anything if they have been *set up* to believe. This has been true since early Egyptians believed, literally, in gods with animal heads and human bodies (Figure 14.8). Ancient Greeks accepted the certainty of centaurs, and the early Chinese came to believe in dragons (possibly predisposed by dinosaur bones they would discover). Today, audiences willingly suspend their own disbelief as we flock to blockbusters based on supernatural heroes (e.g., *Avatar*, *Thor*) (Figure 14.9).

As John Lasseter pointed out, "*in the world of your story, any kind of rules can exist, but there must be rules for your world to be believable. For example, if a character in your story can't fly and then all of a sudden he can fly for no reason, your world and story will lose credibility with your audience. As soon as something looks wrong or out of place, your audience will pop out of your story and think about how weird that looked and you've lost them. The goal is to keep them entertained for the length of your film. When a film achieves this goal, the audience will lose track of time and forget about all their worldly cares...*"[22]

Consistency is the key to believability: Actions must be consistent with the rules of the world, as well as consistent with the personality and traits of the characters. Archer[23] indicates that consistent behaviors of character fall into three categories:

1. *External* behaviors (physical)—a character's manners, dialect, and biological capabilities.
2. *Internal* behaviors (psychological)—a character's personality and beliefs, as well as their personal knowledge of the world around them (i.e., the worlds of Beverly Hills vs. the Ozarks [*Beverly Hillbillies*]).
3. *Uncharacteristic* behaviors/actions—actions the viewer does not accept as *believable*. In *Star Wars: Episode VII*, the Millennium Falcon takes off straightaway, though it has been mothballed for decades. This could have crossed into a *can't happen* moment, breaking the continuity, except for the fact that the viewer has seen it fly before and very much wanted to see it fly again.

This last example straddles a line that Aristole[24] advocated centuries ago. "*For the purposes of (story) a convincing impossibility is preferable to an unconvincing possibility.*" This translates to "believability is more important that real." A believable *plausibility*, something that is unlikely to happen but believed (balloons can float a house away [*Up*]), is more critical than *probable*, something more likely to happen but the viewer doesn't believe it.

This rational is why even if it is something that *really* happened in real life, it *won't* be accepted if it the audience hasn't been set up. In *Toy Story 3*, the viewer is set up to witness Buzz being reprogrammed (plausible) by Lotso to be one of his gang, then Rex resets him but now he is in Spanish mode.

Walt Disney had his own version called "*Plausible Impossible*"[25] he applied to the medium of animation. Things at times were wildly exaggerated to more accurately convey a sense of the action in drawings that were animated (i.e., squash and stretch). The latitude of plausibility has a wider range depending on the medium (flash animation, VR, low res games). In realism, the key is to present it quickly and move on, before a viewer can start to analyze. Weighing what the viewer will believe is an important consideration. It is not unusual for viewers to accept far more in a fantasy story than a modern day, realistic drama.

Believability is built on a foundation of logic. Richard Dansky says, I must ask myself, "*Ok, what would this (character) do (in this situation)?... not, what do I need to have happen next (in the story).*"[26] While character logic makes story creation much more straightforward, it also makes creating interesting characters a bit more challenging.

As a general rule, coincidence kills believability. Yes, coincidences can solve story problems, but more often than not, create a bigger problem by breaking a story's credibility.

> Our characters achieved believability because of their limitations... There is no such thing as sympathy without believability; and there is no such things as real laughter without sympathy.
>
> Chuck Jones[27] (*Looney Tunes*)

Coincidences

Coincidences are built into every story, film, and game. Without them there wouldn't be a plot. A hero and villain just happen to be equally matched adversaries. They have a previous connection to each other (Darth Vader and Luke Skywalker). Characters who need each other just happen to cross paths in the middle of nowhere—old Spock and young Kirk (*Star Trek [2009]*).[28] In *Spiderman*, the premise is built on Peter Parker visiting the one place that has an escaped radioactive spider. The premise also necessitates that he continually runs into acquaintances with pathological jealousy issues, who have access to cutting edge research that turns them into monsters. In that same vein, how many times does the superhero and his nemesis both have a romantic interest in the same heroine (Roxanne [*Megamind*], Gwen [*Spiderman*])?

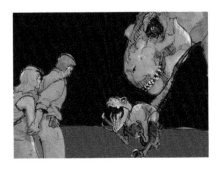

Figure 14.10

T-Rex saves the humans by seizing the raptor at the end of *Jurassic Park*. (Copyright 1993, Universal.)

Coincidence can jumpstart a story or kill it in its tracks. Coincidences are instances, interactions that happen just by chance—that have no causal connection. There is a perception that coincidences are created as a last resort when the storyteller can't figure out how to end the story. When this happens, more often than not, the viewer feels cheated out of a satisfying ending. The key is *when to use* coincidences. As Pixar story artist Emma Coats said, *"Coincidences to get characters into trouble are great; coincidences to get them out of it are cheating."*[29]

Coincidences are a fact of life. By their nature, they are random and viewers know this. Viewers accept the premise of coincidences getting us into trouble. It has happened to everyone—the office gossip who tells others our secrets, or running into someone we are trying to avoid. Yet, most people would be hard pressed to recall the last time a coincidence got them out of trouble. The general rule for coincidence is they can be used in the first half of the story, but not in the second half.

When coincidences are used to solve problems in the second half of a story, they kill believability. There is no cause and effect, which is how viewers extract meaning from the story. The question isn't so much *How* coincidences kill believability, but *When* they do.[30] Problems with Coincidence:

1. When viewers notice coincidences. Viewers hear that voice in their head saying—*"things don't happen that way,"* or the classic *"they wouldn't do that."*
2. When the solution comes out of the blue. This happens when the viewer has not been set up ahead of time with information that would make the actions plausible.
3. When coincidences just *benefit* one person, the one group, the viewer's dislike.
4. When dumb luck rescues the day. There are rare exceptions to this rule. In *Jurassic Park*, where the T-Rex seemingly comes out of nowhere to grab the raptor just before they attack the humans (Figure 14.10). The audience accepts this solution because (1) *the characters have suffered enough* and (2) *viewers are completely engaged in the action* there is no time for them to weigh the odds of plausibility—though they may resent it later upon reflection.

The key to using coincidence is taking advantage of what they do best: (1) turn stories in unanticipated emotional directions, (2) generate surprise, and (3) redirect the action in a different direction.[31] To avoid the destructive side of coincidences, it is vital to plant information early by setting the viewer up, foreshadowing. Foreshadowing sets up the viewer with a plausible reason for something to happen—as opposed to things happening out of the blue. In *Jaws*, the viewer is repeatedly shown scuba air tanks. Brody is warned about the tanks being explosive, and the audience is shown one being pushed into the shark's mouth. At the end of the movie when the tanks blow up the shark, the viewer knows where they came from. The tanks being in the shark's mouth are a fortunate coincidence but because the viewer has been repeatedly set up to their existence they accept the explosive ending.

In horror movies, coincidences are the staple of the genre—but only for the first half of the story. Coincidences are both expected and tolerated at the same time in horror. By the second half of the story, it is essential to forgo coincidences to be able to maintain cause and effect, providing the momentum to get to the end. In *Star Trek: Into Darkness,* the audience is rooting for Kirk to come back to life. When a Tribble shows signs of reanimating itself because of the villain's super-blood, we tolerate the coincidence because the solution is not handed to the characters. They still have to figure out how to use this information to save Kirk.

There is only the perception of coincidences. If the viewer has been sufficiently set up, they will accept even the most outrageous happy accidents. McKee's book, *Story*, contains additional information on coincidences, pages 356–359.[32]

References

1. A. Cuarón, *Story* (Gravity—Blue Ray Supplemental Disc, Location, 2013), Location 1:58.
2. J. Whedon, Joss Whedon's Top 10 Writing Tips Interview by Catherine Bray, http://www.aerogrammestudio.com/2013/03/13/joss-whedons-top-10-writing-tips
3. L. Giannetti, *Understanding Movies* (Englewood Cliffs, New Jersey, Prentice-Hall Inc., 1990), 303.
4. J. Cummings, Jim Cummings on How to Combat the Digital Recession and Lessons to Learn from "South Park" Interview by Sarah Solvarra, *Filmmaker Magazine*, 2014, http://filmmakermagazine.com /84977-ornanas-jim-cummings-on-how-to-combat-the-digital-recession-and-lessons-to-learn-from-south-park/#.VqkkEvH6lUN
5. E. Coats, Pixar's 22 Rules of Storytelling, *Aerogramme Writers' Studio*, 2013, http://www.aerogrammestudio.com/2013/03/07/pixars-22-rules-of-storytelling
6. F. Glebas, *Directing the Story* (Burlington, MA, Focal Press, 2008), 15–18.
7. J. Lambert, *Digital Storytelling* (New York, Routledge, 2012), 66.
8. A. Hitchcock, Quotes, *Goodreads*, https://www.goodreads.com/author/quotes/9420.Alfred_Hitchcock
9. D. Marks, *Transformational Arc*, 197.
10. A Hitchcock, 'Hitchcock, Lessing, and the bomb under the table,' Observation on film art, *David Bordwell's Website on Cinema*, 2013, http://www.davidbordwell.net/blog/2013/11/29/hitchcock-lessing-and-the-bomb-under-the-table/
11. J. Lasseter, Tricks to Animating Characters with a Computer, SIGGRAPH [Conference] (Course 1, Animation Tricks, 1994, Course Notes), https://www.siggraph.org/education/materials/HyperGraph/animation/character_animation/principles/lasseter_s94.htm
12. B. Morgan, *On Story—Screenwriters and Their Craft* (Austin, Texas, University of Texas, 2013), 44.
13. L. Cron, *Wired for Story*, 22.
14. C. Herders, *Fallon*, https://www.fallon.com/case/cat-herders-2
15. R. McKee, *Story*, 147.
16. B. McDonald, *Invisible Ink* (Seattle, Libertary Edition, 2010), 76.
17. S. Kovach, Harrison Ford explained the Story Behind the best scene in 'Indiana Jones', *Business Insider*, 2014, http://www.businessinsider.com/harrison-ford-reddit-ama-2014-4
18. J. Yorke, *Into the Woods*, 135.
19. R. McKee, *Story*, 147–149.
20. J. Vorhaus, *The Comic Toolbox*, (USA, Silman-James Publisher, 1994), 30–46.
21. E. Skolnick, *Video Game*, 73.
22. J. Lasseter, Tricks to Animating Characters with a Computer—Ask Why (online, SIGGRAPH '94, 1994), https://www.siggraph.org/education/materials/HyperGraph/animation/character_animation/principles/lasseter_s94.htm
23. W. Archer, *Play-Making*, 183.
24. A. K. Aristotle, *Poetics—Stephen Halliwell Translation*, 44.
25. W. Disney, 'The Plausible Impossible,' Walt Disney's Wonderful World of Color, *YouTube*, 1956, https://www.youtube.com/watch?v=i1PT8wtJrTs
26. R. Dansky, From Vampires to Vaporware: The terror of being Dansky by Russ Pitts, *Ploygon*, 2013, http://www.polygon.com/features/2013/10/20/4753718/richard-dansky-tom-clancy
27. C. Jones, *Chuck Amuck*, 44.
28. I. Cabe, 6 Insane Coincidences You Didn't Notice Are in Every Movie, *Cracked*, 2016, http://www.cracked.com/article_23592_6-weirdly-specific-things-that-always-happen-in-movies.html
29. E. Coats, 22 Rules to Perfect Storytelling from a Pixar Storyboard Artist Listed by Benjamin Starr, *Visual News*, 2015, http://www.visualnews.com/2015/09/23/22-rules-to-perfect-storytelling-from-a-pixar-storyboard-artist/
30. E. Skolnick, *Video Game Storytelling*, 80.
31. R. McKee, *Story*, 358.
32. R. McKee, *Story*, 356–359.

Index

Printed and bound by CPI Group (UK) Ltd, Croydon, CR0 4YY

22/10/2024

01777635-0012